MW01257969

"The issue of paedobaptism is not merely a topic that is talked about in the ivory tower of church history, but equally delves deep into the life of the church and family. It can be overwhelming to study this subject, requiring the grasp of the exegetical details of numerous texts, biblical theology, systematics, and church history. That is where Goeman's work steps in. This volume is a wonderful guide through the plethora of angles on this issue, not only walking through the arguments, in compelling and concise fashion, but also providing an excellent discussion on the rich significance of this ordinance. This book is an excellent resource to give to those who have questions or are wrestling through the question of infant- versus credobaptism."

Abner Chou, President and John F. MacArthur Endowed Fellow, The Master's University

"The question of whether to baptize their infant children is a significant challenge for many Christian parents. In his new book, *The Baptism Debate*, Peter Goeman carefully examines the best arguments for infant baptism and shows from Scripture that only those who profess faith in Christ should be baptized. Goeman's work is thoroughly researched, clearly written, and exegetically compelling. I couldn't recommend it more highly to anyone who is wrestling with this issue!"

Matt Waymeyer, Associate Pastor, Grace Immanuel Bible Church; Academic Dean, The Expositors Seminary

"Peter Goeman provides a superb resource that fairly critiques the belief in and practice of paedobaptism common in Reformed circles. He also offers a clear understanding of the strong scriptural support for believer's or biblical baptism. Anyone desiring to correctly understand this key issue will find this book a great help for their understanding of God's intentions for His followers."

Michael Grisanti, Professor of Old Testament, The Master's Seminary

"Friendly doctrinal divisions among faithful orthodox believers can be found throughout church history. In our current age of pragmatism and watered-down doctrine, it is refreshing to read an articulate yet gracious defense of a Baptist understanding of baptism. Peter Goeman helpfully lays out the key issues, showing readers how the doctrine of baptism has far-reaching implications for one's system of theology. This volume is a wonderful resource for believers seeking to better understand the full significance of Christian baptism."

Kaspars Ozolins, Assistant Professor of Old Testament Interpretation, The Southern Baptist Theological Seminary

"Peter Goeman clears away the debris of tradition, misinterpretation and speculation so that the sunlight of scripture can illuminate the truth of believer's baptism. With a scholar's mind and a shepherd's heart, he offers a clear and compelling understanding of this significant act in the believer's life."

Stephen Davey, Pastor, The Shepherd's Church; President, Shepherds Theological Seminary

"In a day when doctrinal distinctives are being downplayed and evangelical ecumenism is promoted, it can be very unpopular to insist on biblical accuracy in an area that some might call 'secondary.' Peter Goeman is concerned, however, that Christians who are lovely people can still be wrong! But it is not just a matter of simple disagreement on 'secondary issues' that concerns Goeman. He knows that some doctrines have effects beyond a classroom debate. Such is the practice of infant baptism. Other doctrines are affected by this practice, even soteriology. With all of his evident concern, Goeman does not engage in insults, but in an even-handed discussion of the biblical significance of baptism. I appreciate his informed theological approach and pray that this volume will have a wide effect. His concerns need to be heard."

William Varner, Professor of Biblical Languages and Bible Exposition, The Master's University

The Baptism Debate

The Baptism Debate

Understanding and Evaluating Reformed Infant Baptism

Peter Goeman

SOJOURNER
PRESS

Unless otherwise indicated, all Scripture quotations are taken from The ESV® Bible (The Holy Bible, English Standard Version®) copyright © 2001 by Crossway, a publishing ministry of Good News Publishers. ESV® Text Edition: 2016. The ESV® text has been reproduced in cooperation with and by permission of Good News Publishers. Unauthorized reproduction of this publication is prohibited. All rights reserved.

Cover design by Rob Williams

Interior layout by Andrew "Marcus" Corder

For bulk, special sales, or ministry purchases, please contact us at sales@sojournerpress.org.

The Baptism Debate: Understanding and Evaluating Reformed Infant Baptism
Copyright © 2023 by Peter Goeman
Published by Sojourner Press
Raleigh, NC, 27603
sojournerpress.org

Trade paperback ISBN: 978-1-960255-04-4
Hardcover ISBN: 978-1-960255-05-1
ePub ISBN: 978-1-960255-06-8
Audiobook ISBN: 978-1-960255-07-5

Printed in the United States of America

To my wife, Kinsley.
The fruit of my labor is equally yours.

Contents

Illustrations

Tables

Figures

Acknowledgments

Anyone who writes a book knows there are many people to thank in the process. First of all, it is appropriate that I thank my wife and family for putting up with countless hours of reading, researching, and writing. My wife's name is not listed as a co-author, but in many ways she should be. She is the one who makes writing possible by being a godly wife and mother.

I owe a great debt to the administration and faculty at Shepherds Theological Seminary, who have been completely supportive through the whole process. I am deeply indebted to them for the encouragement and conversations about covenant theology and biblical interpretation which sharpened my thinking.

I also want to thank Aaron Valdizan, who did a great job with the bulk of the editing. He also spent considerable effort to ensure that I was consistent in citations and style. I also received feedback at various stages from Hunter Hays, Nicole Bowal, Collin Marot, Kevin Welch, and Mathew Wronski. Their feedback was tremendously helpful, and they sharpened my writing and thinking in many ways. I am also thankful for Zach Pawlowski, who gave valuable feedback and painstakingly compiled a Scripture index for the book. Finally, Marcus Corder also deserves my immense gratitude for his role in formatting the book and preparing it for publication.

Saving the best for last, I thank our Lord and Savior, Jesus Christ, for giving me the ability and strength to start and finish this task. The Lord gave grace throughout the whole process, and it is fitting that I should end the acknowledgments by attributing the highest praise to the Lord for seeing this work through to completion. May He receive all the glory.

Acknowledgements

Foreword

THE ISSUE OF INFANT baptism continues to be heavily debated in the Christian community. It has rightly been understood that the issue of infant baptism vs. believers' baptism is not an issue in which Christians should break fellowship. Good Christians disagree on this issue and can stand united on the gospel. We can celebrate this fact.

Yet this issue is important and getting baptism right has great significance. Baptism testifies to the reality that the believing sinner has been united with Christ. He or she has died to sin and has been raised to newness of life (see Romans 6). The person is now placed into and is part of the new covenant community, the church, that Jesus established. A new heart and the indwelling ministry of the Holy Spirit have occurred. The conscience has been cleansed. Baptism represents all these realities. Yet infant baptism muddies what baptism conveys. When people are baptized who have not experienced these great truths, the meaning of baptism is lost and confusion ensues. Thus, we need to make sure we understand what biblical baptism is and why it is so important.

That is why this book is needed. Peter Goeman offers an in-depth, *tour de force* case against infant baptism, particularly as found within Covenant Theology. He does so by offering a deep dive into the most important biblical and theological issues associated with the debate. As Goeman shows, there are many substantive reasons against the infant baptism view. And yet, significantly, he also reveals that the main argument against infant baptism is the compelling positive case for believers' baptism.

Few people understand the issues concerning the baptism debate like Peter Goeman. He has deeply studied the issues on both sides and brings a rare clarity to a complex topic.

For those interested in baptism and the baptism debate, this book is a must read. It leaves no Scripture text or theological argument uncovered. It is a serious treatment that both sides of the issue should consider.

Michael J. Vlach
Professor of Theology
Shepherds Theological Seminary

Foreword

The Baptism Debate

Introduction

I BELIEVE INFANT BAPTISM IS unbiblical and harmful to the church. This is obviously a controversial statement, and many will disagree with me (thus, the need for this book). Roman Catholics, Eastern Orthodox, Lutherans, and many Protestant denominations all practice infant baptism (also called paedobaptism), making paedobaptism the most common form of baptism in broader Christendom. However, despite the popularity of infant baptism, I will show in the following pages that it is an unbiblical practice and that the Bible indicates only those who profess faith in Christ should be baptized (a position known as credobaptism).

But first, a word of clarification. Although it would be worthwhile to examine the infant baptism practiced by Roman Catholics, Eastern Orthodox, or Lutherans, this book will primarily analyze what is called Reformed infant baptism (sometimes called covenantal infant baptism). I want to focus on the Reformed understanding of infant baptism for three reasons. First, Reformed theology has the most complicated and robust defense of infant baptism. Second, in contrast to the Roman Catholic understanding of Church tradition, the Reformed paedobaptist recognizes Scripture as the sole and binding authority on baptism. This means we can center our dialogue on Scripture, as it should be. Third, and most practically, I have friends that hold to the Reformed paedobaptist position. Unashamedly, I write to persuade them (and you) that infant baptism is unbiblical. It is my goal to show that Scripture is clear about baptism being only for believers, and that the Reformed arguments for infant baptism are lacking.

To facilitate this conversation, I have divided this book into eight chapters. In the first chapter, I set up what is perhaps the defining question concerning infant baptism—what is the relationship between faith and baptism? I show that a biblical analysis demands a strong connection between faith and baptism. I also show that the early church historically emphasized faith and baptism through the Reformation. It was not until the 16th century with the writings of Ulrich Zwingli that there was any attempt to separate baptism from faith. The Reformed paedobaptist is eager to separate faith and baptism, because if faith is linked with baptism, then it would be natural to question infant baptism.

Having raised the issue of faith and baptism, in the second chapter I summarize the Reformed framework of covenant theology. Understanding the Reformed argument for paedobaptism is impossible without understanding covenant theology. Thus, this chapter briefly outlines the contours of covenant theology and summarizes how this theological system forms the basis for infant baptism.

Following the summary of covenant theology, the third chapter launches a thorough analysis of the focal point of covenant theology—the covenant of grace. Because the Reformed paedobaptist position completely depends on the belief in a covenant of grace, I discuss the arguments for the covenant of grace. I argue that the Reformed paedobaptist understanding of the covenant of grace is fallacious and we should abandon it as evidence for infant baptism.

The fourth chapter discusses the argument for one people of God, which is said to be the same in both Old and New Testaments. The Reformed proposition that there is one people of God is a crucial component of the argument for infant baptism. If the nation of Israel and the church are the same, the entrance requirement could conceivably be the same. However, I seek to show in this chapter that, although both Jew and Gentile are incorporated into the church, Israel keeps a special role and function in God's plan. Observing the difference between Jew and Gentile challenges the idea that the entrance requirement into Israel and the church are the same.

The fifth chapter deserves a significant amount of attention because it addresses the most important argument for infant baptism from a Reformed perspective. In this chapter, I address the fundamental argument that baptism has replaced circumcision and the two signs are essentially equal in signifying acceptance into the covenant community. After analyzing the Reformed viewpoint, I argue that circumcision and baptism are distinct in their descriptions and significance.

The sixth chapter deals with household baptisms and corporate headship. The Reformed paedobaptist argues that when the head of the household embraces Christ, the rest of the family would also be baptized in solidarity with the head of the household. However, I show how these household arguments are short-sighted and do not fully consider the biblical evidence.

In the seventh chapter, I deal with the mode and significance of baptism. While chapters two through six deal with negative critiques of the Reformed paedobaptist argumentation, this seventh chapter provides a positive presentation about the meaning of baptism. I walk through the biblical theology of baptism, spending significant time on the New Testament description of baptism. The definition of baptism in the New Testament contradicts the paedobaptist position, making it the strongest argument against infant baptism.

Finally, in the eighth chapter I briefly summarize why this book is important and why I took the effort to write it. Although baptism is often relegated to a secondary issue, there are significant ramifications for this doctrine in the life of the church. Thus, in the final chapter I encourage the believer to love baptism and to embrace the bible's teaching on the subject.

Admittedly, not everyone will like this book. I have tried to present and evaluate the Reformed paedobaptist position fairly, but not every Reformed paedobaptist explains things the same way or uses the same passages the same way. Nevertheless, I have attempted to use well-known sources to represent the best of the Reformed paedobaptist arguments, but obviously it is not possible to include every paedobaptist on every issue.

Although there is always more that could be said about baptism, I believe this book provides an excellent summary of the Reformed paedobaptist position. I also think I have provided solid, biblical arguments for why we should reject the Reformed paedobaptist position. Thus, I pray God uses this book to challenge those holding to a paedobaptist position and to encourage others by helping them understand the biblical significance of baptism.

Chapter 1

The Relationship between Faith and Baptism

ALTHOUGH THERE ARE MANY ways we could start our discussion on baptism, I believe the most profitable starting point is the historic question of how faith and baptism relate. The reason for this approach is that there is an abundance of biblical and historical evidence on the relationship between faith and baptism. If faith is a prerequisite for baptism, then this point has immense implications for infant baptism. On the other hand, if faith is not a prerequisite for baptism, then we have removed the most significant problem for the Reformed paedobaptist.

Reformed paedobaptist Louis Berkhof clearly defines the importance of the relationship between faith and baptism with the following summary:

> The most important objection to infant baptism raised by the Baptists, is that, according to Scripture, baptism is conditioned on an active faith revealing itself in a creditable profession. Now it is perfectly true that the Bible points to faith as a prerequisite for baptism, Mark 16:16; Acts 10:44–48; 16:14, 15, 31, 34. If this means that the recipient of baptism must *in all cases* give manifestations of an active faith before baptism, then children are naturally excluded. But though the Bible clearly indicates that only those adults who believed were baptized, it nowhere lays down the rule that an active faith is absolutely essential for the reception of baptism.[1]

This quote by Berkhof summarizes the issue well. If faith is an essential requirement for baptism, it is difficult to argue that we can baptize infants. Thus, for most Reformed paedobaptists, faith cannot be a prerequisite for baptism (at least in the case of infant baptism). Notable Reformed theologian, R.C. Sproul, summarizes the issue this way:

---

1 Louis Berkhof, *Systematic Theology* (Grand Rapids: Eerdmans, 1938), 637.

> The most common argument against infant baptism is that it signifies things that flow from faith, and since infants are not capable of expressing or embracing faith, they should not receive the sign. But if that argument were correct, it would nullify the legitimacy of circumcision in the Old Testament. If we reject infant baptism on the basis of the principle that a sign that involves faith must never be given until after faith is present, we also negate the legitimacy of circumcision in the Old Testament.[2]

We will look at the Reformed paedobaptist presupposition that there is a link between baptism and circumcision later. In this chapter, I simply want to highlight Sproul's acknowledgment that the relationship between faith and baptism is a genuine issue. Historically, the church has recognized an essential relationship between faith and baptism. Even those in the early church who embraced paedobaptism accepted the importance of faith in the baptism process.

This chapter will begin with a brief survey of biblical texts which demonstrate an essential connection between faith and baptism. We will then explore a selected portion of early historical sources which show that the early church recognized the importance of faith and baptism. Finally, we will explore why there was a divorce between faith and baptism during the time of the Reformation.

Faith and Baptism in Scripture

Let us begin by briefly surveying key Scripture passages about baptism to highlight the faith language that is used. We will discuss many of these passages more thoroughly in later chapters. Our goal here is to highlight the faith and believing language that is used or implied in these crucial baptism texts.

Baptism in the Book of Acts

The book of Acts often takes a prominent place in the baptism debate because it mentions entire households being baptized, which presumably could have included infants. We will discuss the idea of household baptisms in a later chapter. Here I want to point out the intrinsic link between faith and baptism in the book of Acts.

---

2 R. C. Sproul, *What Is Baptism?*, The Crucial Questions Series 11 (Orlando, FL: Reformation Trust, 2011), 63.

As the following chart demonstrates, within the baptism passages of Acts, belief and faith are intrinsic to every text except one.[3] The only exception is the baptism of Lydia and her family recorded in Acts 16:11–15. However, this passage does nothing to discourage us from assuming belief played a prominent role in the narrative.[4]

Table 1.1. Baptism in the Book of Acts

Passage	Summary	Biblical Text
2:38, 41	Peter calls the Jewish nation to repent and be baptized and "those who received his word were baptized … about 3,000 souls."	"Repent and be baptized every one of you in the name of Jesus Christ for the forgiveness of your sins, and you will receive the gift of the Holy Spirit" (v. 38).
8:12–13	Men and women are identified as being baptized after belief. Simon also is said to believe and be baptized (v. 13).	"But when they believed Philip … they were baptized, both men and women. Even Simon himself believed, and after being baptized he continued with Philip" (v. 12–13a).
8:35–38	Philip explains the gospel, and the eunuch asks to be baptized when he sees water (belief is not mentioned, but seems to be implied—i.e., narrative compression).	"See, here is water! What prevents me from being baptized?" (v. 37).
10:34–48	Peter proclaims forgiveness of sins to "everyone who believes in him" (v. 43), and after the Gentiles had received the Holy Spirit (implied that they believed), they were baptized.	"'Can anyone withhold water for baptizing these people, who have received the Holy Spirit just as we have?' And he commanded them to be baptized in the name of Jesus Christ" (vv. 47–48).

3 The words for the verb "believe" (πιστεύω), the noun "faith" (πίστις), and the adjective "faithful" (πιστός) are all cognates in Greek referring to the same broad concept of faith or the working out of faith in belief.

4 Although the passage does not say Lydia believed, it does say she asked the apostles to stay at her house if they found her to be faithful to the Lord. One would assume this action implies that she expected them to agree she had showed faith and repentance as evidence of a new life in Christ. It would be difficult to argue that Lydia had not already expressed faith in the message Paul preached prior to her baptism. I am not aware of any paedobaptists who would challenge that point.

Passage	Summary	Biblical Text
16:11–15	Lydia responds because God "opened her heart" and she and her household are baptized. She then invites the apostles to stay at her house if they deemed her "faithful to the Lord."	"And after she was baptized, and her household as well" (v. 15).
16:30–34	Paul proclaims the need to "believe in the Lord Jesus" for salvation. The jailer believes, and his entire household rejoices that he had believed (v. 34).	"... and he was baptized at once, he and all his family.... And he rejoiced along with his entire household that he had believed in God" (vv. 33–34).
18:8	Crispus believed in the Lord (with his entire household also believing). The text implies that he was baptized.	"And many of the Corinthians hearing Paul believed and were baptized" (v. 8b).
19:1–7	John's disciples are baptized as followers of Jesus after being convinced to believe in Jesus.	"'John baptized with the baptism of repentance, telling the people to believe in the one who was to come after him, that is, Jesus.' On hearing this, they were baptized in the name of the Lord Jesus" (vv. 4–5).

As we can see by surveying the information on the baptism passages of Acts above, there is certainly a link between faith and baptism, a point even Reformed paedobaptists will acknowledge. However, they will often argue that this emphasis on faith and baptism is because of the nature of "missionary baptisms"—i.e., unbelievers from unbelieving families putting their faith in Christ.[5] Although this is possible, one also needs to account for how the rest of the New Testament talks about the relationship between faith and baptism.

5 Brownson writes, "Here it is important to remember that the earliest church, as witnessed in the New Testament, was in a missionary situation where the dominant pattern was conversion to the faith. It is thus not surprising that the baptism of those who have come to faith is the norm in the book of Acts, and elsewhere in the New Testament to a significant degree. But this fact tells us nothing about infant baptism in itself" (James V. Brownson, *The Promise of Baptism: An Introduction to Baptism in Scripture and the Reformed Tradition* [Grand Rapids: Eerdmans, 2007], 168).

1 Corinthians 12:13

> For in one Spirit we were all baptized into one body—Jews or Greeks, slaves or free—and all were made to drink of one Spirit.

This verse powerfully links the concept of baptism and faith through the operation of the Spirit. The context of 1 Corinthians 12 shows that those who drink of one Spirit here in verse 13 are those who say "Jesus is Lord" by the power of the Spirit (12:3). Likewise, these are also the believers who participate in gifts from the Spirit for the good of the church (12:4, 7). Thus, Paul's argument is that all who are baptized are also participants in the Spirit. In other words, those who are believers have also received the Spirit. Although the term "faith" is not present here in 1 Corinthians 12:13, Pauline theology clearly links the reception of the Spirit with the exercise of faith (Gal 3:2, 5, 14).

The key point of 1 Corinthians 12:13 is that *all* members of the church were baptized into one body and *all* were recipients of the Spirit (a process which only takes place through faith). Although some interpreters would like to distinguish water baptism and Spirit baptism in this passage, Schreiner notes, "Paul himself was not interested in distinguishing them from one another in this verse since both are associated with the transition from the old life to the new."[6] Commenting on this verse, the eminent Reformed paedobaptist, John Calvin, states the following:

> Here there is a proof brought forward from the effect of baptism. "We are," says he, "engrafted by baptism into Christ's body, so that we are by a mutual link bound together as members, and live one and the same life. Hence every one, that would remain in the Church of Christ, must necessarily cultivate this fellowship." He speaks, however, of the baptism of believers, which is efficacious through the grace of the Spirit, for, in the case of many [i.e., chil-

6 Thomas R. Schreiner, "Baptism in the Epistles: An Initiation Rite for Believers," in *Believer's Baptism: Sign of the New Covenant in Christ*, ed. Thomas R. Schreiner and Shawn D. Wright, NAC Studies in Bible & Theology (Nashville, TN: B & H Academic, 2006), 72. See also, G. R. Beasley-Murray, *Baptism in the New Testament* (New York: St Martin's Press, 1962), 168–69. Supporting the viewpoint that spiritual baptism can be distinguished from water baptism, see Douglas Wilson, *To a Thousand Generations: Infant Baptism—Covenant Mercy for the People of God* (Moscow, ID: Canon Press, 1996), 50–51. Wilson is not primarily discussing 1 Corinthians 12:13, but he provides an argument for distinguishing between Spirit and water baptism which I ultimately find unconvincing.

> dren], baptism is merely in the letter—the symbol without the reality; but believers, along with the sacrament, receive the reality.[7]

Calvin must qualify the text because of his belief in infant baptism. As we will discuss in the following chapters, for the Reformed paedobaptists, there are intentional baptisms of some people [i.e., infants] for whom 1 Corinthians 12:13 is not reality. However, the context of 1 Corinthians 12 would seem to indicate that Paul expects all in the church to experience the unity in the Spirit through baptism—a process which in Pauline theology assumes the exercise of faith.

Galatians 3:26–27

> For in Christ Jesus you are all sons of God, through faith. For as many of you as were baptized into Christ have put on Christ.

As noted in our discussion of 1 Corinthians 12, Paul's theology in Galatians 3 connects the reception of the Spirit and the exercise of faith (cf. Gal 3:2, 5, 14). But as Paul develops the theme of faith, we see a specific link between the Christian identity as sons of God through faith and baptism.

After identifying the Galatian church as "sons of God" (v. 26), Paul further clarifies the identity of the "sons of God," in the following verse, "as many of you as were baptized."[8] In other words, Paul's argument is that those who have been baptized are sons of God through faith.[9]

Paul's terminology of putting on Christ is the language of a believer becoming like Christ (cf. Eph 4:24; Col 3:10).[10] All those who have been baptized into Christ have also put on Christ. If the churches of Galatia baptized infants, could Paul have said that those infants were sons of God through faith, and that those infants had put on Christ? In a similar manner to 1 Corinthians 12:13, Calvin comments on this passage:

> But the argument, that, because they have been baptized, they have put on Christ, appears weak; for how far is baptism from being efficacious in all? Is it reasonable that the grace of the Holy Spirit should be so closely linked to an external symbol? Does not

---

7 John Calvin and William Pringle, *Commentaries on the Epistles of Paul the Apostle to the Corinthians* (Bellingham, WA: Logos Bible Software, 2010), 406.

8 Richard N. Longenecker, *Galatians*, Word Biblical Commentary 41 (Dallas: Word, 1990), 155.

9 Thomas R. Schreiner, *Galatians*, Zondervan Exegetical Commentary on the New Testament (Grand Rapids: Zondervan, 2010), 256.

10 Longenecker, *Galatians*, 156.

> the uniform doctrine of Scripture, as well as experience, appear to confute this statement? I answer, it is customary with Paul to treat of the sacraments in two points of view. When he is dealing with hypocrites, in whom the mere symbol awakens pride, he then proclaims loudly the emptiness and worthlessness of the outward symbol, and denounces, in strong terms, their foolish confidence.... When, on the other hand, he addresses believers, who make a proper use of the symbols, he then views them in connexion [sp] with the truth—which they represent.[11]

Again, Calvin must heavily qualify Paul's point. Calvin argues that baptism is not as efficacious as Paul seems to imply. Although the text seems to assume all who are baptized are recipients of God's salvific grace, that would certainly be problematic for the Reformed paedobaptist. However, a straight-forward reading of Galatians 3 links baptism and faith. The text states that those who have been baptized are the ones who have put on Christ—and they are the sons of God.

1 Peter 3:21

> Baptism, which corresponds to this, now saves you, not as a removal of dirt from the body but as an appeal (ἐπερώτημα) to God for a good conscience, through the resurrection of Jesus Christ ...

This verse "is the nearest approach to a definition of baptism that the NT affords."[12] Although we will revisit this verse later in defining the importance of baptism, it is in keeping with our theme to recognize Peter defines baptism as, "an appeal (ἐπερώτημα) to God for a good conscience." The word "appeal" (ἐπερώτημα) is also translated as "pledge" in some translations. There are good arguments on both sides, and the issue is not an easy one.[13] However, in either interpretation, we must understand baptism as a volitional outworking of faith. As Schreiner notes, "Whether Peter speaks of an appeal or a pledge, baptism does not save apart from the commitment of the one being baptized."[14]

---

11 John Calvin and William Pringle, *Commentaries on the Epistles of Paul to the Galatians and Ephesians* (Bellingham, WA: Logos Bible Software, 2010), 111.

12 James D. G. Dunn, *Baptism in the Holy Spirit* (London: SCM Press, 1970), 219.

13 For a helpful survey of the evidence, see Thomas R. Schreiner, *1, 2 Peter, Jude*, The New American Commentary 37 (Nashville, TN: Broadman & Holman, 2003), 195–97.

14 Schreiner, "Baptism in the Epistles," 70.

This verse then is problematic for the Reformed paedobaptist. Schreiner continues, "What is said here does not fit with infant baptism, for infants cannot appeal to God for a good conscience or pledge to maintain a good conscience before God."[15] Although 1 Peter 3:21 does not mention faith explicitly, the text is loaded with the implicit necessity of faith. Peter's definition of baptism here assumes the volitional expression of commitment to God. Therefore, this verse is problematic for the paedobaptist since infants cannot express volitional commitment.

Ephesians 4:4–5

> There is one body and one Spirit—just as you were called to the one hope that belongs to your call—one Lord, one faith, one baptism.

In Ephesians 4:1–3, Paul admonishes the Ephesian believers to walk in unity. Ephesians 4:4–6 then provides the basis for the unity to which Paul calls all believers in 4:1–3.[16] These verses provide short, concise statements that would have been recognized as valid by all the believers in Ephesus.[17] At the head of these statements, Paul identifies the church as one unified body. The labeling of the church as one body naturally leads to the declaration that there is "one Spirit," since the Spirit is He who incorporates believers into that one body (cf. 1 Cor 12:13).[18]

In 4:5, Paul declares that there is one Lord (a reference to Christ), one faith, and one baptism. Paul's reference to one faith and one baptism reveals that his expectation is that all believers have a unified set of beliefs and a unified experience of baptism into Christ. Schreiner rightly states, "They have all shared a common saving experience by being immersed into Christ, and Paul assumes that all believers have been baptized."[19]

I have included this text in the discussion to highlight the natural combination of faith and baptism. Paul's discussion in Ephesians 4 seems to presume the audience would recognize that these three phrases go together: one Lord, one faith, one baptism.

---

15 Ibid., 71.

16 Clinton E. Arnold, *Ephesians*, Zondervan Exegetical Commentary on the New Testament (Grand Rapids: Zondervan, 2010), 227–28.

17 Ibid., 232.

18 Ibid., 233.

19 Schreiner, "Baptism in the Epistles," 71.

Colossians 2:11–12

> In him also you were circumcised with a circumcision made without hands, by putting off the body of the flesh, by the circumcision of Christ, having been buried with him in baptism, in which you were also raised with him through faith in the powerful working of God, who raised him from the dead.

Reformed paedobaptists often use this passage to argue that baptism has replaced circumcision (an argument we will address in chapter five). At this point, I simply want to point out that Paul directly connects faith and baptism here.

Paul explicitly says that believers have "been buried with [Christ] in baptism." This baptism is further defined as "in which you were also raised with him *through faith*" (emphasis added). Here again, as we have repeatedly seen in the New Testament, we have Paul linking the expression of faith by the believer with the experience of baptism. In the words of Beasley-Murray, "faith is integrated into the baptismal event. In baptism the baptized is raised through faith."[20]

Comparing the New Testament Descriptions of Faith and Baptism

We have observed that the New Testament regularly links faith and baptism together. This is clear from the examples in Acts and in Paul's descriptions of baptism in the Epistles. However, looking at the specific baptism texts is not the only way to show that faith and baptism are linked.

Another support for the link between baptism and faith can be seen by comparing and contrasting the descriptions of faith and baptism. Specifically, when we compare those gifts that God gives to those who exercise faith with the gifts He gives to those who are baptized, we see that they are the same. In other words, those gifts which are promised through faith are also promised through baptism. Note the similarities displayed in the following chart.[21]

---

20 Beasley-Murray, *Baptism in the New Testament*, 154.

21 This chart is taken without edit from Anthony R. Cross, "Faith-Baptism: The Key to an Evangelical Baptismal Sacramentalism," in *Truth That Never Dies*, ed. Nigel G. Wright (Cambridge, UK: The Lutterworth Press, 2014), 35. Cross composes this chart to summarize the data presented by G. R. Beasley-Murray.

Table 1.2. The Gifts Promised to Faith and Baptism

Gift of God	Faith	Baptism
Forgiveness	Rom 4:5–8; 1 John 1:9	Acts 2:38; 22:16
Justification	Rom 3–5 (e.g., 3:28); Gal 2–3 (e.g., 3:11)	1 Cor 6:11
Union with Christ	Eph 3:17	Gal 3:27; Rom 6:3, 5, 8
Being crucified with Christ	Gal 2:19–20	Rom 6:2–11 (esp. 3–4, 6)
Death and Resurrection	Gal 2:19–20	Rom 6:2–11 (esp. 3–4, 5–6 and 8; Col 2:12)
Sonship	John 1:12	Gal 3:26–27
Holy Spirit	Gal 3:2–5, 13–14	Acts 2:38; 1 Cor 12:13
Entry in the church	Acts 5:14; Gal 3:6–7	Gal 3:27; 1 Cor 12:13
Regeneration and life	John 3:14–16; 20:31	Titus 3:5; John 3:5
The kingdom and eternal life	Mark 10:15; John 3:14–16	1 Cor 6:9–11; Acts 22:16
Salvation	Rom 1:16; John 3:16	1 Peter 3:21

As the chart above illustrates, faith and baptism are so connected that you can talk about them almost interchangeably. Some paedobaptists even acknowledge this point. For example, paedobaptist James Brownson writes:

> Scripture repeatedly links baptism and faith, minimizing neither faith nor the importance of baptism. Indeed, almost all the blessings that Scripture speaks of as flowing from faith are also spoken of as flowing from baptism, including cleansing, justification, union with Christ, adoption, membership in the body of Christ, giving of the Holy Spirit, and the inheritance of the Kingdom of God.[22]

In the New Testament, it is unquestionably the default to talk about baptism and faith in the same breath. They are intrinsically linked in the narratives of Acts, as well as in the Epistles. The church has historically recognized this essential link between faith and baptism. It was not until the Reformation that this connection between faith and baptism was seriously

22 Brownson, *The Promise of Baptism*, 88.

challenged. Thus, we now turn to a brief survey of church history to highlight the early church's view of faith and baptism.

Faith and Baptism in the Early Church

As the above section showed, the New Testament consistently links faith and baptism together. This seems to be the understanding of the early church as well. Admittedly, the evidence on baptism in the early church is quite varied. Instruction on clothing, procedures, catechisms, and motivations for baptisms all differ in some degree. Yet, there is a strong and outspoken unity on faith and baptism in early church writings.

The goal of this section is to briefly address a few sources to highlight the fact that the early church viewed faith as an integral part of the baptism process. Some of the following sources cited are paedobaptists. Although many of these paedobaptists did not explain how infant baptism relates to the belief that faith is integral to baptism, they still provide evidence that the early church did indeed consider faith and baptism to be linked.

Mark 16:15–16

> And he said to them, "Go into all the world and proclaim the gospel to the whole creation. Whoever believes and is baptized will be saved, but whoever does not believe will be condemned."

I did not include this text in the previous section on Scripture and faith because I am not convinced that Mark 16:15–16 is original to Mark.[23] Although present in most English translations, these verses are part of the longer ending of Mark (16:9–20), which many scholars believe was a later addition to the Gospel, which originally ended at 16:8.[24]

However, even if those verses are not original to Mark, this longer ending of Mark shows an early Christian understanding of the link between faith and baptism. Edwards notes that this ending must be dated to at least the very beginning of the second century.[25] Thus, although it is

23 In this, I agree with Daniel M. Doriani, "Matthew 28:18–20 and the Institution of Baptism," in *The Case for Covenantal Infant Baptism*, ed. Gregg Strawbridge (Phillipsburg, NJ: P&R Publishing, 2003), 43–47. However, Doriani does not think the text contributes to our understanding of baptism at all, while I would say it is a very early witness of at least some in the church linking faith and baptism.

24 James R. Edwards, *The Gospel According to Mark*, Pillar New Testament Commentary (Grand Rapids: Eerdmans, 2002), 499.

25 "Although the longer ending is clearly secondary, it is nevertheless very old. The earliest witnesses to the longer ending come from the *Epistula Apostolorum* 9–10 (c. 145), perhaps

unlikely that this text was originally part of Mark's Gospel, it is a very early testimony of what the church believed about faith and baptism.

In Mark 16:16, the phrase, "Whoever believes and is baptized will be saved," indicates that the same individual is in view. In other words, to be saved one must have believed *and* have been baptized (cf. Acts 2:38). As Collins notes, "The linking of believing and being baptized reflects widespread practice in the communities of those who accepted Jesus as the messiah or as Lord."[26] Mark 16:16 provides a very early witness of the link between faith and baptism.

Didache 7:1, 4

> Concerning baptism, baptize in this way: after you have reviewed all these things, baptize into the name of the Father and of the Son and of the Holy Spirit in running water.... Prior to baptism, let the one who baptizes and the baptizand fast, and others if they are able. Instruct the baptizand to fast one or two days beforehand.[27]

The *Didache* is one of the earliest Christian sources we have. Although some date its composition to as early as 50 AD, it was likely written between 80 and 110 AD.[28] The *Didache* is a valuable resource and witness to early church life, not only due to its early date but also because it reads as a manual to guide church function.

Although the entire section on baptism is worth studying in its entirety (*Didache* 7:1–4), the pertinent observation for us is that the manual clearly expects a Christian to have come to grips with the gravity of baptism before partaking in it. Although the *Didache* does not explicitly mention faith or belief in the section on baptism, clearly faith was an essential part of the community experience (cf. 10:2; 16:2, 5). The recitation and fasting requirements expected of the baptismal candidate assume a profession of faith.

According to the *Didache*, the candidate for baptism was first required to take part in a baptismal catechism (7:1, "Having first recited all these things..."). Wilhite argues that the first six chapters of the *Didache* are most

---

Justin Martyr (*Apol.* 1.45; c. 155), Tatian's *Diatessaron* (c. 170), and Irenaeus (*Adv. Haer.* 3.9–12; c. 180)" (Edwards, *The Gospel According to Mark*, 499).

26 Adela Yarbro Collins, *Mark: A Commentary on the Gospel of Mark*, Hermeneia (Minneapolis, MN: Fortress Press, 2007), 810.

27 Translation from Shawn J. Wilhite, *The Didache: A Commentary* (Eugene, OR: Cascade Books, 2019), xxxvii.

28 Ibid., 18–22.

likely the material that the baptismal candidate would have recited.[29] In addition to the catechismal recitation, the *Didache* instructs the candidate to "fast beforehand for one or two days." These details assume we are talking about someone who is volitionally involved in exercising his faith through baptism.

Still, it is possible for one to raise the objection that the *Didache* could have only adult converts in mind. However, it is, in the words of Jewett, "highly implausible" that the *Didache*, with all of its concern for church function, would be produced by a community of early paedobaptists "who just happen to say nothing" about the procedures of infant baptism.[30]

Epistle of Barnabas, 11:8, 11

> Ye perceive how He pointed out the water and the cross at the same time. For this is the meaning; Blessed are they that set their hope on the cross, and go down into the water.... This He saith, because we go down into the water laden with sins and filth, and rise up from it bearing fruit in the heart, resting our fear and hope on Jesus in the spirit. *And whosoever shall eat of these shall live for ever;* He meaneth this; whosoever, saith He, shall hear these things spoken and shall believe, shall live for ever.[31]

The *Epistle of Barnabas* is another well-known Christian work from the end of the first century or the beginning of the second century.[32] Although *Barnabas* is most well-known for its allegorical and typological interpretations, it also makes a brief foray into the subject of baptism. *Barnabas* notes that those who "set their hope on the cross" also "go down into the water." He also concludes that these individuals "hear these things" and "believe," securing their eternal life. Thus, we have another testimony of the early church linking volitional belief and baptism.

---

29 Ibid., 166–69.

30 Paul K. Jewett, *Infant Baptism and the Covenant of Grace: An Appraisal of the Argument That as Infants Were Once Circumcised, so They Should Now Be Baptized* (Eugene, OR: Wipf and Stock Publishers, 1999), 40–41.

31 Joseph Barber Lightfoot and J. R. Harmer, *The Apostolic Fathers* (London: Macmillan and Co., 1891), 280.

32 Treat notes, "Since Barnabas 16:3 refers to the destruction of the temple, Barnabas must be written after 70 c.e. It must be written before its first indisputable use in Clement of Alexandria, ca. 190. Since 16:4 expects the temple to be rebuilt, it was most likely written before Hadrian built a Roman temple on the site ca. 135" (Jay Curry Treat, "Barnabas, Epistle Of," in *The Anchor Yale Bible Dictionary*, vol. 1, ed. David Noel Freedman [New York: Doubleday, 1992], 613).

Aristides, *The Apology of Aristides*, 15

> Further, if one or other of them have bondmen and bondwomen or children, through love towards them they persuade them to become Christians, and when they have done so, they call them brethren without distinction.[33]

Aristides was an early Christian apologist who wrote from Athens. He defended and explained Christianity to Emperor Hadrian around 124 AD.[34] In his lengthy explanation of who the Christians are, Artistides notes how Christians persuade their servants and children to become Christians. Although he does not mention baptism in this text, it is appropriate to include since Aristides explains the relationship between Christians and their children. Aristides says that, in the Christian community, Christians seek to persuade their slaves and their children to become Christians.

The fact that Aristides explicitly says that Christians seek to persuade bondmen, bondwomen, and children is a soft argument for believer's baptism. Only after a slave or a child was persuaded to become a Christian were they then embraced as "brethren without distinction." Before that time, the slaves and children were presumably *not* treated as brethren.

Aristides does not provide direct evidence of a link between faith and baptism. Nevertheless, this text shows that the Christian community expected children to exercise faith in Christ before they were considered "brethren without distinction." This is contrary to the practice of some Reformed paedobaptists who view children as full-fledged Christians from birth, even prior to a confession of faith.[35]

---

33 Aristides of Athens, "The Apology of Aristides," in *The Ante-Nicene Fathers*, vol. 9, *The Gospel of Peter, the Diatessaron of Tatian, the Apocalypse of Peter, the Visio Pauli, the Apocalypses of the Virgil and Sedrach, the Testament of Abraham, the Acts of Xanthippe and Polyxena, the Narrative of Zosimus, the Apology of Aristides, the Epistles of Clement (Complete Text), Origen's Commentary on John, Books I–X, and Commentary on Matthew, Books I, II, and X–XIV*, ed. Allan Menzies, trans. D. M. Kay (New York: Christian Literature Company, 1897), 277.

34 Robert M. Grant, "Aristides," in *The Anchor Yale Bible Dictionary*, vol. 1, ed. David Noel Freedman, (New York: Doubleday, 1992), 382.

35 For example, Sproul writes, "But our assumption, based on the covenant promises of God, is that the child is in, all the way in, until he or she gives contrary evidence and is eventually excommunicated" (R. C. Sproul Jr., "In Jesus' Name, Amen," in *The Case for Covenantal Infant Baptism*, ed. Gregg Strawbridge [Phillipsburg, NJ: P&R Publishing, 2003], 307–8). We will discuss this kind of view in more detail in chapter six.

Justin Martyr, 1st Apology, LXI

> As many as are persuaded and believe that what we teach and say is true, and undertake to be able to live accordingly, are instructed to pray and to entreat God with fasting, for the remission of their sins that are past, we praying and fasting with them. Then they are brought by us where there is water, and are regenerated in the same manner in which we were ourselves regenerated.[36]

Justin Martyr is one of the most well-known second century church fathers. Justin was likely the most significant apologist for Christianity in the second century until his death around 165 AD.[37] In his explanation about baptism, after individuals are persuaded and come to believe the truth, Justin instructs them to pray and fast, after which time they are brought to the waters of baptism. Clearly faith and baptism are related in Justin's defense of baptism. We also observe again the early church practice of catechizing individuals *before* baptism (cf. *Didache* 7:1).

Tertullian, On Repentance, VI

> That *baptismal* washing is a sealing of faith, which faith is begun and is commended by the faith of repentance. We are not washed *in order that* we *may* cease sinning, but *because* we *have* ceased, since in *heart* we have *been* bathed already.[38]

Tertullian (ca. 160–225 AD) has been called the father of Latin Theology and wrote prolifically in the Latin language on many theological subjects. As is clear from the above quote, Tertullian clearly emphasizes a strong connection between faith and baptism. He even goes so far as to describe baptism as the "sealing of faith." He also links baptism with the "faith of repentance."

Tertullian is best known in baptism debates because he is regarded as the first undisputed evidence that infant baptism was being practiced in the

36 Justin Martyr, "The First Apology of Justin," in *The Ante-Nicene Fathers*, vol. 1, *The Apostolic Fathers with Justin Martyr and Irenaeus*, ed. Alexander Roberts, James Donaldson, and A. Cleveland Coxe (Buffalo, NY: Christian Literature Company, 1885), 183.

37 Robert M. Grant, "Justin Martyr," in *The Anchor Yale Bible Dictionary*, vol. 3, ed. David Noel Freedman (New York: Doubleday, 1992), 1133–34.

38 Tertullian, "On Repentance," in *The Ante-Nicene Fathers,* vol. 3, *Latin Christianity: Its Founder, Tertullian,* ed. Alexander Roberts, James Donaldson, and A. Cleveland Coxe, trans. S. Thelwall (Buffalo, NY: Christian Literature Company, 1885), 662.

early third century.[39] In his extensive treatise on baptism, which he wrote between 200 and 206 AD,[40] Tertullian acknowledged the practice of infant baptism, but argued that it was preferable to wait to baptize children until they "know how to 'ask' for salvation." He writes:

> And so, according to the circumstances and disposition, and even age, of each individual, the delay of baptism is preferable; principally, however, in the case of little children.... Let them "come," then, while they are growing up; let them "come" while they are learning, while they are learning whither to come; let them become Christians when they have become able to know Christ.... Let them know how to "ask" for salvation, that you may seem (at least) to have given "to him that asketh." ... If any understand the weighty import of baptism, they will fear its reception more than its delay: sound faith is secure of salvation.[41]

In this passage Tertullian argues that it is preferable to delay baptism until the candidate understands the "weighty import of baptism." Tertullian goes on to argue, "sound faith is secure of salvation." Although some implications of Tertullian's statements can be debated, the main point is obvious. In the words of Jewett, "Tertullian's fundamental point is clear enough: it is better to wait until one is ready to live what he professes in baptism than to repudiate that profession by subsequent wickedness of life."[42] So, although Tertullian acknowledges some churches practicing infant baptism, he preferred to connect a "sound faith" with the process of baptism.

Cyprian, Epistle LXXV (§12)

> In the sacraments of salvation, when necessity compels, and God bestows His mercy, the divine methods confer the whole benefit on believers; nor ought it to trouble any one that sick people seem to be sprinkled or affused, when they obtain the Lord's grace.... Whence it appears that the sprinkling also of water prevails equally with the washing of salvation; and that when this is done in

39 Peter J. Leithart, "Infant Baptism in History: An Unfinished Tragicomedy," in *The Case for Covenantal Infant Baptism*, ed. Gregg Strawbridge (Phillipsburg, NJ: P&R Publishing, 2003), 246.

40 Jewett, *Infant Baptism and the Covenant of Grace*, 20.

41 Tertullian, "On Baptism," in *The Ante-Nicene Fathers*, vol. 3, *Latin Christianity: Its Founder, Tertullian*, ed. Alexander Roberts, James Donaldson, and A. Cleveland Coxe, trans. S. Thelwall (Buffalo, NY: Christian Literature Company, 1885), 678.

42 Jewett, *Infant Baptism and the Covenant of Grace*, 22.

> the Church, where the faith both of receiver and giver is sound, all things hold and may be consummated and perfected by the majesty of the Lord and by the truth of faith.[43]

Cyprian of Carthage (200–258 AD) overlapped with Tertullian. They were even from the same city! Cyprian undoubtedly supported the practice of infant baptism. Around 251 or 253 AD, Cyprian was involved with a church council that discussed whether infant baptism should be delayed until the eighth day.[44] One wonders why, if infant baptism was the regular practice of the church since its inception, the church in the third century still had not answered the basic question of when an infant should be baptized. Regardless, it is enough to note that Cyprian gives his answer to Fidus in *Epistle LVIII*, showing clear support for the baptism of infants.

For our purposes, we note that in the above quote (*Epistle LXXV*) Cyprian argues that faith of both the candidate for baptism *and* the one who baptizes is important. For example, in the previous section (§11) he notes, "But if heretics and schismatics baptized without have not the Holy Spirit, and therefore hands are imposed on them among us, that *here* may be received what *there* neither is nor can be given; it is plain, also, that remission of sins cannot be given by those who, it is certain, have not the Holy Spirit."[45] To summarize, Cyprian argues that if a heretic baptizes someone, that individual will not receive the Holy Spirit, nor the forgiveness of sins! That leads to Cyprian's statement a few lines later, that true baptism is, "where the faith both of receiver and giver is sound." Unfortunately, Cyprian does not describe how faith and infant baptism go together. However, Cyprian clearly believes faith is essentially related to baptism—both for the baptismal candidate and the one baptizing.

Basil, On the Holy Spirit, XII

> Faith and baptism are two kindred and inseparable ways of salvation: faith is perfected through baptism, baptism is established through faith, and both are completed by the same names. For as we believe in the Father and the Son and the Holy Ghost, so are we also baptized in the name of the Father and of the Son and

43 Cyprian of Carthage, "The Epistles of Cyprian," in *The Ante-Nicene Fathers*, vol. 5, *Fathers of the Third Century: Hippolytus, Cyprian, Novatian, Appendix*, ed. Alexander Roberts, James Donaldson, and A. Cleveland Coxe, trans. Robert Ernest Wallis (Buffalo, NY: Christian Literature Company, 1886), 401.

44 Jewett, *Infant Baptism and the Covenant of Grace*, 18.

45 Cyprian of Carthage, "The Epistles of Cyprian," 400.

> of the Holy Ghost: first comes the confession, introducing us to salvation, and baptism follows, setting the seal upon our assent.[46]

Basil, the first of the three major Cappadocian theologians (Basil, Gregory of Nyssa, and Gregory of Nazianzus), served as bishop of Caesarea from 370 to 379 AD. As the above quote illustrates, Basil strongly emphasized the connection between faith and baptism, calling them inseparable. Furthermore, Basil emphasized that a confession of faith was a prerequisite to baptism.

Gregory of Nyssa, On the Baptism of Christ: A Sermon for the Day of the Lights

> And we in receiving Baptism, in imitation of our Lord and Teacher and Guide, are not indeed buried in the earth (for this is the shelter of the body that is entirely dead, covering the infirmity and decay of our nature), but coming to the element akin to earth, to water, we conceal ourselves in that as the Saviour did in the earth: and by doing this thrice we represent for ourselves that grace of the Resurrection which was wrought in three days: and this we do, not receiving the sacrament in silence, but while there are spoken over us the Names of the Three Sacred Persons on Whom we believed, in Whom we also hope, from Whom comes to us both the fact of our present and the fact of our future existence.[47]

Gregory, brother of Basil, was bishop of Nyssa from 372 until his death (ca. 395 AD).[48] Baptists often cite Gregory as evidence that immersion was practiced in the early church because of his description of baptism being an imitation of being buried in the earth and concealed by the water "as the Saviour did in the earth."

Although we will discuss the mode of baptism in chapter seven, here I simply wish to observe that Gregory gave significant prominence to faith

46 Basil of Caesarea, "The Book of Saint Basil on the Spirit," in *A Select Library of the Nicene and Post-Nicene Fathers of the Christian Church, Second Series*, vol. 8, *St. Basil: Letters and Select Works*, ed. Philip Schaff and Henry Wace, trans. Blomfield Jackson (New York: Christian Literature Company, 1895), 18.

47 Gregory of Nyssa, "On the Baptism of Christ," in *A Select Library of the Nicene and Post-Nicene Fathers of the Christian Church, Second Series*, vol. 5, *Gregory of Nyssa: Dogmatic Treatises, Etc.*, ed. Philip Schaff and Henry Wace, trans. Henry Austin Wilson (New York: Christian Literature Company, 1893), 520.

48 Everett Ferguson, *Baptism in the Early Church: History, Theology, and Liturgy in the First Five Centuries* (Grand Rapids: Eerdmans, 2009), 603.

as a necessity for baptism. Besides his description quoted above, we read that those who are baptized have believed in the "Three Sacred Persons." In another of his writings, *The Great Catechism* (Ch XXXIII), Gregory stated that baptism required prayer, the invocation of heavenly grace, water, and faith.[49] We find a similar statement in his work, *Against Those Who Defer Baptism*, "Every place belongs to the Master, and all water is suitable for the use of baptism, if only it finds faith in the one receiving it and the blessing of the priest who sanctifies it."[50] For Gregory of Nyssa, it was like his brother Basil had said, "Faith and baptism are two kindred and inseparable ways of salvation."

Gregory of Nazianzus

Gregory of Nazianzus, friend of Basil, is the third of the Cappadocian fathers. He served a brief tenure as bishop of Constantinople (379–381 AD) and was largely in agreement theologically with Basil and Gregory of Nyssa. When encouraging others to embrace baptism, like his fellow Cappadocian leaders, he emphasized the confession of faith which precedes baptism: "Seize the opportunity; rejoice greatly in the blessing; and having spoken be baptized; and having been baptized be saved."[51]

At this point it is helpful to point out that each of the three major Cappadocian fathers emphasized faith in relationship to baptism. Ferguson notes that they each talk about sickbed baptisms and they each highlight the need to make a proclamation of faith before baptism.[52]

Few early church sources before Augustine deal with the potential problem of infant baptism and the relationship of faith. Gregory of Na-

---

49 Gregory of Nyssa, "The Great Catechism," in *A Select Library of the Nicene and Post-Nicene Fathers of the Christian Church, Second Series*, vol. 5, *Gregory of Nyssa: Dogmatic Treatises, Etc.*, ed. Philip Schaff and Henry Wace, trans. William Moore (New York: Christian Literature Company, 1893), 501.

50 Jacques-Paul Migne, ed., *Patrologia Graeca* [= *Patrologiae Cursus Completus*: Series Graeca] (Paris, 1863), 46:421D, cited in Ferguson, *Baptism in the Early Church*, 607.

51 Gregory Nazianzen, "Select Orations of Saint Gregory Nazianzen," in *A Select Library of the Nicene and Post-Nicene Fathers of the Christian Church, Second Series,* vol. 7, *S. Cyril of Jerusalem, S. Gregory Nazianzen*, ed. Philip Schaff and Henry Wace, trans. Charles Gordon Browne and James Edward Swallow (New York: Christian Literature Company, 1894), 369.

52 Ferguson writes, "All of these accounts of sickbed baptism emphasize the importance of the candidate being able to speak the words of faith. This emphasis accords with the summaries of the baptismal process given by each preacher: being taught, having faith in the heart, and receiving the seal of the Spirit (Basil); faith and baptism (the Nyssene); 'having spoken, be baptized; and being baptized, be saved' (Nazianzen)" (Everett Ferguson, "Exhortations to Baptism in the Cappadocians," in *The Early Church at Work and Worship, Volume 2: Catechesis, Baptism, Eschatology, and Martyrdom* [London: James Clarke, 2014], 105).

zianzus is one of those few exceptions. Regarding the infant baptism happening during his day, he advises the following:

> What have you to say about those who are still children, and conscious neither of the loss nor of the grace? Are we to baptize them too? Certainly, if any danger presses. For it is better that they should be unconsciously sanctified than that they should depart unsealed and uninitiated....
>
> But in respect of others [where there is no danger] I give my advice to wait till the end of the third year, or a little more or less, when they may be able to listen and to answer something about the Sacrament; that, even though they do not perfectly understand it, yet at any rate they may know the outlines; and then to sanctify them in soul and body with the great sacrament of our consecration. For this is how the matter stands; at that time they begin to be responsible for their lives, when reason is matured, and they learn the mystery of life (for of sins of ignorance owing to their tender years they have no account to give), and it is far more profitable on all accounts to be fortified by the Font, because of the sudden assaults of danger that befall us, stronger than our helpers.[53]

Like other early church sources, Gregory acknowledges the practice of infant baptism at the end of the fourth century. However, it seems noteworthy that Gregory teaches that it is best to wait to baptize children until they can understand the significance of baptism and "begin to be responsible for their lives." Gregory of Nazianzus seems to attempt some sort of balancing act by saying infant baptism is allowable, but that it should only be used in situations of danger (i.e., the child is about to die). Gregory prefers that children be able to confess their own faith at the time of their baptism.

Summary of the Early Church

Usually when interpreters analyze the historical evidence of the early church, it is in search of the first references to paedobaptism in order to find out whether infant baptism was the norm or the exception. Although such an endeavor is a worthwhile project,[54] I have focused this survey on

53 Gregory Nazianzen, "Select Orations of Saint Gregory Nazianzen," 370.

54 See, for example, Ferguson, *Baptism in the Early Church*, 199–816; Jewett, *Infant Baptism and the Covenant of Grace*, 13–45.

the early church teaching that baptism and faith were fundamentally related. The sources have shown that we can easily establish this point.

Some may sweep away the biblical and early church evidence by claiming most of these passages qualify as "missionary baptisms"—i.e., they are focused on the salvation of an individual from a non-Christian family. However, some of these passages, especially the texts from Tertullian and Gregory of Nazianzus, suggest waiting to baptize children so that the child may know what it is he is doing. In the words of Gregory, it is preferable that the children "may be able to listen and to answer something about the Sacrament." Similarly, one of the earliest testimonies we have of a Christian mindset is that of *Aristides*, who mentions that it was a common practice for early Christians to persuade their children to become Christians prior to welcoming them as brethren.

As the previous material illustrates, both the New Testament and the early church clearly testify that faith was central to the baptismal process. However, apparently because of the prevalence of infant baptism from at least the third century on, theologians sensed the need to talk about the relationship between faith and paedobaptism. Thus, we find a full discussion of this issue during the fifth century in the writings of Augustine.

Augustine and the Medieval Catholic Church

Augustine is perhaps the most well-known church theologian of all time. It is difficult to overstate the effect of Augustine on theology and western thought. Augustine made vast contributions on the issues of election, predestination, free will, and a myriad of other subjects. The question of how faith and infant baptism relate was also an issue that Augustine deemed important enough to address.

In his writings on baptism, after explaining that baptism belongs to those who repent of their sins, Augustine addresses the obvious problem of *what* infants are repenting *from*. He writes, "Now, inasmuch as infants are not held bound by any sins of their own actual life, it is the guilt of original sin which is healed in them by the grace of Him who saves them by the laver of regeneration."[55] So, for Augustine, although infants have committed no sin, they must repent of original sin that was passed down through

55 Augustine of Hippo, "A Treatise on the Merits and Forgiveness of Sins, and on the Baptism of Infants," in *A Select Library of the Nicene and Post-Nicene Fathers of the Christian Church, First Series*, vol. 5, *Saint Augustin: Anti-Pelagian Writings*, ed. Philip Schaff, trans. Peter Holmes (New York: Christian Literature Company, 1887), 24.

Adam. By being baptized, the infant secures justification in the presence of God. Augustine states it this way:

> If, however, the infant departs from the present life after he has received baptism, the guilt in which he was involved by original sin being done away, he shall be made perfect in that light of truth, which, remaining unchangeable for evermore, illumines the justified in the presence of their Creator. For sins alone separate between men and God; and these are done away by Christ's grace, through whom, as Mediator, we are reconciled, when He justifies the ungodly.[56]

Obviously, someone could raise the objection that it is not really repentance if infants have no volitional ability to confess and forsake sin on their own. To this Augustine replies:

> Some one will say: How then are mere infants called to repentance? How can such as they repent of anything? The answer to this is: If they must not be called penitents because they have not the sense of repenting, neither must they be called believers, because they likewise have not the sense of believing. But if they are rightly called believers, because they in a certain sense profess faith by the words of their parents, why are they not also held to be before that penitents when they are shown to renounce the devil and this world by the profession again of the same parents?[57]

We must take careful note of Augustine's point here. His argument presumes the necessity of belief and repentance in baptism. But, since the child is incapable, Augustine argues that the parent's words of faith and penitence are attributed to the child. Theologically, this phenomenon is called *fides aliena*, the faith of others (or, an alien faith). Elsewhere Augustine clarified that this concept only applied to infants and not to others who could confess their own faith.

> Therefore, when others take the vows for [infants], that the celebration of the sacrament may be complete in their behalf, it is unquestionably of avail for their dedication to God, because they cannot answer for themselves. But if another were to answer for one who could answer for himself, it would not be of the same avail. In accordance with which rule, we find in the gospel what

56 Ibid.

57 Ibid.

> strikes every one as natural when he reads it, "He is of age, he shall speak for himself."[58]

Unsurprisingly, the concept of *fides aliena* prompted some significant debate among theologians. Although *fides aliena* solves the problem of how infant baptism relates to faith, numerous other difficulties arise because of this view. For example, who is it that believes on behalf of the infant?

> If *fides aliena* solves the problem of the infant's lack of faith, it opens up a new question: who actually does the believing? The early scholastics reckoned with the possibility that parents or sponsors may not really believe. In this case, the act of believing devolves upon the church as a whole, as Augustine had said.[59] But what if the entire church was in error? Then, said the early scholastics, it is the faith of the *ecclesia triumphans*, the church already in heaven, that suffices. But the church triumphant does not need faith; how can it "believe"? Answer: its faith is on deposit in the treasury of merits. So the theologians spun out the strands that came from the Pandora's box that Augustine had opened.[60]

The problematic theological consequences of Augustine's *fides aliena* led to an alternative viewpoint, called *fides infusa baptisme*, a special "virtue or power infused by baptism."[61] Continuing with the attempt to resolve the connection of faith and infant baptism, medieval thinkers like Peter Lombard proposed the idea that the church conferred faith on the infant through the act of baptism.[62] This viewpoint found significant support among theologians. Thomas Aquinas, the great medieval theologian,

---

58 Augustine of Hippo, "On Baptism, against the Donatists," in *A Select Library of the Nicene and Post-Nicene Fathers of the Christian Church, First Series*, vol. 4, *St. Augustin: The Writings against the Manichaeans and against the Donatists*, ed. Philip Schaff, trans. J. R. King (Buffalo, NY: Christian Literature Company, 1887), 462.

59 "And that this takes place in the case of infants, through the sacrament of baptism, is not doubted by mother Church, which uses for them the heart and mouth of a mother, that they may be imbued with the sacred mysteries, seeing that they cannot as yet with their own heart 'believe unto righteousness,' nor with their own mouth make 'confession unto salvation'" (Augustine of Hippo, "A Treatise on the Merits and Forgiveness of Sins, and on the Baptism of Infants," 30).

60 Jonathan H. Rainbow, "'Confessor Baptism': The Baptismal Doctrine of the Early Anabaptists," in *Believer's Baptism: Sign of the New Covenant in Christ*, ed. Thomas R. Schreiner and Shawn D. Wright, NAC Studies in Bible & Theology (Nashville, TN: B & H Academic, 2006), 191.

61 Ibid.

62 Ibid. Rainbow cites A. M. Landgraf, *Dogmengeschichte der Frühscholastik, Dritter Teil: Die Lehre von den Sakramenten* (Regensburg: Verlag Friedrich Pustet, 1954), 323, as a scholar

seemed to support this viewpoint. In his *Summa Theologiae*, Aquinas argued that "children believe, not by their own act, but by the faith of the Church, which is applied to them: by the power of which faith, grace and virtues are bestowed on them" (*Summa Theologiae*, Q 69, A 6).

Although *fides infusa* became a popular view in the Catholic Church, like its predecessor *fides aliena* it suffered from problems. The most obvious problem of *fides infusa* was that "faith cannot be both the prerequisite for baptism and the gift bestowed by baptism."[63]

It is not my goal to fully evaluate the development of *fides aliena* or *fides infusa* here. Rather, my goal is to make the simple point that, from Augustine through the medieval period, the prevailing opinion was that faith somehow related to baptism. Even in infant baptism, theologians embraced the idea that faith was integral to the baptism process.

Although theologians could easily account for the exercise of volitional faith prior to baptism in adult converts, they heavily debated the relationship between faith and infant baptism. This debate led to two prevailing views—neither of which denied the relationship between faith and baptism, but only tried to make sense of it. It was into the world of *fides aliena* and *fides infusa* that Martin Luther was born. Luther added another viewpoint of how faith and infant baptism could relate.

Luther and Individual Faith[64]

Martin Luther (1483–1546) is one of the most well-known figures of the Reformation. Importantly, he pointed out the theological deviation of the Roman Catholic Church and helped get the Bible into the hands of the German-speaking people. Although Luther broke away from the Roman Catholic Church in many key areas (one such area being justification by faith alone),[65] he largely embraced Rome's view of infant baptism.[66] How-

---

who claims *fides infusa* was the "distinctive contribution" of scholastic thought concerning the relationship between faith and baptism.

63 Ibid.

64 Much of the information on Luther's early life was brought to my attention by Rainbow, "'Confessor Baptism,'" 192–94.

65 For an interesting analysis of how Luther's view of baptism seems to compromise his doctrine of *sola fide*, see D. Patrick Ramsey, "Sola Fide Compromised? Martin Luther and the Doctrine of Baptism," *Themelios* 34, no. 2 (2009): 179–93.

66 Some have argued that Luther's similarity to Rome on the issue of baptism being a work of regeneration conflicts with his emphasis on justification by faith alone. For example, see Ramsey, "Sola Fide Compromised?," 179–93.

ever, one of the major differences in Luther's view of baptism, including infant baptism, was the key ingredient of individual faith—at least initially.

In 1520, Luther spoke adamantly about the connection between faith and baptism. He noted, "For unless faith is present or is conferred in baptism, baptism will profit us nothing."[67] The belief that faith was a volitional expression of the individual in baptism was essential to Luther's theology of baptism. Thus, in contrast to the traditional *fides aliena* or *fides infusa* position, Luther argued for *fides propria*, the necessity of one's own expression of faith. The need for individual and personal faith was one of the most significant themes in Luther's theology and extended beyond baptism to apply to other areas, including the mass.[68]

Luther saw no problem with *fides infantium*, an infant having his own faith. In the early 1520s, Luther wrote in defense of infant baptism with the concrete statement, "The infants themselves believe in baptism, and have their own faith."[69] In defending this idea to the Bohemian Brethren, Luther pointed to the baptismal liturgy, where the minister asks whether the infant believes. In the liturgy, the sponsor answers in the affirmative, and Luther points out that if the child doesn't believe, then the answer would be a lie.[70] Thus, for Luther it was important to acknowledge that the child really is expressing faith at the time of baptism. Although individual faith for the infant was essential to Luther initially, things changed when he began to argue with the Anabaptists.

Luther and the Anabaptist Movement

The Reformation cry of *ad fontes* (to the sources) sparked a renewed assessment of traditional doctrines through the lens of *sola scriptura* (scripture alone). The doctrines of salvation, the papacy, indulgences, and the mass all received critical evaluation through the lens of Scripture. But it did not

---

67 Martin Luther, "The Babylonian Captivity of the Church, 1520," in *Luther's Works: Volume 36 Word and Sacrament II*, trans. A. T. W. Steinhäuser, Frederick C. Ahrens, and Abdel Ross Wentz (Philadelphia, PA: Fortress Press, 1959), 59. Luther later writes, "For the power of baptism depends not so much on the faith or use of the one who confers it as on the faith or use of the one who receives it" (Luther, "The Babylonian Captivity of the Church, 1520," 64).

68 Luther writes, "No one can observe or hear mass for another, but each one for himself alone" (Martin Luther, "A Treatise on the New Testament, That Is, the Holy Mass, 1520," in *Luther's Works: Volume 35 Word and Sacrament I*, trans. Jeremiah J. Schindel and E. Theodore Bachmann [Philadelphia, PA: Fortress Press, 1960], 94).

69 Quoted in Karl Brinkel, *Die Lehre Luthers von der fides infantium bei der Kindertaufe* (Berlin: Evangelische Verlagsanstatt, 1958), 41. *Die kinder ynn der tauffe selb glauben und eygen glauben haben.*

70 Brinkel, *Die Lehre Luthers*, 44. *Darumb mus es auch selbs gleuben, oder die paten mussen liegen, wenn sie sagen an seyner stat, "Ich gleube."*

stop there. Those who were referred to by their detractors as the Anabaptists critically evaluated paedobaptism as a non-biblical practice. Unsurprisingly, one of the chief arguments they used was that faith was linked with baptism in Scripture; thus, how could an infant exercise faith?

It is difficult to understate the disdain with which Luther and other Reformers viewed the Anabaptists.[71] The Reformers viewed the Anabaptists as troublemakers who were impeding God's work in the church. But because the Anabaptists were using arguments that persuaded many Christians, they needed to be addressed.

In 1528, Luther took up the challenge to defend paedobaptism against the Anabaptists. In defending paedobaptism against the Anabaptists, Luther argued differently than he had in the early 1520s.[72] Although Luther had argued earlier that faith had an essential place in baptism, when writing against the Anabaptists, Luther notes, "Whoever bases baptism on the faith of the one to be baptized can never baptize anyone."[73] A little while later, Luther also says, "Since there is no difference in baptism whether lack of faith precedes or follows, baptism doesn't depend on faith."[74] And perhaps most shocking of all, Luther writes, "Even if they could establish that children are without faith when they are baptized, it would make no difference to me."[75]

It is difficult to say whether Luther's baptismal theology changed dramatically or he simply was overemphasizing a point in his rhetoric against the Anabaptists.[76] If he was claiming faith had no relationship to baptism, then he would not only be undergoing a massive change of personal theology but also departing from the historic position of the church, including the teaching of theological giants like Augustine and Aquinas. In any case, Luther's writing on faith and baptism changed because of pressure from the Anabaptists. They forced him to address the issue of faith and baptism concerning infants, and signs of inconsistency began to show in his

---

71 For example, see Larry D. Pettegrew, "Israel and the Dark Side of the Reformation," in *Forsaking Israel: How It Happened and Why It Matters*, 2nd ed. (The Woodlands, TX: Kress Biblical Resources, 2021), 75–106; Leonard Verduin, *The Reformers and Their Stepchildren* (Grand Rapids: Eerdmans, 1964).

72 Rainbow, "'Confessor Baptism,'" 195.

73 Martin Luther, "Concerning Rebaptism, 1528," in *Luther's Works: Volume 40 Church and Ministry II*, trans. Conrad Bergendoff (Philadelphia, PA: Fortress Press, 1958), 240.

74 Ibid., 248.

75 Ibid., 246.

76 Rainbow assumes that "Concerning Rebaptism" was "not a substantial shift" in Luther's baptismal theology, but rather simply a less-than-careful response to the Anabaptist movement (Rainbow, "'Confessor Baptism,'" 196).

arguments. Luther was not the only Reformer who had to deal with this Anabaptist argument.

Ulrich Zwingli and the Separation of Faith and Baptism

The conflict that Luther experienced in Germany with the Anabaptists also existed elsewhere. In Zurich, Ulrich Zwingli apparently started out as an ally of the Anabaptist movement, rejecting infant baptism.[77] Early on in his ministry, Zwingli noted his distaste for practicing infant baptism: "Nothing grieves me more than that at the present I have to baptize children, for I know it ought not to be done."[78] Elsewhere, Zwingli writes, "I leave baptism untouched, I call it neither right nor wrong; if we were to baptize as Christ instituted it then we would not baptize any person until he has reached the years of discretion; for I find it nowhere written that infant baptism is to be practiced...."[79]

If Zwingli was convinced infant baptism was unbiblical, why did he continue to support it? In one place, Zwingli appears to note concern over losing his stipend. He writes, "If however I were to terminate the practice then I fear that I would lose my prebend [stipend]."[80] Elsewhere he notes, "But on account of the possibility of offence I omit preaching this; it is better not to preach it until the world is ready to take it."[81] According to Blaurock, a contemporary of Zwingli, one reason Zwingli did not continue to support the Anabaptist view was because he did not want an uprising to break out among the people.[82]

---

77 Pettegrew, "Israel and the Dark Side of the Reformation," 82. Rainbow cites the personal testimony of Balthasar Hubmaier, "Ein Gespräch (1526)," in *Quellen zur Geschichte der Täufer* (Gütersloh, Germany: Gerd Mohn, 1962), 9:186. Hubmaier claimed that on May 1, 1523, Zwingli and Hubmaier stood together in Zurich and agreed that the practice of infant baptism should be discontinued (Rainbow, "'Confessor Baptism,'" 189).

78 Leonard von Muralt and Walter Schmid, *Quellen zur Geschichte der Täufer in der Schweiz, I Band* (Zürich: S. Hirzel, 1952), 184ff, cited in Verduin, *The Reformers and Their Stepchildren*, 198.

79 Cited in Verduin, *The Reformers and Their Stepchildren*, 199. Verduin's work, *The Reformers and Their Stepchildren*, is largely the product of Verduin's time spent in Europe in 1950. He examined many of Zwingli's writings which have not been translated into English. He has provided many of his own translations, and sometimes does not cite where he obtained Zwingli's quote.

80 Ibid.

81 Ibid.

82 George Blaurock, "The Beginnings of the Anabaptist Reformation Reminiscences of George Blaurock," in *Spiritual and Anabaptist Writers*, ed. George H. Williams and Angel M. Mergal (Philadelphia, PA: Westminster Press, 1957), 43. Verduin notes, "It is quite apparent that what restrained Zwingli from introducing believers' baptism was the consideration that

The evidence seems to indicate that Zwingli entertained the Anabaptist position initially, but later abandoned it. Balthasar Hubmaier, a man who once held a friendship with Zwingli before being shunned because of his Anabaptist views, writes to Zwingli, "You used to hold to the same ideas, wrote and preached them from the pulpit openly; many hundreds of people have heard it from your mouth."[83] Although the Anabaptists once counted Zwingli as a friend and ally, he ultimately became one of their staunchest opponents.[84]

Zwingli and the Formulation of Covenant Theology

Theologians have historically viewed Zwingli as the founder of Reformed covenant theology.[85] It was primarily in response to the Anabaptists that Zwingli formulated his covenant theology so clearly.[86] Interestingly enough, when Zwingli first wrote in defense of infant baptism, he avoided referring to covenant theology or to the continuity between the testaments.[87] However, the increased pressure from the Anabaptists compelled Zwingli to use new argumentation. In so doing, Zwingli departed from the normal paedobaptist arguments and embraced a different kind of argumentation. Zwingli himself realized he was employing a new understanding of baptism. He writes:

> In this matter of baptism—if I may be pardoned for saying it—I can only conclude that all the doctors have been in error from the time of the apostles. This is a serious and weighty assertion,

---

such a baptism would tend to divide society—the one thing that men of sacralist conviction cannot allow" (Verduin, *The Reformers and Their Stepchildren*, 200).

83 Balthasar Hubmaier, *Quellen zur Geschichte der Täufer, IX Band, Balthasar Hubmaiers Schriften von Westin-Gergsten* (Gütersloh, Germany: Gerd Mohn, 1962), 186, cited in Verduin, *The Reformers and Their Stepchildren*, 200. Zwingli doesn't seem to deny these statements. Rather, Zwingli affirms that he had once thought baptism should not be given to infants. He writes, "After it had been rashly accepted that the sign testifies to the faith then men had to assail infant baptism. For, how could baptism testify to the faith in the case of little children, seeing they cannot believe. This error had misled also me some years ago and made me think it were better not to baptize little ones until they had grown up" (Ulrich Zwingli, *Corpus Reformatorum*, 91:241, cited in Verduin, *The Reformers and Their Stepchildren*, 201).

84 Pettegrew, "Israel and the Dark Side of the Reformation," 83.

85 Ibid., 80; Lyle D. Bierma, *German Calvinism in the Confessional Age: The Covenant Theology of Caspar Olevianus* (Grand Rapids: Baker, 1996), 31.

86 Lillback writes, "It must be admitted, then, that the struggle with the Anabaptists did cause the Reformed to begin to use the covenant concept of unity of Old and New Testament to bolster their argument for infant baptism" (Peter A. Lillback, *The Binding of God: Calvin's Role in the Development of Covenant Theology* [Grand Rapids: Baker Academic, 2001], 95).

87 Ibid., 89.

> and I make it with such reluctance that had I not been compelled to do so by contentious spirits, I would have preferred to keep silence.... At many points we shall have to read a different path from that taken either by ancient or more modern writers or by our own contemporaries.[88]

What was this new form of argumentation—argumentation which took a different path from ancient or modern writers? It was the divorce between the material and the spiritual. Specifically, in the case of baptism, baptism (as the material, external) was separated from faith (as the spiritual, internal).[89] Zwingli regularly took passages that spoke of baptism and argued that they were referring to Spirit baptism, not water baptism.[90] Faith could relate to Spirit baptism, but not to water baptism. In an unprecedented turn, "Zwingli did what nobody had yet done: he severed baptism from faith."[91]

Zwingli argued that both papists and Anabaptists put too much emphasis on baptism, which he viewed as a mere external rite.[92] In order to account for biblical passages which linked faith and baptism, Zwingli would often interpret the reference to baptism as a figurative saying that was symbolic of faith.[93] Rainbow remarks:

> What Zwingli achieved was a marvelously clever and persuasive way to reject the suspicious devices of previous paedobaptist argumentation, *fides aliena*, *fides infusa*, *fides infantium*, and the like, and at the same time to maintain infant baptism against the Anabaptists. But this solution had as its price the integrity of Zwingli's exegesis of the baptismal passages of the NT and the very signif-

88 Ulrich Zwingli, *Of Baptism*, in *Zwingli and Bullinger*, Library of Christian Classics, vol. 24, trans. G. W. Bromiley (Philadelphia, PA: Westminster, 1953), 130.

89 Jeffrey D. Johnson, *The Fatal Flaw of the Theology Behind Infant Baptism* (Conway, AR: Free Grace Press, 2010), 11–12.

90 As an example, paedobaptist Fesko notes that Zwingli argued Romans 6:1–4 was not talking about water baptism, but the internal baptism of the Spirit (J. V. Fesko, *Word, Water, and Spirit: A Reformed Perspective on Baptism* [Grand Rapids: Reformation Heritage Books, 2010], 61). See Ulrich Zwingli, "Friendly Exegesis (1527)," in *Huldrych Zwingli: Writings*, ed. E. J Furcha and H. Wayne Pipkin (Allison Park, PA: Pickwick, 1984), 2.292.

91 Rainbow, "'Confessor Baptism,'" 197.

92 Ibid., 198.

93 Ulrich Zwingli, *Antwort über Balthasar Hubmaiers Taufüchlein*, in *Huldreich Zwinglis Sämtliche Werke*, ed. Emil Egli et al. (Leipzig: Verlag von Heinsius Nachfolger, 1927), 4:619.

> icance of baptism itself. For if baptism is a mere external thing, disconnected from salvation, why practice it at all?[94]

Once Zwingli had divorced faith from baptism, he then employed a revolutionary argument for paedobaptism against the Anabaptists.[95] He argued for a unified covenant between the Old and New Testaments. Children were granted entrance into this covenant through circumcision in the Old Testament and baptism in the New Testament. Although quite revolutionary at that time, this belief in a unified covenant has become the dominant argument for paedobaptism in Reformed churches today. Consequently, the connection between faith and baptism has been severely strained in Reformed churches, and in many cases completely separated. We will discuss the Reformed paedobaptist arguments for a unified covenant in chapter three. But at this point, we have raised the foundational question: what is the relationship between faith and baptism?

The Decision Which Must Be Made: How Does Faith Relate to Baptism?

If faith is integral to baptism, then there is a significant dilemma for the paedobaptist position. This is because the biblical picture of faith includes volitional confession and a change of lifestyle. In Douglas Campbell's definitive study on faith in Paul's writings, he writes, "Whatever else scholars think that faith in Paul was, all agree it had an overt confessional dimension."[96] However, although the confessional element is essential, it is not the only element of faith. Faith is not to be viewed as merely an entry criterion, but as a way of life for the believer.[97] After examining some of the key texts on faith in Paul, Campbell summarizes:

> We learn from all this then that Christian faith, in the context of the community and the various forms of nurturing activity present within it, is intimately connected to, if it is not identical with, Christian knowing or thinking.... Christian believing is for Paul

94 Rainbow, "'Confessor Baptism,'" 199.

95 Lillback, *The Binding of God*, 95.

96 Douglas A. Campbell, "Participation and Faith in Paul," in "*In Christ*" *in Paul: Explorations in Paul's Theology of Union and Participation*, ed. Michael J. Thate, Kevin J. Vanhoozer, and Constantine R. Campbell, Wissenschaftliche Untersuchungen zum Neuen Testament 2. Reihe 384 (Tübingen, Germany: Mohr Siebeck, 2014), 37.

97 This is not simply a Baptist point. As an example of paedobaptist agreement with this, see Brownson, *The Promise of Baptism*, 85–87.

> apparently both comprehensive and ethical, and even emotional; it is an entire mind or mentality.[98]

In other words, the biblical picture of faith is not just something to be believed. It is a mindset or worldview. Faith carries with it a commitment to do good works. In the simple, yet profound theology of James, faith without works is dead (James 2:17). If faith is integral to baptism—which seems to be the foundational New Testament position, as well as the majority position held throughout most of church history—this is a significant predicament for any paedobaptist position, since infants are incapable of committing to anything. Thus, when addressing the relationship between faith and baptism, there are essentially five options that a paedobaptist can choose from.[99]

First, one could reject the connection between faith and baptism. Ironically, Reformed traditions that have historically emphasized the need for justification by faith are the ones that occasionally reject the connection between faith and baptism, even though their historic confessions have acknowledged that connection. For example, the *Canons of Dort* note, "We, therefore, by being baptized, do confess our faith, and are bound to give unto God obedience, mortification of the flesh, and newness of life."[100] Or, again, the *Anglican Catechism* frames it this way:

> *Ques.* What is required of persons to be baptized?
>
> *Ans.* Repentance, whereby they forsake sin; and Faith, whereby they steadfastly believe the promises of God made to them in that Sacrament.[101]

Second, one could hold to *fides aliena*, a vicarious faith. Although a popular position because of Roman Catholic influence, Reformed paedobaptists have been hesitant to embrace such a position for a variety of good, biblical reasons. Believing that one fallible human can vicariously

98 Campbell, "Participation and Faith in Paul," 43–44.

99 I have summarized the major options, although I acknowledge there are other viewpoints that subdivide some of these categories. For example, Johnson organizes the different paedobaptist viewpoints into eight categories: (1) *Fides Aliena*; (2) *Fides Infusa*; (3) *Fides Infantium*; (4) *Sacramental Symbolism*; (5) *Pre-credobaptism*; (6) *Presumptive Regeneration*; (7) *Baptismal Regeneration*; (8) *Paedofaith*. For a full explanation and summary of these positions, see Johnson, *The Fatal Flaw*, 4–19.

100 Philip Schaff, *The Creeds of Christendom, with a History and Critical Notes: The Evangelical Protestant Creeds, with Translations* (New York: Harper & Brothers, 1882), 890.

101 Ibid., 521.

stand in the place of another's faith is fraught with theological danger. Although Augustine taught that this could only happen with infants, if there is no biblical evidence either way for vicarious faith, why stop at infants? The Roman Catholic Church certainly did not.

Third, one could hold to a *fides infusa* position, the belief that faith is given at the point of baptism. This is an unattractive position since the New Testament predominantly treats faith as a prerequisite to baptism. It is difficult to argue that faith results *from* baptism, while also being the prerequisite *for* baptism.

Fourth, one could hold to *fides propria* or *fides infantium*, the viewpoint that infants themselves somehow believe. This is the standard position of the Lutheran Church. Of course, it is difficult to see how infants could exercise a life-changing volitional commitment to God. Usually, the principal argument for this view is that faith is a gift of God, so God could give faith to an infant. While faith is certainly a gift from God (cf. Eph 2:8–9), faith is *also* clearly a volitional belief that facilitates action. Faith and commitment go hand in hand, so it is difficult to see how infants could demonstrate an intentional, volitional commitment to Christ.

Finally, one could view the baptism of adults as a different kind of baptism than that of infants. Or perhaps, as some would claim, it is the same baptism, just a different application. Whereas adults are baptized on the profession of faith, infants are baptized on the possibility of a future faith. This is, in my mind, the most preferable option for the Reformed paedobaptist. Calvin seems to prefer this option. He notes:

> We firmly deny that such ought to be baptized unless their conversion and faith have been observed, at least, so far as men can judge. *But it is perfectly clear that infants ought to be put in another category*, for in ancient times if anyone joined himself in religious fellowship with Israel, he had to be taught the Lord's covenant and instructed in the law before he could be marked with circumcision, because he was of foreign nationality, that is, alien to the people of Israel, with whom the covenant, which circumcision sanctioned, had been made.[102]

For Calvin, there is a categorical difference between infant baptism and adult baptism. In his understanding, adult baptism symbolizes present

102 John Calvin, *Institutes of the Christian Religion*, ed. John T. McNeill, trans. Ford Lewis Battles, The Library of Christian Classics 1 (Louisville, KY: Westminster John Knox Press, 2011), 1346. Emphasis added.

faith, repentance and union with Christ; while "infants are baptized into future repentance and faith."[103]

In general, paedobaptist proponents argue against the idea of different kinds of baptisms. For example, John Murray notes that baptism, "has one import and it bears this same import whether it is dispensed to adults or to infants. It signifies union with Christ, purifying from the pollution of sin by the regeneration of the Spirit, and purifying from the guilt of sin by the blood of Christ. It can have no other import for infants than this."[104]

However, it is an inescapable conclusion that there is a significant difference between infant baptism and the baptism which is described in the New Testament and in the church confessions. The New Testament and the early church talk about the necessity of faith as a prerequisite of baptism. Jewett describes the paedobaptist conundrum perfectly, "Whether he makes infants an exception to the requirement of Scripture that faith precede baptism, or holds to faith by proxy, or admits that infant baptism is an incomplete form of the sacrament, he is espousing notions alien to the New Testament."[105]

Conclusion

The relationship between faith and baptism is one of the most foundational issues in the baptism debate. The New Testament evidence and the early church testimony is essentially unanimous on the connection between faith and baptism. Those who were baptized in the New Testament believed on the Lord and publicly confessed that belief. The New Testament idea of faith was a volitional expression that resulted in a changed life.

The relationship between faith and baptism leads to a dilemma of how faith can work with infant baptism. This dilemma has prompted much writing and discussion. Augustine was instrumental in his formulation of the concept of *fides aliena*, the idea that another person's faith is credited to an infant when baptized (whether that be the faith of a sponsor or of the church itself). Because of the problems of *fides aliena*, many in the medieval church embraced *fides infusa*, the idea that baptism attributed some virtue or benefit of faith to the infant. Luther differed from those who came before him by proposing *fides propria* or *fides infantium*, the idea that the infants themselves truly believed in some sense during the baptismal process.

---

103 Ibid., 1343.

104 John Murray, *Christian Baptism* (Phillipsburg, NJ: P&R Publishing, 1980), 41.

105 Jewett, *Infant Baptism and the Covenant of Grace*, 184.

Although Luther's later writings downplayed the importance of faith in baptism (because of his arguments with the Anabaptists), it was not until Ulrich Zwingli that faith was radically severed from baptism. By doing so, Zwingli revolutionized the paedobaptist argument through his systematization of covenant theology. Zwingli paved the way for future Reformed paedobaptist argumentation. In the following chapters, we will analyze the Reformed argument for paedobaptism that defends infant baptism without a personal expression of faith.

Chapter 2

Understanding the Reformed Paedobaptist Position

As we noted last chapter, Zwingli revolutionized the arguments for paedobaptism. Largely because of Zwingli and Calvin, Reformed paedobaptists today use distinct arguments for paedobaptism that differ from those used in Lutheran or Catholic churches. Once Zwingli separated faith from baptism, the argument for paedobaptism also changed. Today, systematic covenant theology has become the centerpiece for the Reformed paedobaptist argument. Thus, we will spend this chapter summarizing and laying out the basics of covenant theology and how it relates to infant baptism.[1]

The Foundational Elements of Covenant Theology

Adherents of covenant theology claim it to be the natural outworking of God's covenantal relationship with humanity.[2] Few would disagree with that general statement, but proponents of covenant theology often debate the finer details. Although most historians view Zwingli as the originator of covenant theology,[3] it developed into a full-fledged system through the

1 We will be necessarily brief in this chapter, but for a fuller treatment of the connection between covenant theology and infant baptism, see Stephen J. Wellum, "Baptism and the Relationship between the Covenants," in *Believer's Baptism: Sign of the New Covenant in Christ*, ed. Thomas R. Schreiner and Shawn D. Wright, NAC Studies in Bible & Theology (Nashville, TN: B & H Academic, 2006), 97–162.

2 Michael Horton, *Introducing Covenant Theology* (Grand Rapids: Baker Books, 2006), 1–14.

3 Lillback notes, "Calvin is not the initiator of covenant theology, since this honor must really fall to Zwingli. He is not the designer of the first paradigm of covenant thought, since this distinction falls to Bulllinger" (Lillback, *The Binding of God*, 311).

contributions of Zwingli's successors.[4] As covenant theology developed into a system, there emerged a broad agreement on the central components of covenant theology. Covenant theologian, Michael Horton, summarizes:

> A broad consensus emerged in this Reformed (federal) theology with respect to the existence in Scripture of three distinct covenants: the covenant of redemption (*pactum salutis*), the covenant of creation (*foederus naturae*), and the covenant of grace (*foederus gratiae*). The other covenants in Scripture (Noahic, Abrahamic, Mosaic, Davidic) are all grouped under these broader arrangements.[5]

These three covenants—the covenant of redemption, the covenant of creation (more often called the covenant of works)[6], and the covenant of grace—form the basis of covenant theology.

We can define the covenant of redemption as "an eternal pact between the persons of the Trinity. The Father elects a people in the Son as their mediator to be brought to saving faith through the Spirit. Thus, this covenant made by the Trinity in eternity already takes the fall of the human race into account."[7] Or, in the words of Berkhof, "The covenant of redemption may be defined as *the agreement between the Father, giving the Son as Head and Redeemer of the elect, and the Son, voluntarily taking the place of those whom the Father had given Him.*"[8] In other words, this is the pre-Fall covenantal agreement between the members of the Trinity to save the elect.

The second significant covenant in covenant theology is the covenant of works. Whereas the covenant of redemption is within the Godhead, the covenant of works is between humanity and God. The Westminster Confession (7.2) defines this covenant as follows: "The first covenant made with man was a covenant of works, wherein life was promised to Adam, and in him to his posterity, upon condition of perfect and personal obedience." Obviously, Adam failed to keep this covenant and thereby failed to secure eternal life for himself and his posterity. According to Frame, the covenant of works is essential to covenant theology primarily because

---

4 To trace the historical development of covenant theology, see the fine work of Pettegrew, "Israel and the Dark Side of the Reformation," 78–105.

5 Horton, *Introducing Covenant Theology*, 70.

6 The covenant of works has been referred to as covenant of creation, works, Edenic covenant, or Adamic covenant.

7 Horton, *Introducing Covenant Theology*, 70.

8 Berkhof, *Systematic Theology*, 271. Emphasis in original.

human beings are identified as covenant breakers in Adam. Additionally, human beings see God's perfect standard, which only Jesus can fulfill on our behalf.[9]

The final covenant which makes up the foundation of covenant theology is the covenant of grace. Berkhof defines the covenant of grace as "that gracious agreement between the offended God and the offending but elect sinner, in which God promises salvation through faith in Christ, and the sinner accepts this believingly, promising a life of faith and obedience."[10] The Westminster Confession (7.3) defines and compares this covenant to the covenant of works as follows:

> Man by his fall having made himself incapable of life by that covenant [the covenant of works], the Lord was pleased to make a second, commonly called the covenant of grace: wherein he freely offered unto sinners life and salvation by Jesus Christ, requiring of them faith in him that they may be saved, and promising to give unto all those that are ordained unto life his Holy Spirit, to make them willing and able to believe.

Importantly, covenant theology views the covenant of grace as a unified covenant spanning both Old and New Testaments, although it shows up in various administrations.[11] Zwingli describes this covenant as follows, "God therefore made no other covenant with the miserable race of man than that he had already conceived before man was formed. One and the same testament has always been in force."[12]

This one covenant of grace has many administrations, but it must be essentially the same throughout Old and New Testaments, according to covenant theology.[13] Frame notes, "Scripture mentions covenants that God made with Noah, Abraham, and others. Theologians have gathered these covenants together under a master title that includes all of them: the

9 John Frame, *Systematic Theology: An Introduction to Christian Belief* (Phillipsburg, NJ: P&R Publishing, 2013), 119.

10 Berkhof, *Systematic Theology*, 277. Emphasis in original has been removed.

11 Notably, many within the Reformed Baptist tradition would say the covenant of grace is to be equated *only* with the new covenant. We are concerned primarily with the Reformed paedobaptist position here.

12 Ulrich Zwingli, *Selected Works of Huldreich Zwingli*, ed. Samuel Macauley, trans. Lawrence A. McClouth, Henry Preble, and George W. Gilmore (Philadelphia, PA: University of Pennsylvania, 1901), 234.

13 Berkhof, *Systematic Theology*, 279; Cornelis P. Venema, "Covenant Theology and Baptism," in *The Case for Covenantal Infant Baptism*, ed. Gregg Strawbridge (Phillipsburg, NJ: P&R Publishing, 2003), 217.

covenant of grace."[14] Thus, although Scripture speaks of multiple covenants, covenant theologians view these covenants as a manifestation of the one, unified covenant of grace between God and humanity.

Covenant Theology and Infant Baptism

Reformed paedobaptists are not shy to assert that their defense of infant baptism relies on covenant theology. In fact, although many Baptists take issue with infant baptism not being mentioned anywhere in Scripture, this is really a simplistic understanding of the Reformed position. In reality, for the Reformed paedobaptist, the entire debate centers on the unified covenant of grace.[15] Note the words of paedobaptist theologian, Cornelis Venema:

> This debate can be reduced to one principal question: Does the covenant of grace in its New Testament administration embrace the children of believing parents just as it did in the Old Testament administration? However complex and diverse the arguments, pro and con, on the subject of infant baptism may be, this remains the overriding issue. Precisely because the debate between paedobaptists and Baptists centers on the doctrine of the covenant of grace, particularly the similarity and dissimilarity of the covenant in its Old and New Testament administrations, *it can hardly be resolved merely by appealing to specific biblical texts*.[16]

Similarly, in Robert Booth's book, *Children of the Promise*, he outlines the essentials for a defense of infant baptism as follows:

1. *Covenant Theology*. Throughout the Bible, God relates to his people by way of a covenant of grace. Covenant theology provides the basic framework for rightly interpreting Scripture.

---

14 Frame, *Systematic Theology: An Introduction to Christian Belief*, 119. Emphasis in original.

15 Collins explains, "The concept of the covenant of grace developed during the Reformation in part due to the Anabaptists' challenges to infant baptism. By asserting the unity of the covenant of grace under different administrations, Zwingli and others were able to argue for continuity between the circumcision of covenant children under the Abrahamic and Mosaic covenants and the baptism of covenant children under the new covenant. A unified covenant of grace also ensured that there is one way of salvation in every era of redemptive history" (Brian Collins, "The Covenants of Grace," in *Lexham Survey of Theology*, ed. Mark Ward et al. [Bellingham, WA: Lexham Press, 2018]).

16 Venema, "Covenant Theology and Baptism," 202. Emphasis added.

2. *Continuity of the Covenant of Grace*. The Bible teaches one and the same way of salvation in both the Old and the New Testaments, despite some different outward requirements.
3. *Continuity of the People of God*. Since there is one covenant of grace between God and man, there is one continuous people of God (the church) in the Old and New Testaments.
4. *Continuity of the Covenant Signs*. Baptism is the sign of the covenant in the New Testament, just as circumcision was the sign of the covenant in the Old Testament.
5. *Continuity of Households*. Whole households are included in God's redemptive covenant.[17]

The covenant of grace is essential to the Reformed argument because it provides a lens through which continuity can be established between the Old and New Testaments. If the sign of the covenant in the Old Testament was circumcision, then it is reasonable that baptism would be the manifestation of the covenant sign in the New Testament. If it is the same covenant, then the need for a similar application of the covenant sign remains. In this view, baptism has replaced circumcision as the sign of the covenant of grace.

According to such logic, what can be said about circumcision also applies to baptism. Specifically, that the sign applies not only to believers but also to their children. One of the best explanations of this connection is that of B.B. Warfield, who notes:

> The argument in a nutshell is simply this: God established His Church in the days of Abraham and put children into it. They must remain there until He puts them out. He has nowhere put them out. They are still then members of His Church and as such entitled to its ordinances. Among these ordinances is baptism, which standing in similar place in the New Dispensation to circumcision in the Old, is like it to be given to children.[18]

For the covenant theologian, because the covenant is the same and the God of the covenant is the same, we would expect God to deal with households and their children rather than *only* individuals. In other words,

---

17 Robert R. Booth, *Children of the Promise: The Biblical Case for Infant Baptism* (Phillipsburg, NJ: P&R Publishing, 1995), 8.

18 Benjamin Breckinridge Warfield, "The Polemics of Infant Baptism," in *Studies in Theology* (New York: Oxford University Press, 1932), 408.

God has obligated himself through a covenant to work with individuals *and* their households. Therefore, for the Reformed paedobaptist, not only would it be strange if infants were ignored in the New Testament while they were an integral part of the covenant community in the Old Testament, it would also violate God's covenant promise. Holding the covenant of grace as the key theological principle leads some Reformed paedobaptists, like Doug Wilson, to say, "The debate about infant baptism is fundamentally a debate about *children*, and not really a debate about baptism at all."[19] Reformed paedobaptists ask a valid question. If children had a place in the covenant of grace in the Old Testament, why should we remove them from the covenant of grace in the New Testament?

Not only is a unified covenant of grace essential to the Reformed paedobaptist argument, but, as Warfield's quote illustrates, another key assumption is the unity of the people of God in both Old and New Testaments. Put another way, the Reformed argument for paedobaptism assumes no distinction between Israel in the Old Testament and the church in the New Testament.

Covenant theologians view this unity of the people of God so strongly that they will regularly refer to Israel as the "church of the Old Testament." Because of this assumed continuity between Israel and the church, there is an expectation that the new covenant community is mixed (i.e., made up of believers *and* unbelievers), just like the Old Testament covenant community. In other words, for Reformed paedobaptists there is a difference between the elect (those saved) and those who are a part of the covenant community (the church).

To summarize, the Reformed argument for paedobaptism rests on two foundational realities: (1) the unity of the covenant of grace between the Old and New Testaments and (2) the unity of the people of God. These foundational realities lead to the idea that the sign of the covenant of grace is essentially the same, and that God acts with His people in the same way. If He has covenanted with them by the *same* covenant, as argued by covenant theologians, then we would expect the *same* participants.

19 Douglas Wilson, "Baptism and Children: Their Place in the Old and New Testaments," in *The Case for Covenantal Infant Baptism*, ed. Gregg Strawbridge (Phillipsburg, NJ: P&R Publishing, 2003), 287.

Figure 2.1. Reformed Paedobaptist Framework

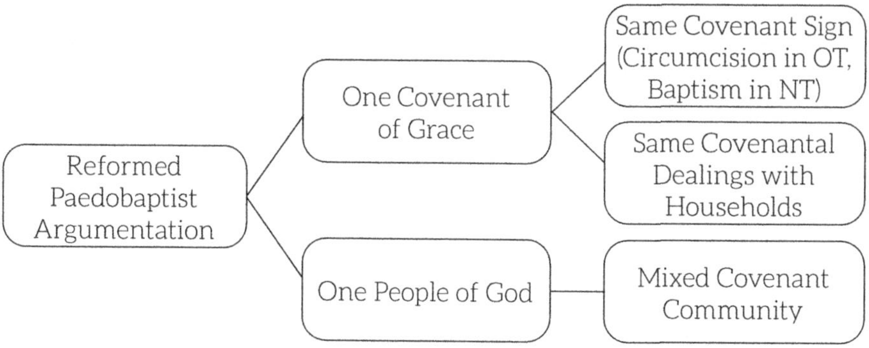

Conclusion

In this chapter, I have briefly outlined the Reformed argument for paedobaptism with no critical evaluation. I have given an overview of the covenantal system, for it is through this system that the Reformed paedobaptist argues for infant baptism. The Reformed paedobaptist position entirely depends on the theological concept of the covenant of grace and the idea that there is no distinction between Israel and the church. If either of those realities is invalid, it poses a serious problem for the Reformed paedobaptist position. In the coming chapters, I will provide a detailed analysis of the Reformed paedobaptist position in each of the above areas and will provide a thorough critical evaluation.

Chapter 3

Paedobaptism and the Covenant of Grace

Now that we understand the framework of covenant theology, we can understand the crux of the Reformed argument for paedobaptism. Within this argument, the central component is the covenant of grace. Reformed paedobaptists themselves are adamant about this point. For example, paedobaptist Robert Booth writes, "There are also other evidences in the pages of Scripture that support the truth of infant baptism. Nevertheless, *the foundation of the argument consists of the unified covenant of grace evident in the Scriptures of the Old and New Testaments.*"[1]

The covenant of grace is essential to the Reformed position on paedobaptism for many reasons. Primarily, it provides the theological connection between circumcision and baptism, so that "baptism and circumcision have essentially the same meaning."[2] Additionally, it provides a theological framework for understanding a continuity in the people of God within the Old and New Testaments. Finally, the framework of the covenant of grace also underlies the idea that God covenants with households, not just individuals.[3] Clearly, this is an important concept to understand.

Many Baptists have historically argued against paedobaptism while simultaneously embracing covenant theology and the covenant of grace.[4]

---

1 Booth, *Children of the Promise*, 10. Emphasis in original. Likewise, Venema says, "This debate can be reduced to one principal question: Does the covenant of grace in its New Testament administration embrace the children of believing parents just as it did in its Old Testament administration? However complex and diverse the arguments, pro and con, on the subject of infant baptism may be, this remains the overriding issue" (Venema, "Covenant Theology and Baptism," 202).

2 Mark E. Ross, "Baptism and Circumcision as Signs and Seals," in *The Case for Covenantal Infant Baptism*, ed. Gregg Strawbridge (Phillipsburg, NJ: P&R Publishing, 2003), 100.

3 The specific issues of circumcision's relationship to baptism and the significance of households will be dealt with in detail in later chapters.

4 For modern examples of such defenses, see Richard C. Barcellos, ed., *Recovering a Covenantal Heritage: Essays in Baptist Covenant Theology* (Palmdale, CA: RBAP, 2014); Jewett, *Infant*

So, I am not claiming that one must adopt infant baptism if he holds to a covenant of grace. However, the Reformed paedobaptist arguments would have no foundation without a distinct understanding of the covenant of grace. Since a unified covenant of grace is *the* primary argument for Reformed paedobaptism, in this chapter we will spend significant effort analyzing whether this is a valid theological construct.

The Covenant of Grace as One Covenant

As noted in the last chapter, covenant theologians argue for the unity between the Old and New Testaments by appealing to one covenant—the covenant of grace—which appears in various manifestations. Zwingli was the architect for this kind of argumentation, developing it to counter the claims made by the Anabaptists. Zwingli claimed that there had always been just one covenant. In his words, "God therefore made no other covenant with the miserable race of man than that he had already conceived before man was formed. One and the same testament has always been in force."[5]

But Zwingli's assertion that there is only one covenant was open to challenge. After all, if there was only one covenant in both Old and New Testaments, why does Scripture seem to speak of multiple covenants (e.g., Heb 8, 2 Cor 3; Gal 4–5)? To explain these passages, Zwingli states, "Two covenants are spoken of, not that they are two diverse covenants, for this would necessitate not only two diverse people, but also two gods."[6] In other words, even though the Scriptures talk about multiple covenants, this is not the reality.

Again, Zwingli writes, "Paul speaks of two testaments, but the one he calls a testament by a misuse of language, when he wishes them to be understood who ... betrayed the light and Christ himself. Paul therefore called the way of these a testament, not that it was a true testament, but by a copying or imitation of those who so named it."[7] As we can see, the

---

Baptism and the Covenant of Grace. Older defenses include the fine work of Nehemiah Coxe, *A Discourse of the Covenants That God Made with Men before the Law: Wherein, the Covenant of Circumcision Is More Largely Handled, and the Invalidity of the Plea for Paedobaptism Taken from Thence Discovered* (London: John Darby, 1681). Many Reformed Baptists view the covenant of grace as identical with the new covenant, and not formally operational until Christ's sacrifice on the cross.

5 Zwingli, *Selected Works of Huldreich Zwingli*, 234.

6 Ibid., 228.

7 Ibid., 228–29.

concept of a singular covenant is so important to Zwingli that he attributes a "misuse of language" to the Apostle Paul.

Few modern Reformed paedobaptists would be as bold as Zwingli in their assertions. Yet, modern Reformed paedobaptists also assume a singular covenant in texts which refer to plurality. For example, in response to Romans 9:4, "They are Israelites, and to them belong ... the covenants [pl.]," Venema says, "However diverse and particular may be the various dispensations or administrations of the covenant of grace—so that we may even speak of 'covenants' in the plural (Rom 9:4)—they do not differ as to substance."[8] In other words, Venema argues that there is one covenant of grace; and when Scripture refers to a plurality of covenants, it is really only referring to different manifestations of that one covenant.

There are at least two problems with this line of thinking. First, there is the problem of falsifiability. The standard that Zwingli and Venema use for their interpretation is untestable, and their conclusion is assumed preemptively. They presuppose a unified covenant of grace in the texts. And even when there is mention of multiple covenants, they explain it away as a reference to various administrations of the same covenant. Thus, there is no way to disprove the idea of a singular covenant. The very evidence which would prove multiple covenants is used as evidence for a singular covenant. Second, and more significantly, this presuppositional reading of these texts seems to ignore the more natural reading. Texts that distinguish between the various covenants should be read as evidence for different covenants. Covenants exist separately, with unique terms and obligations. In the words of Paul, "even with a man-made covenant, no one annuls it or adds to it once it has been ratified" (Gal 3:15).

The Reformed Paedobaptist Defense of the Covenant of Grace

The Reformed paedobaptist argument relies on the essential sameness of the covenant of grace. It is one covenant that manifests differently through other covenants. However, Scripture regularly speaks of multiple covenants as being cooperative (Heb 8; 2 Cor 3; Gal 4–5; Rom 9:4; Eph 2:12, etc.). Thus, the burden of proof is on the Reformed paedobaptist to defend the idea that there is one overarching covenant of grace that is "essentially the same in all dispensations."[9]

8 Venema, "Covenant Theology and Baptism," 216.

9 Berkhof, *Systematic Theology*, 279.

Cornelis Venema has taken up the challenge and has offered a defense of the covenant of grace.[10] His defense is beneficial because he provides objective criteria for examining the covenants of Scripture. We can group his primary evidence for a covenant of grace into four categories: (1) the same promise of life and salvation, (2) the same mediator, (3) the same gospel, and (4) the same obligations.

The Same Promise of Life and Salvation

Venema begins his defense of the covenant of grace as a valid theological category by arguing that each successive covenant contains the same promise of life and salvation. Venema writes:

> First, the covenant promise of life and salvation is described in the same way throughout the Scriptures. When God first entered into an everlasting covenant with Abraham, he promised to be God to him and to his seed after him (Gen 17:7). This language is used of the covenant made at Sinai under Moses (Exod 19:5; 20:1), of the covenant made on the plains of Moab (Deut 29:13), of the covenant with David (2 Sam 7:14), and of the new covenant in Christ (Jer 31:33; Heb 8:10).[11]

In a similar description, Berkhof writes:

> The summary expression of the covenant is the same throughout, both in the Old and New Testament: "I will be thy God." It is the expression of the essential content of the covenant with Abraham, Gen. 17:7, of the Sinaitic covenant, Ex. 19:5; 20:1, of the covenant of the Plains of Moab, Deut. 29:13, of the Davidic covenant, 2 Sam. 7:14, and of the new covenant, Jer. 31:33; Heb. 8:10.[12]

The point for both Venema and Berkhof is that God describes His relationship with His people the same way in each manifestation of the covenant. Reformed paedobaptists view this as proof that the various covenants are manifestations of one unified covenant.

---

10 Venema, "Covenant Theology and Baptism," 201–29. Ursinus provides an older defense and argues that the covenant is "one in substance, but two-fold in circumstances" (Zacharias Ursinus, *The Commentary of Zacharias Ursinus on the Heidelberg Catechism*, trans. G. W. Williard [Cincinnati, OH: T. P. Bucher, 1851], 98–99). His arguments are more generic, and therefore, less helpful than Venema's arguments. Therefore, I will focus on Venema's presentation.

11 Venema, "Covenant Theology and Baptism," 216.

12 Berkhof, *Systematic Theology*, 279.

There are two substantial responses to this argument. First, a comparison of the language of the covenants shows some dissimilarities within the covenants. Both Venema and Berkhof imply that the covenant texts include "I will be your God" language. However, we see meaningful differences if we compare the actual language from the passages they cite.

Table 3.1. Comparison of Covenantal Language

Gen 17:7	"And I will establish my covenant between me and you and your offspring after you throughout their generations for an everlasting covenant, *to be God to you and to your offspring after you.*"
Exod 19:5	"Now therefore, if you will indeed obey my voice and keep my covenant, you shall be *my treasured possession* among all peoples, for all the earth is mine."
Exod 20:1	"I am the Lord *your God,* who brought you out of the land of Egypt, out of the house of slavery."
Deut 29:13	"That he may establish you today as *his people,* and that *he may be your God,* as he promised you, and as he swore to your fathers, to Abraham, to Isaac, and to Jacob."
2 Sam 7:14	"*I will be to him a father, and he shall be to me a son.* When he commits iniquity, I will discipline him with the rod of men, with the stripes of the sons of men …"
Jer 31:33; Heb 8:10	"For this is the covenant that I will make with the house of Israel after those days, declares the Lord: I will put my law within them, and I will write it on their hearts. *And I will be their God, and they shall be my people.*"

Although I am sympathetic to the idea of connections between these covenants, it is far too simplistic to assume that the language "I will be your God" is equivalent with phrases like, "my treasured possession" or "I will be to him a father." These phrases carry their own nuances and are not simply interchangeable. For example, ancient texts often referred to kings in the ancient world as "sons" of their respective deities.[13] This well-known sonship description emphasized representative rule by the king on behalf of his deity. So, for example, the promise in 2 Samuel 7:14 is a promise of dynastic rule on behalf of God, whereas Genesis 17:7 affirms God's rela-

13 Adela Yarbro Collins and John J. Collins, *King and Messiah as Son of God: Divine, Human, and Angelic Messianic Figures* (Grand Rapids: Eerdmans, 2008), 1–9. For example, see Ivan Engnell, *Studies in Divine Kingship in the Ancient Near East*, 2nd ed. (Oxford: Basil Black-

tionship in the context of promised progeny, land, and blessing. Thus, it is not accurate to say these passages use the same language to talk about the same covenant promise. Although it is true that there is thematic overlap between the covenants in Scripture, one must also be sensitive to the differences between the covenants.

Second, even when there is similar language used within covenants, this is evidence of *how* God typically makes covenants, not evidence that each covenant is a manifestation of the covenant of grace. One of the clearest examples of this point is the priestly covenant in Numbers 25:10–13.[14]

The priestly covenant is so named because we see God grant Phinehas a covenant for his faithful service to Yahweh. This covenant is a promise of continuing priestly service for Phinehas and his descendants. Importantly, this covenant uses the same language as other, more well-known covenants. For example, God promises the covenant will be "to him [Phinehas] and to his descendants" (v. 13a), a phrase found in the Noahic and Abrahamic covenants (cf. Gen 9:9; 13:15; 15:18; 17:7). The priestly covenant is also called a "perpetual" (עוֹלָם) covenant, which is the same terminology used of the Noahic covenant (Gen 9:16), Abrahamic covenant (Gen 17:13, 19), and the new covenant (Jer 32:40). God also calls the priestly covenant a "covenant of peace" (Num 25:12b), which is the same phraseology used for the new covenant in Ezekiel 37:26a. According to the understanding of Venema and other covenant theologians, the priestly covenant should also be a manifestation of the covenant of grace given the use of the same language found in other covenants. Yet I am unaware of any covenant theologian who would affirm that. Rather, most covenant theologians ignore this primary example of God making a covenant with Phinehas. However, the priestly covenant is powerful evidence that similarity of language does not necessitate a unifying covenant of grace.

The Same Mediator

The second evidence for the covenant of grace is that, according to Venema, the covenant mediator is the same across every administration. Venema writes, "Second, the Mediator of the covenant is the same in every dispensation or administration of the covenant of grace. Jesus Christ, ac-

---

well, 1967), 58. Engnell points out that the Hittite king is often referred to as the son of the weather-god.

14 For more on the priestly covenant, see Irvin A. Busenitz, "Introduction to the Biblical Covenants: The Noahic Covenant and the Priestly Covenant," *The Master's Seminary Journal* 10, no. 2 (Fall 1999): 186–89.

cording to the writer of Hebrews, is 'the same yesterday and today and forever' (13:8)."[15]

In addition to the above quote, Venema also points to 1 Timothy 2:5 to argue that there is only one mediator between God and man.[16] But the argument that Jesus is the same mediator in every administration of the covenant of grace is weak. In trying to argue for one unified covenant of grace, Venema wipes out the mediatorial distinctions between the covenants. He refers to Hebrews 13:8, that Jesus Christ is "the same yesterday and today and forever," as a prooftext for his argument. However, he does not cite Hebrews 3:1–6 or 8:5–6, which teach that Jesus's new covenant mediatorial role is superior to that of Moses.

In the overall argument of Hebrews, the author compares Moses and Jesus as covenant mediators. The author unquestionably views Christ as better than Moses (Heb 3:1–6), who is described as the mediator of the old covenant (e.g., Heb 9:19). So too, in Hebrews 8:6, we read, "But as it is, Christ has obtained a ministry that is as much more excellent than the old as the covenant he mediates is better, since it is enacted on better promises."[17] Thus, it is central to the theology of Hebrews that Jesus is the better new covenant mediator, and this description is contrasted with Moses, who was the mediator of the old covenant.[18]

Other Scriptures also compare the mediatorial roles of Moses and Jesus. For example, John writes, "For the law was given through Moses; grace and truth came through Jesus Christ" (John 1:17). Similarly, in

---

15 Venema, "Covenant Theology and Baptism," 216.

16 Ibid., 217. Commenting on 1 Timothy 2:5, Booth notes, "This means that Jesus Christ is the Mediator of the covenant in both the Old and New Testaments" (Randy Booth, "Covenant Transition," in *The Case for Covenantal Infant Baptism*, ed. Gregg Strawbridge [Phillipsburg, NJ: P&R Publishing, 2003], 195).

17 "The measure of that superiority is expressed with a comparison based on Jesus' entrance into the heavenly sanctuary as the mediator of a superior covenant. In Hebrews the theologically significant word μεσίτης, 'mediator,' is always associated with the new covenant (8:6; 9:15; 12:24; cf. 7:22). The new covenant required a new mediator. By his life of perfect obedience and his death, Jesus inaugurated the new covenant of Jer 31:31–34. His entrance into the heavenly sanctuary guarantees God's acceptance of his sacrifice and the actualization of the provisions of the superior covenant he mediated" (William L. Lane, *Hebrews 1–8*, Word Biblical Commentary 47a [Nashville, TN: Thomas Nelson, 1991], 208).

18 "This characterization of 'covenant mediator' (διαθήκης μεσίτης) is of great significance for covenant Christology (cf. 8:6; 9:15; 12:24). Jesus establishes a new relationship between God and his people in that his atoning death makes possible new soteriological provisions from God. In this, Christ parallels Moses as the 'mediator of the first covenant'" (Peter Gräbe, "The New Covenant and Christian Identity in Hebrews," in *A Cloud of Witnesses: The Theology of Hebrews in Its Ancient Contexts*, ed. Richard Bauckham et al. [New York: T&T Clark, 2008], 123).

2 Corinthians 3:7–18, Paul insinuates a significant difference between the ministry of Moses and that of Jesus.

Clearly the Bible labels Jesus as the mediator of the new covenant, and Moses is recognized as the mediator of the old covenant. So how do Reformed paedobaptists synthesize this apparent contradiction? Early covenant theologian Zacharias Ursinus writes, "[Moses] was a Mediator only as a type of Christ, who was even then already Mediator, but is now the only Mediator without any type."[19] In other words, Christ was the real mediator because Moses was only a type. However, this explanation suffers from a lack of texts which describe Christ being the mediator of the old covenant. Furthermore, why would a new covenant even be necessary if Christ was already the mediator of the old covenant? This viewpoint disregards the straightforward statements of Moses being the mediator of the old covenant. In summary, one cannot use the idea that Christ is the mediator of both old and new covenants as evidence for a unified covenant of grace.

The Same Gospel

Venema's third argument for a unified covenant of grace is that the same gospel and means of salvation is present in both Old and New Testaments. He writes, "Third, the gospel preached in the old covenant is the same as the gospel preached in the new covenant."[20]

Venema is completely correct that the gospel never changes. It has been the same throughout history. The same grace of God saved everyone who expressed faith, whether Adam, David, Paul, or any of us. However, the fact that salvation is always by grace through faith doesn't contribute to the discussion of whether there is a covenant of grace.

Reformed paedobaptists will usually argue that the gospel was the same in both old and new covenants, and this allegedly shows that the biblical covenants are a manifestation of one covenant of grace. But God's way of salvation (grace through faith) was operative from the time of Adam to Noah and beyond. God even saved those outside the stipulations of the old covenant. For example, faith presumably saved Job and Melchizedek, though they were outside the Abrahamic covenant. We could say the same thing about Naaman (2 Kgs 5), or many others who expressed faith in God while being outside of God's covenant with Israel. So, to argue that the same gospel existed in the old and new covenants does not prove they are

19 Ursinus, *The Commentary of Zacharias Ursinus on the Heidelberg Catechism*, 99.

20 Venema, "Covenant Theology and Baptism," 217.

manifestations of the covenant of grace. It is simply correct to observe that God saves people the same way in every age.

The Same Obligations

The final claim made by Venema is that the same covenant obligations exist across the covenants. He writes, "Fourth, the obligation of the covenant of grace is essentially the same throughout the course of its various and successive administrations."[21]

It is difficult to understand what Venema means by this statement. Clearly the obligations of the Mosaic covenant, "You shall therefore keep my statutes and my rules; if a person does them, he shall live by them: I am the Lord" (Lev 18:5), differ drastically from the obligations of the new covenant, "For the whole law is fulfilled in one word: 'You shall love your neighbor as yourself'" (Gal 5:14). The dietary obligations of the Mosaic covenant are no longer applicable to those under the new covenant (Deut 14; cf. Mark 7:18–19; Acts 10:9–16; Rom 14:1–4). Similarly, the Mosaic Sabbath restrictions are also done away with in the new covenant (Exod 20:8–11; cf. Rom 14:5–7; Col 2:16–17). It is impossible to argue that the obligations between the Mosaic and new covenants are the same. The covenant obligations differ significantly.

This is evident even beyond the comparison of the Mosaic and new covenants. For example, those living under the Noahic covenant had fewer obligations than the Mosaic covenant (e.g., no dietary restrictions, etc.). Venema cannot be saying that there are no differences in obligations between the covenants, because that would be nonsense.

In context, what Venema seems to be arguing is similar to his third point—the obligations of faith in God for salvation are the same across history. Venema writes, "The gracious promise of the covenant precedes the giving of the law, thereby teaching us that salvation is by grace alone through faith alone, and not on account of the righteousness of works."[22] In other words, salvation always comes through faith, never by works. Although this is undoubtedly true, it is not an argument for the universality of the covenant of grace. It is simply a restatement of Venema's third argument: that God saves by grace through faith. Furthermore, the way Venema states his case ignores the actual issue. There *are* genuine differences

21 Ibid.

22 Ibid.

of covenant obligations between the various covenants.[23] These differences demonstrate a multifaceted plan of God that has purposes that extend beyond salvation.

Although I agree with Venema that God's plan of salvation is the same throughout all time, I am unconvinced by his arguments that, "the covenant of grace, throughout its successive and diverse administrations, is essentially one and the same covenant."[24] I believe Venema and other Reformed paedobaptists force the covenant of grace construct onto the biblical covenants. Just because salvation is the same in every age does not mean the covenants are manifestations of one covenant of grace. Furthermore, I believe the scriptural evidence describes a variety of unique, specialized covenants that testify to a multifaceted and complex plan of God.[25]

A Positive Argument for the Uniqueness of the Covenants

One of the most persuasive arguments against the covenant of grace is an analysis of how Scripture describes the various covenants as unique and distinct. If we can demonstrate that the Bible speaks of multiple covenants that operate coextensively, each having a unique function and purpose, then it would be difficult to argue that the biblical covenants are manifestations of one covenant of grace. In this section, I will present a positive case for unique and distinct covenants, and I will attempt to show that how these covenants interact with one another precludes the concept of one overarching covenant of grace.

---

23 For example, there is no indication Sabbath observance was required from Noah to Moses (Noahic and Abrahamic covenants). During the administration of the Mosaic covenant, however, Sabbath observance was a moral issue, and a failure to observe the requirement meant execution (cf. Exod 20:8–11; Num 15:32–36). However, under the administration of the new covenant, the Sabbath is no longer a requirement (cf. Col 2:16–17; Rom 14:5–6). These calendrical differences are one illustration of the various differing obligations within the covenants.

24 Venema, "Covenant Theology and Baptism," 217.

25 On this point, Niehaus writes, "More recently, some scholars have seen all God's covenants as one, but can only accomplish their goal by blurring over the distinctions that make the covenants different. Such an approach, although it has found favor recently in some quarters, is truly a form of idealism that can succeed only by abstracting a few things common to all covenants (e.g., that God has provided for his vassals in the past, that he requires certain things of them in the present, and that he promises to provide for them in the future) and declaring all the covenants to be one because they share those elements. Although a full discussion of the issues would require more space than is appropriate here, the failure of this approach is most easily illustrated when we consider the basic differences between the Common Grace covenants and the Special Grace covenants. The two sets of covenants are different in their provisions and in their promises. The Noahic covenant, for example, does not offer a way of eternal salvation for anyone—although all people live under it" (Jeffrey J. Niehaus, *Biblical Theology: The Common Grace Covenants*, vol. 1 [Bellingham, WA: Lexham Press, 2014], 224–25).

Scripture Speaks of Covenants as a Plurality

This may seem like an obvious starting place, but I believe it sets a strong foundation for expectation. In contrast to many of the statements that are made by Reformed paedobaptists, the New Testament speaks of a diversity of covenants. For example, as already referred to, Romans 9:4 says, "They are Israelites, and to them belong the adoption, the glory, the covenants, the giving of the law, the worship, and the promises." Of importance to our argument is the fact that the terms "covenants" (αἱ διαθῆκαι) and "promises" (αἱ ἐπαγγελίαι) are both plural. Moo points out that Paul's reference to covenants (plural) is most naturally a reference to the covenants mentioned in the Old Testament (e.g., Noahic, Abrahamic, Mosaic, Davidic). Other non-biblical Jewish sources also use the plural to refer to the different covenants that Israel had received (cf. Sir 44:12, 18; Wis 18:22; 2 Macc 8:15).[26] Paul's point is that God gave the nation of Israel unique privileges through a variety of covenants and promises.

Similarly, Ephesians 2:12 reads, "Remember that you were at that time separated from Christ, alienated from the commonwealth of Israel and strangers to the covenants of promise, having no hope and without God in the world." F. F. Bruce notes that the plural "covenants" here refers to the Abrahamic, Mosaic, and Davidic covenants.[27] As with Romans 9:4, the point of Ephesians 2:12 is that through multiple covenants God had given the nation of Israel special privileges that had not been given to the Gentiles.

This seems to be a powerful argument against the idea of a covenant of grace. Gentiles could be saved in the Old Testament through faith, yet Romans 9:4 and Ephesians 2:12 highlight the special privileges Israel had through a covenantal relationship with God. Israel received multiple covenants that operated for a variety of purposes.

The Priestly Covenant is a Distinct Covenant

The priestly covenant (Num 25:10–13) is an oft-ignored but essential component to consider in this debate. Within the context of Numbers 25, Israel had "yoked himself to Baal of Peor," engaging in vile idolatry (v. 3). The Lord brought a plague upon the people of Israel to punish them, until Phinehas, Aaron's grandson, stopped the plague by killing a man of Israel

26 Douglas Moo, *The Epistle to the Romans*, 2nd ed., New International Commentary on the New Testament (Grand Rapids: Eerdmans, 2018), 583–84.

27 F. F. Bruce, *The Epistles to the Colossians, to Philemon, and to the Ephesians*, New International Commentary on the New Testament (Grand Rapids: Eerdmans, 1984), 293.

and his seductress (vv. 7–8). Considering Phinehas's actions, the text notes God's promise in Numbers 25:10–13:

> And the Lord said to Moses, "Phinehas the son of Eleazar, son of Aaron the priest, has turned back my wrath from the people of Israel, in that he was jealous with my jealousy among them, so that I did not consume the people of Israel in my jealousy. Therefore say, 'Behold, I give to him my covenant of peace, and it shall be to him and to his descendants after him the covenant of a perpetual priesthood, because he was jealous for his God and made atonement for the people of Israel.'"

As mentioned earlier, we see this covenant uses language often associated with the covenant of grace. First, this covenant promises a "perpetual priesthood," which uses the same term elsewhere translated as "everlasting" (עוֹלָם). This is the same language used in the Noahic covenant (Gen 9:12, 16), the Abrahamic covenant (Gen 17:7–8), and the Davidic covenant (2 Sam 7:13, 16). Second, God gave this priestly covenant not just to Phinehas, but to his descendants (Num 25:13). This promise follows the same structure as the Abrahamic and Davidic covenants (Gen 17:7; 2 Sam 7:12). Finally, the priestly covenant is also called a "covenant of peace" (Num 25:12b), which is the same phraseology used of the new covenant (Ezek 37:26a). Covenant theologians hardly mentioned the priestly covenant, but it contains the same elements found in the other biblically significant covenants.

Although some might wish to connect the priestly covenant with the Mosaic covenant, the priestly covenant is to be viewed as distinct from the Mosaic covenant. The prophets reveal that the priestly covenant continues in operation parallel with the new covenant. For example, priests from Zadok's line, who are descendants of Phinehas (1 Chron 6:50–53), will serve in the future temple described by Ezekiel (Ezek 44:15; 48:11).[28] Similarly, Jeremiah 33:17–18 talks about the timelessness of the Davidic covenant and Levitical covenant side by side. This point is even more concretely made in Jeremiah 33:20–21 where God says that neither "my covenant with David," nor "my covenant with the Levitical priests my ministers," can be broken.

Although proponents of covenant theology often ignore the priestly covenant, it is important enough in Israelite theology that it finds continuity along with the Davidic and new covenants. The priestly covenant deals strictly with the Levitical priesthood and does not pertain to God's

28 Busenitz, "Introduction to the Biblical Covenants," 188.

salvation promise. Therefore, one cannot use it as evidence for a covenant of grace, even though it uses similar language to the other covenants. The priestly covenant is evidence that there are multiple covenants in operation which serve a variety of purposes. They are not to be viewed as different manifestations of a covenant of grace.

Biblical Authors Apply the Covenants of Scripture Coextensively and Uniquely

Another important argument for the uniqueness of the covenants is that the Bible describes them as operating coextensively and concurrently. The biblical authors regularly describe the covenants as operating in plurality, with each covenant contributing something unique to the biblical storyline. Nowhere is it hinted at that we should view these covenants as manifestations of one covenant. The covenants are not interchangeable, but unique. The Bible consistently references multiple covenants within one given text to emphasize the particular ramifications of those specific covenants.

For example, Isaiah 24:4–5 says that all the earth has broken the "everlasting covenant." This reference to a generic covenant with the world seems to fit best with the Noahic covenant,[29] although it could be a reference to the obligatory relationship between creature and Creator.[30] In either case, Isaiah grounds his condemnation in this general covenant. However, when addressing the nation of Israel, Isaiah writes from within the framework of the Mosaic covenant. The Mosaic covenant forms the basis of Isaiah's covenant lawsuit in Isaiah 1.[31] Thus, Isaiah is showing awareness of multiple covenants operating simultaneously. The Noahic covenant provides the ground for generic condemnation of the nations, and the Mosaic covenant establishes the reason for Israel's indictment.

We find more examples of authors emphasizing different covenants operating during the same timeframe in the psalms. As Craigie has observed, "the psalmists are covenant writers," and their "knowledge of God is rooted in covenant."[32] However, this covenant reflection is not tied to a covenant of grace but to the revealed biblical covenants. For example,

---

29 John D. W. Watts, *Isaiah 1–33*, rev. ed., Word Biblical Commentary 24 (Nashville, TN: Thomas Nelson, 2005), 378.

30 Michael J. Vlach, *He Will Reign Forever: A Biblical Theology of the Kingdom of God* (Silverton, OR: Lampion Press, 2017), 165.

31 Watts, *Isaiah 1–33*, 23.

32 Peter C. Craigie, *Psalms 1–50*, 2nd ed., Word Biblical Commentary 19 (Nashville, TN: Thomas Nelson, 2004), 40.

Psalm 105:8–11 clearly interprets history in light of the covenant with Abraham, Isaac, and Jacob. Psalm 106:45 also likely refers to the Abrahamic covenant, providing the basis for God's faithfulness to Israel. David quotes both psalms in 1 Chronicles 16:8–36, which shows that, even if he was not the author of those psalms, he knew about and applied them to the present situation. David is also the author of Psalm 103:17–18, which is a reference to the Mosaic covenant. We can also add Psalm 2 and Psalm 110 to David's writings, which are reflections on the application of the Davidic covenant. Therefore, we see that David writes about and meditates on at least three covenants: the Abrahamic (Psalm 105; 106), the Mosaic (Psalm 103), and the Davidic (Psalm 2; 110). He takes those specific covenants and applies their promises to distinct circumstances. This is just one example of how the psalms show awareness of multiple covenants in operation, each with a variety of specific ramifications.

Out of the many other examples, we can observe one last instance of the coextensive nature of the biblical covenants in Jeremiah 33:20–21, which I alluded to before, but will now quote in full:

> Thus says the Lord: If you can break my covenant with the day and my covenant with the night, so that day and night will not come at their appointed time, then also my covenant with David my servant may be broken, so that he shall not have a son to reign on his throne, and my covenant with the Levitical priests my ministers.

This text refers to three coextensive and cooperative covenants.[33] There is the Noahic covenant ("my covenant with the day … and night"), the Davidic covenant ("my covenant with David"), and the priestly covenant ("my covenant with the Levitical priests"). God's message in this text *assumes* the coextensive nature of these covenants. God assures the people of Israel that the Davidic and priestly covenants will continue, each finding fulfillment of their specific promises. The foundation for this assurance is based on the continuity of the Noahic covenant, a covenant that has its own unique contribution of promised daily continuity. Given the flow and argument of the text, it seems improbable that Jeremiah would agree that each of the covenants mentioned in Jeremiah 33 is a manifestation of one covenant of grace.

33 Interestingly, Vlach notes that there are at least four unconditional covenants (perhaps five) mentioned in Jeremiah 30–33: the new covenant (31:31–34); Davidic covenant (33:14–17); Priestly covenant (33:18); Noahic covenant (33:19–22); and perhaps the Abrahamic covenant (30:22) (Vlach, *He Will Reign Forever*, 188–91).

The New Testament Distinguishes the Mosaic Covenant from the Abrahamic Covenant

One way to highlight the uniqueness of each covenant is to observe how the New Testament describes them. The New Testament differentiates between the Abrahamic and Mosaic covenants, calling the Mosaic covenant the old covenant, which is done away with in Christ. The Abrahamic and Mosaic covenants are not identical, but distinct covenants.

We see this position clearly articulated in Galatians 3:15–17. Paul states that the giving of the Law, "does not annul a covenant previously ratified by God" (v. 17). In context, Paul is comparing the giving of the Law (the Mosaic covenant) and the previous covenant (the Abrahamic covenant). For Paul, the Mosaic covenant did not nullify the Abrahamic promise.[34] The two covenants existed simultaneously.

Importantly, the New Testament highlights the fact that the new covenant has replaced the Mosaic covenant. Hebrews 8:13 says, "In speaking of a new covenant, he makes the first one obsolete. And what is becoming obsolete and growing old is ready to vanish away." Which first covenant is obsolete? The context of Hebrews 9 makes it clear, "Now even the first covenant had regulations for worship and an earthly place of holiness" (v. 1). Which covenant had "regulations for worship and an early place of holiness?" This must refer to the covenant God made with Israel at Mount Sinai, commonly known as the Mosaic covenant. Thus, for the author of Hebrews, the new covenant has replaced the Mosaic covenant.

Similarly, Paul contrasts the new covenant glories with the glory of the Mosaic covenant in 2 Corinthians 3:7–11. Paul contrasts the new covenant against the "ministry of death, carved in letters on stone" (v. 7), which is an explicit reference to the Mosaic covenant. Paul points out that the ministry of the Spirit (i.e., the new covenant) is far superior. As Schreiner observes, "The new covenant is superior to the old, for the glory of Christ outshines the glory of Moses (2 Cor 3:10–11)."[35]

As we can see, the New Testament regularly contrasts the new covenant and the Mosaic covenant, which is often called the old covenant. One reason this is important to understand is because the Reformed paedobaptist will typically argue that the old covenant is essentially synonymous with the Abrahamic covenant. For example, when Booth talks about the old covenant, he talks about the blessings and promises made to Abra-

---

34 Schreiner, *Galatians*, 230.

35 Thomas R. Schreiner, *Paul, Apostle of God's Glory in Christ* (Westmont, IL: IVP Academic, 2006), 26.

ham.[36] When covenant theologians appeal to circumcision as the old covenant sign, this assumes the Abrahamic covenant is in view. There is, in the mind of the Reformed paedobaptist, a direct connection between the Abrahamic covenant and the new covenant. In fact, they are usually considered essentially the same. In the words of Berkhof:

> The covenant made with Abraham was primarily a *spiritual* covenant, though it also had a national aspect, and of this spiritual covenant circumcision was a sign and seal.... This covenant is still in force and is essentially identical with the "new covenant" of the present dispensation. The unity and continuity of the covenant in both dispensations follows from the fact that the Mediator is the same; the condition is the same, namely, faith; and the blessings are the same, namely, justification, regeneration, spiritual gifts, and eternal life.[37]

In other words, for the Reformed paedobaptist, the new covenant is essentially identical with the old covenant (i.e., the Abrahamic covenant), both being similar manifestations of the covenant of grace. Thus, baptism (the sign of the new covenant) can replace circumcision (the sign of the Abrahamic covenant).

However, as noted above, the New Testament identifies the Mosaic covenant as the old covenant, not the Abrahamic. The New Testament marks a distinction between the Mosaic and the Abrahamic covenants (cf. Gal 3:15–17). The Abrahamic covenant continues to stand in the New Testament, while the new covenant replaces the Mosaic covenant. Thus, the New Testament's distinction between the Mosaic and Abrahamic covenants is another positive argument for the unique functionality of the covenants.

Two Completely New Aspects of the New Covenant

One of the best ways to show that the new covenant is unique and different from the preceding covenants is to highlight the completely original aspects of the new covenant. This contrasts with the Reformed paedobaptist, who of necessity views the new covenant as essentially synonymous with the Abrahamic covenant.[38] For the Reformed paedobaptist, the new covenant is not brand new but a renewal of something already in exis-

36 Booth, "Covenant Transition," 178–79, 182.

37 Berkhof, *Systematic Theology*, 632–33. Emphasis in original.

38 Booth, "Covenant Transition," 175.

tence.[39] Reformed paedobaptists usually describe any newness of the new covenant as a reference to *external* aspects only. For example, Jeffrey Niell notes, "The newness of the new covenant pertains to the external aspects, the outward administration, of the covenant of grace. The new covenant is not new in its nature of membership."[40]

Is there any actual newness in the new covenant? Examining the texts concerning the new covenant, I will argue that there are significant differences between the old and new covenants, confirming that the new covenant is distinct from any of the covenants that came before it.[41] Although we can observe a variety of these qualitative differences, I will focus on two. First, the regenerative capacity of the new covenant changes from that under the old covenant. Second, the indwelling ministry of the Holy Spirit differs significantly under the new covenant.

1. The Complete Regenerative Capacity of the New Covenant

In Jeremiah 31:31–34, we have the clearest Old Testament annunciation of the new covenant. This passage is even more critical because Hebrews quotes it in 8:8–12 as evidence that the old covenant was inferior and has been replaced by the new covenant. Jeremiah 31:31–34 reads as follows:

> Behold, the days are coming, declares the Lord, when I will make a new covenant with the house of Israel and the house of Judah, not like the covenant that I made with their fathers on the day when I took them by the hand to bring them out of the land of Egypt, my covenant that they broke, though I was their husband, declares the Lord. For this is the covenant that I will make with the house of Israel after those days, declares the Lord: I will put my law within them, and I will write it on their hearts. And I will be their God, and they shall be my people. And no longer shall each one teach his neighbor and each his brother, saying, 'Know the Lord,' for they shall all know me, from the least of them to the

---

39 In the words of Booth, "The transition from the old covenant to the new covenant is a smooth unfolding of God's redemptive plan, because the two covenants are organically connected—they are essentially one covenant of grace" (Booth, "Covenant Transition," 199).

40 Jeffrey D. Niell, "The Newness of the New Covenant," in *The Case for Covenantal Infant Baptism*, ed. Gregg Strawbridge (Phillipsburg, NJ: P&R Publishing, 2003), 155.

41 It should be noted here that this is one of the classic arguments by Reformed Baptists who hold to a covenant of grace. Reformed Baptists typically argue that the change from old to new covenant is drastic and brings with it significant changes to the participants. For an example of this argumentation, see James R. White, "The Newness of the New Covenant (Part 2)," in *Recovering a Covenantal Heritage: Essays in Baptist Covenant Theology*, ed. Richard C. Barcellos (Palmdale, CA: RBAP, 2014), 360–82.

greatest, declares the Lord. For I will forgive their iniquity, and I will remember their sin no more.

We should note, first of all, that the Lord says the new covenant will be "not like the covenant I made with their fathers." The implication is that we should expect dissimilarity between the Mosaic and the new covenant.

As part of this new covenant, God promises that "no longer shall each one teach his neighbor and each his brother, saying, 'Know the Lord,' for they shall all know me, from the least of them to the greatest, declares the Lord" (Jer 31:34a). Scholars have understood the phrase, "they shall all know me," in a variety of ways.

Niell interprets the phrase, "they shall all know me," in Jeremiah 31:34 (cf. Heb 8:11) as referring to the cessation of the Levitical priesthood.[42] He writes, "The conclusion that the Levitical priesthood and its attendant duties are in view is based on the immediate context and an understanding of the place and function of the priests in the old covenant administration of the covenant of grace."[43] Niell argues for this viewpoint because the priests typically had a special relationship before the Lord, which involved teaching and instructing others about Yahweh. In the old covenant, those who were laypeople could not approach God in the same way as the priests. Thus, the distinction of the new covenant, according to Niell, is that everyone ("from the least to the greatest of them") will now know God in the same way the Levitical priests did.

Although not the majority position among Reformed paedobaptists, it is worth making some comments on Niell's view.[44] First, the phraseology of "knowing" someone often has relational implications in both the Old Testament (e.g., Gen 4:1; Ps 88:9 [8]; Amos 3:2, etc.) and the New Testament (e.g., Matt 11:27; Luke 2:44; John 17:3; 1 Cor 1:21, etc.). Typically, when a person is the object of a verb of knowledge, a relationship is in view. Thus, for Niell to argue that special Levitical knowledge is in view here is not the most natural interpretation of this phrase.

Furthermore, the context of the new covenant passages forbids such an interpretation. Most scholars agree that Jeremiah 30–33 forms one unit in Jeremiah. This section is often called, "The Book of Consolation," due

42 Niell, "The Newness of the New Covenant," 147–53.

43 Ibid., 148.

44 For a full response to Niell's discussion on the newness of the new covenant, see White, "The Newness of the New Covenant (Part 2)," 360–74.

to the hope and encouragement found within.[45] Inside this section, while discussing the guarantee of Israel's future, God promises twice that the Levitical priests will continue to serve (Jer 33:18, 22). Therefore, it would be most unnatural to see Jeremiah 33:34 as promising the Levitical priesthood will end, while in the same section Jeremiah promises the priesthood will continue alongside the Davidic covenant.

Richard Pratt represents a second, and much more popular, view among Reformed paedobaptists. Referring to the same phrase, "they shall all know me," Pratt writes, "In a word, to know God as Jeremiah spoke of it would be to receive eternal salvation. In the covenant of which Jeremiah spoke, salvation would come to each participant. *There would be no exceptions*."[46] For Pratt, and most Reformed paedobaptists, there is agreement with non-paedobaptists that the knowledge spoken of here in Jeremiah 31:34 is salvific knowledge.

However, this is potentially problematic for the Reformed paedobaptist. If the new covenant promises each new covenant member will be regenerate ("they shall all know me"), how can one consider infants as covenant members? Pratt alerts his readers to the issue when he says, "How can we believe in infant baptism when God himself said that the new covenant would be inviolable, internalized, and include only those who know the Lord?"[47]

The crux of Pratt's argument is that, although Jeremiah 31:34 refers to an entirely regenerate covenant community, that promise will only find complete fulfillment at the return of Christ. In Pratt's words, "Once Christ returns, it will not be possible to break the new covenant and thereby to enter into another exile. Before that time, however, participants in the new covenant can break the new covenant."[48] In other words, new covenant participants in today's church can (and often do) break the covenant by apostatizing into unbelief. However, after Christ comes, the fullness of the new covenant will be present, and there will be no more covenant break-

45 Walter C. Kaiser Jr., *Walking the Ancient Paths: A Commentary on Jeremiah* (Bellingham, WA: Lexham Press, 2019), 336.

46 Richard L. Pratt Jr., "Infant Baptism in the New Covenant," in *The Case for Covenantal Infant Baptism*, ed. Gregg Strawbridge (Phillipsburg, NJ: P&R Publishing, 2003), 161. Emphasis added.

47 Ibid.

48 Ibid., 169.

ers.[49] Thus, according to Pratt, the new covenant, like the old covenant, continues to be a mixed community until the return of Christ.

Pratt argues for this position by pointing to a threefold fulfillment pattern in Jeremiah 31. He argues that the new covenant includes three aspects:

- Future planting of God's people in the land (vv. 27–30)
- Future new covenant with God's people (vv. 31–37)
- Future rebuilding and permanence of the holy city (vv. 38–40)[50]

Pratt explains:

> Because the New Testament does not explicitly apply this threefold fulfillment pattern to Jeremiah's prophecy of the new covenant, the fulfillment of that particular prophecy is often misunderstood. Often interpreters approach this text as if the new covenant was realized in its fullness when Christ first came to earth, but this is a serious error. Christ has not yet completed the restoration, and thus we have not yet obtained the promised blessings in full. The new covenant was inaugurated in Christ's first coming; it progresses in part during the continuation of Christ's kingdom; but it will reach complete fulfillment only when Christ returns in the consummation of all things. We must approach Jeremiah 31:31–34 just as we approach all prophecies regarding the restoration after exile: with the understanding that the restoration of the kingdom and the renewal of the covenant will not be complete until Jesus returns.[51]

I agree with Pratt that the new covenant has not been completely fulfilled at this point in history.[52] The restoration of the land to Israel has not taken place yet (Jer 33:11b; cf. Ezek 36:24). Additionally, the nation of Israel is not "one nation in the land" with "one king over them all" (Ezek 37:22). Even in the New Testament, well after the death of Christ, Paul viewed the restoration of Israel to be a future event as per the promise of

49 "Until the consummation, the new covenant will continue to be a mixture of true believers and sanctified unbelievers" (Pratt, "Infant Baptism in the New Covenant," 173).

50 Ibid., 164.

51 Ibid., 168–69.

52 Contra White, who argues, "We suggest that any concept of partiality stands in direct opposition to the apologetic thrust of the writer himself. If we take the inspired interpretation of the New Testament as our norm, we must reject the partial fulfillment theory based upon the usage of the text itself" (White, "The Newness of the New Covenant (Part 2)," 380).

additional difference between the old and new covenants. Ezekiel 36:25–27 reads as follows:

> I will sprinkle clean water on you, and you shall be clean from all your uncleannesses, and from all your idols I will cleanse you. And I will give you a new heart, and a new spirit I will put within you. And I will remove the heart of stone from your flesh and give you a heart of flesh. And I will put my Spirit within you, and cause you to walk in my statutes and be careful to obey my rules.

Ezekiel prophesies that, in contrast to the old covenant experience, where many of the individuals did not obey the Lord, God will "cause you to walk in my statutes and be careful to obey my rules" (v. 27b). The key component for why this will happen in the future is the indwelling ministry of the Spirit for each covenant member.

In the Old Testament, God dwelled with His people in the tabernacle and temple. However, in the New Testament, God gives His Spirit to each covenant member.[61] This, of course, does not mean the Holy Spirit was not active in the Old Testament.[62] Rather, Scripture recognizes a distinction in the ministry of the Holy Spirit under the old covenant compared to the Spirit's ministry in the new covenant.[63]

A survey of the Old Testament shows a variety of differences between the new covenant age and the ministry of the Holy Spirit experienced by those under the old covenant.[64] First, the coming of the Spirit upon individuals in the Old Testament was apparently unrelated to the individual's spiritual qualities.[65] For example, the Spirit empowered Saul in 1 Samuel 10:10 and 11:6, even though Saul's character was highly questionable at that point. Similarly, the Spirit of God came upon wicked Balaam to prophesy blessing upon Israel (Num 24:2). Second, when the Spirit's operative power is in view, it was a unique empowerment of a political leader

61 For a full defense of this position, see James M. Hamilton Jr., *God's Indwelling Presence: The Holy Spirit in the Old & New Testaments*, New American Commentary Studies in Bible and Theology (Nashville, TN: B&H Academic, 2006). Hamilton argues that the personal indwelling ministry of the Holy Spirit is a new covenant phenomenon.

62 For example, see John F. Walvoord, "The Work of the Holy Spirit in the Old Testament," *Bibliotheca Sacra* 97, no. 388 (October 1940): 410–34.

63 Larry Pettegrew, *The New Covenant Ministry of the Holy Spirit* (The Woodlands, TX: Kress Biblical Resources, 2013).

64 Hamilton Jr., *God's Indwelling Presence*, 25–56; John F. Walvoord, *The Holy Spirit*, 3rd ed. (Grand Rapids: Zondervan, 1958), 72–73.

65 Walvoord, *The Holy Spirit*, 72.

assembly in Corinth, Paul identifies each church member as God's temple, the Spirit indwelling each one (1 Cor 3:16–17). Paul uses this identity as the temple of the Holy Spirit to motivate those in the church to keep themselves from sexual sin (1 Cor 6:19–20). Not only does Scripture assume that new covenant members have the Holy Spirit, but Paul describes their initiation into the Spirit as happening through baptism (1 Cor 12:13; Eph 4:4–6).[71]

It is worth emphasizing that the New Testament describes each member of the church as having the Spirit. Importantly, the Spirit's absence indicates that one does not have a relationship with Christ. One of the clearest examples of this is Romans 8:9, "Anyone who does not have the Spirit of Christ does not belong to him."

The simple message of Romans 8:9—that those who do not have the Spirit do not belong to Christ—demonstrates an inconsistency in the Reformed paedobaptist position. Although infants are not saved and do not have the Spirit, the Reformed paedobaptist typically views baptized infants as belonging to God in Christ. For example, Brownson writes, "For both believers and baptized children, baptism is the public mark upon them, signifying that they belong to God in Jesus Christ."[72] As another example, paedobaptist Daniel Doriani encourages parents to speak the following words to their baptized children:

> We baptized you when you were little, too. We promised to raise you to trust Jesus. The pastor put water on your head. We use water for washing, and when we baptized you, we asked God to wash away your sins. The pastor said "In the name of the Father and of the Son and of the Holy Spirit" for you, too. That means that he asked God to be your God. Now you belong to him.[73]

Although Reformed paedobaptists may claim that an infant's baptism brings that child into a relationship with Christ, Scripture speaks against such an idea. For the New Testament writers, the Spirit's presence is essential for new covenant members. This affirmation matches the unified prophetic voice of the Old Testament (cf. Isa 32:15; Ezek 36:27; 39:29; Joel 2:28–29). Conversely, according to the New Testament, the Spirit's *absence* indicates someone does not belong to Christ (cf. Rom 8:9; Jude 19).

---

71 Additionally, Galatians links the reception of the Spirit to the exercise of faith (Gal 3:2, 5; cf. Eph 1:13). Galatians also emphasizes the connection between being a son of God and the reception of the Spirit (Gal 4:6).

72 Brownson, *The Promise of Baptism*, 101.

73 Doriani, "Matthew 28:18–20 and the Institution of Baptism," 42.

The implication of the Holy Spirit's explicit link with the new covenant is twofold. First, there is a significant difference between the indwelling of the Holy Spirit in the new covenant and the lack of permanent indwelling in the old covenant. Therefore, it is incorrect to view the old and new covenants as essentially the same, with only external differences. The new covenant indwelling of the Holy Spirit differs significantly from any other covenant. Second, the New Testament describes each new covenant member as having the indwelling presence of the Spirit. Thus, we cannot view unregenerate infants who do not have the indwelling Spirit as members of the new covenant.

Given the above argument, it should come as no surprise that most Reformed paedobaptists would, of necessity, assert that the ministry of the Holy Spirit is the same in both Old and New Testaments.[74] For example, B.B. Warfield writes, "The Spirit of God of the Old Testament performs all the functions which are ascribed to the Holy Ghost of the New Testament, and bears all the same characteristics. They are conceived alike both in their nature and in their operations."[75] Similarly, John Owen, writes, "The indwelling of the Spirit is the great and solemn promise of the covenant of grace."[76] Owen points to David as an example that the Spirit "doth so dwell in and remain with the saints."[77] Similar to Warfield and Owen, Sinclair Ferguson notes that the difference between old covenant believers being indwelled by the Spirit and new covenant believers is, "not in the manner of his dwelling so much as in the capacity in which he indwells."[78]

---

74 However, not every Reformed paedobaptist argues that the Holy Spirit's ministry is essentially the same in the old and new covenants. Although disagreement is uncommon among Reformed adherents, a few exceptions exist. Notably, Michael Horton, "'The Lord and Giver of Life': The Holy Spirit in Redemptive History," *Journal of the Evangelical Theological Society* 62, no. 1 (2019): 53; R. C. Sproul, *Who Is the Holy Spirit?*, The Crucial Questions Series 13 (Orlando, FL: Reformation Trust, 2012), 58.

Additionally, there are non-paedobaptist interpreters who would see the Spirit's indwelling ministry as the same in both covenants. For example, Walter C. Kaiser Jr., "The Indwelling Presence of the Holy Spirit in the Old Testament," *Evangelical Quarterly* 82, no. 4 (2010): 308–15; Robert V. McCabe, "Were Old Testament Believers Indwelt by the Spirit?," *Detroit Baptist Theological Seminary Journal* 9 (2004): 215–64.

75 Benjamin Breckinridge Warfield, "The Spirit of God in the Old Testament," in *Biblical and Theological Studies* (Philadelphia, PA: Presbyterian and Reformed, 1952), 8.

76 John Owen, *The Doctrine of the Saints Perseverance Explained and Confirmed* [1654], vol. 11 of *The Works of John Owen*, ed. W. G. Gould (London: Johnstone & Hunter, 1850–53; reprint, Edinburgh: Banner of Truth Trust, 1965), 330.

77 Ibid., 331.

78 Sinclair B. Ferguson, *The Holy Spirit* (Downers Grove, IL: InterVarsity Press, 1997), 68.

However, as noted above, the Old Testament prophets and New Testament discourse clearly indicate a difference between the new covenant indwelling ministry of the Spirit and the experience of believers under the old covenant. If the Spirit's role in the new covenant differs from the old covenant experience, then it is difficult to argue for essential sameness between the old and new covenants. The qualitative and significant differences in the new covenant experience prevent viewing these covenants as the same covenant of grace. Furthermore, if Spirit-indwelling is the expectation for every member of the new covenant in the church, then this is a convincing argument against including children in the covenant through infant baptism. Infants cannot be considered new covenant members without the presence of the Holy Spirit. And the Holy Spirit comes through the exercise of faith (Gal 3:2, 5, 14).

Conclusion

Reformed paedobaptists argue that we should view the various covenants in Scripture as manifestations of one covenant of grace. I have argued in this chapter against the idea of one unified covenant of grace. Although God's plan of salvation is the same in the Old and New Testaments, there is no evidence that we should view the covenants of Scripture as various manifestations of a singular covenant of grace.[79] If the covenant of grace is not a valid category, this theological conclusion carries with it important consequences.

First, because the old and new covenants are distinct covenants, this puts the burden of proof on the Reformed paedobaptist to prove that infants are to be granted full membership under the new covenant. Because of the covenant dissimilarities, one cannot simply assume that the old and new covenant are the same. The new covenant carries with it some significant qualitative differences that are not merely external.

Second, if the covenant of grace is not a valid category, the view that baptism has replaced circumcision is questionable.[80] Reformed paedobaptists often promote the connection between infant circumcision and baptism as a powerful argument for infant baptism. However, one of the primary reasons they view this connection so strongly is because of the presupposed unity of the covenant of grace. If the covenant of grace is not

79 See Jeffrey J. Niehaus, "An Argument Against Theologically Constructed Covenants," *Journal of the Evangelical Theological Society* 50, no. 2 (June 2007): 259–273.

80 We will discuss this issue in chapter five.

a valid construct, the paradigm of baptism replacing circumcision is on shaky ground.

As discussed in the first chapter, Ulrich Zwingli began to formulate and emphasize one singular covenant of grace between the Old and New Testaments as a way of arguing against the Anabaptists. Since Zwingli, Reformed paedobaptists have used the covenant of grace argument as their primary support for infant baptism. In this chapter, I have shown that the idea of one unifying covenant of grace does not fit with the biblical evidence. It is far more consistent to recognize multiple biblical covenants instituted by God for many purposes—all of which facilitate His plan to save a people for Himself and glorify His name.

Chapter 4

Paedobaptism and the One People of God

As we saw in chapter two, for the Reformed paedobaptist, the argument for paedobaptism depends on covenant theology. A central piece of the Reformed paedobaptist understanding of covenant theology is one unified covenant across the testaments. This singular covenant is called the covenant of grace. Reformed paedobaptists understand this covenant of grace to be manifested in various ways throughout history in the biblical covenants. They view the old and new covenants as essentially the same, with an equivalent covenant sign (circumcision in the old, and baptism in the new).

Having dealt with the foundational belief of a unified covenant of grace in the previous chapter, we now consider a second critical argument for the Reformed paedobaptist. Most Reformed paedobaptists believe that there is one continuous people of God in both Old and New Testaments. For the typical Reformed paedobaptist, there is no distinction between the church and Israel.

Does it Matter if There Is a Distinction between the Church and Israel?

Some readers may wonder why this point relates to paedobaptism. To see how it relates, one simply needs to follow the Reformed paedobaptist logic. For example, take the argument for paedobaptism by B. B. Warfield. He writes:

> The argument in a nutshell is simply this: God established His Church in the days of Abraham and put children into it. They must remain there until He puts them out. He has nowhere put them out. They are still then members of His Church and as such entitled to its ordinances. Among these ordinances is baptism,

which standing in similar place in the New Dispensation to circumcision in the Old, is like it to be given to children.[1]

Notice Warfield's foundational point—children belonged to the church in the days of Abraham, and there has been no change or instruction since that time to put children out of the church today. Therefore, the church (as it exists in both Old and New Testaments) must continue to include children.

In even more bold terms, Warfield writes:

> It is true that there is no express command to baptize infants in the New Testament, no express record of the baptism of infants, and no passages so stringently implying it that we must infer from them that infants were baptized. If such warrant as this were necessary to justify the usage we should have to leave it incompletely justified. But the lack of this express warrant is something far short of forbidding the rite; and if the continuity of the Church through all ages can be made good, the warrant for infant baptism is not to be sought in the New Testament but in the Old Testament, when the Church was instituted, and nothing short of an actual forbidding of it in the New Testament would warrant our omitting it now. As Lightfoot expressed it long ago, "It is not forbidden" in the New Testament to "baptize infants—therefore, they are to be baptized."[2]

In this quote, Warfield argues that the church of the New Testament must practice infant baptism, "if the continuity of the Church through all ages can be made good." In other words, if Old Testament Israel and the New Testament church are the same, then infant baptism should be practiced. For Warfield, himself a stalwart paedobaptist, one cannot find evidence for infant baptism in the New Testament. However, that is inconsequential because "the warrant for infant baptism is not to be sought in the New Testament but in the Old Testament."

Although many paedobaptists would not state the case as strongly as Warfield, they would agree with him about the importance of the continuity between Israel and the church. For example, Booth writes, "Since God has not changed the terms of church membership, new covenant believers and their children are likewise included in his church.... The people of

1 Warfield, "The Polemics of Infant Baptism," 408.

2 Ibid., 399–400.

God in the Old Testament and the people of God in the New Testament are one and the same people."[3]

Charles Hodge also acknowledges the importance of this argument when he writes:

> If children are to be deprived of a birthright which they have enjoyed ever since there was a Church on earth, there must be some positive command for their exclusion, or some clearly revealed change in the conditions of membership, which renders such exclusion necessary. It need hardly be said that Christ did not give any command no longer to consider the children of believers as members of the Church, neither has there been any change in the conditions of church-membership which necessarily works their exclusion. Those conditions are now what they were from the beginning.[4]

As these quotes illustrate, for the Reformed paedobaptist, there is one people of God. This one people of God are the same in both Old and New Testaments, unified under the same covenant of grace. Therefore, because the people of God and the covenant are the same, the Reformed paedobaptist expects the covenant sign to continue to apply in the same way to believers and their children. For the Reformed paedobaptist, the covenant sign is circumcision in the old covenant and baptism in the new covenant. It is a logical argument built on the theological framework of the covenant of grace and the unity of the people of God.

I would propose that it is a logical necessity for the Reformed paedobaptist position to hold to a unified people of God in both Old and New Testaments. This is not to say everyone who equates Israel and the church must believe in infant baptism. After all, many Reformed Baptists do not distinguish between Israel and the church. Nor is it correct to say that every paedobaptist has historically equated Israel and the church. However, if one recognizes a distinction between Israel and the church, it becomes inconsistent to argue for the Reformed understanding of paedobaptism, since the argument rests on the continuity of one covenant *and* one people of God.

If Israel and the church are distinct entities, then this opens the possibility that God may have a distinct purpose for both Israel and the church. Furthermore, if there are distinct purposes for Israel and the church, then

3 Booth, *Children of the Promise*, 73.

4 Charles Hodge, *Systematic Theology*, vol. 3 (Oak Harbor, WA: Logos Research Systems, 1997), 556.

the sign which revealed Israelite identity (circumcision), need not correspond to the sign of entrance into the church (baptism).[5] If Israel and the church are distinct in Scripture, then one must talk about entrance requirements for each entity. One cannot presume that the conditions of entrance for Israel and the church are the same.

A Biblical Case for a Distinction between Israel and the Church

Given the focus of this book on baptism, it is not possible to do a thorough analysis into all the differences between Israel and the church. Others have already done masterful, full-length treatments on the issue.[6] However, for our purposes, I would like to point out three brief lines of evidence that argue for a distinction between the church and Israel.

Old Testament Prophecy of Israel's Exile and Restoration

From the very outset of Israel's existence, God taught Israel that they would ultimately disobey God and go into exile. We find this message firmly entrenched in the Law itself. For example, Moses prophesies in Deuteronomy 4:25–31 that the people of Israel will live in the land, act corruptly, anger the Lord, and be cast into exile.[7] However, Moses is confident that the future exile would not be the end for Israel. He tells Israel in Deuteronomy 4:29, that after exile, "you will seek the Lord your God, and you will find him, for you will seek him with all your heart and all your soul."[8] Moses then promises the people of Israel that, "When you are in tribulation, and all these things come upon you in the latter days, you will return to the LORD your God and obey his voice" (v. 30). These verses speak of a future time when Israel will experience "all these things." It is especially important to note the phrase "latter days," which highlights the eschatological implications of this section.[9]

5 We will discuss the link between circumcision and baptism in the next chapter.

6 For example, see Michael J. Vlach, *Has the Church Replaced Israel? A Theological Evaluation* (Nashville, TN: Broadman & Holman, 2010).

7 Another important passage to be aware of is Leviticus 26:40–45, which clearly stipulates the pattern of Israel's exile and repentance.

8 Translation is my own. For a full explanation of Deuteronomy 4:25–31, along with a defense of the above translation, see Peter J. Goeman, "Towards a New Proposal for Translating the Conjunction כִּי in Deuteronomy 4.29," *The Bible Translator* 71, no. 2 (2020): 158–78.

9 G. K. Beale, *A New Testament Biblical Theology: The Unfolding of the Old Testament in the New* (Grand Rapids: Baker Academic, 2011), 92–102; Peter J. Goeman, "Implications of the Kingdom in Acts 3:19–21," *The Master's Seminary Journal* 26, no. 1 (2015): 81–82.

The final chapters of Deuteronomy repeat this message of exile and restoration (cf. Deut 30:1–10). The major difference between 4:25–31 and 30:1–10 is the in-depth treatment of the cause of Israel's repentance and restoration. In Deuteronomy 30, God himself will circumcise the hearts of the people and their offspring, "so that you will love the LORD your God with all your heart and with all your soul, that you may live" (30:6). God will enable the nation to obey, and they will obey and return to their land.

This Mosaic expectation of Israel's treachery, exile, and repentance that leads to restoration also shows up in the prophetic literature. Although it is impossible to discuss the vast volume of prophetic commentary on Israel's future restoration,[10] a few passages will suffice.

A primary example from the Minor Prophets is Hosea 3:4–5. These verses teach, "the children of Israel shall dwell many days without king or prince, without sacrifice or pillar, without ephod or household gods. Afterward the children of Israel shall return and seek the Lord their God, and David their king, and they shall come in fear to the Lord and to his goodness in the latter days." Identical to Deuteronomy 4:30, we find the phrase, "in the latter days" here.[11] Keeping with the themes foretold in Deuteronomy, Hosea prophesies that Israel will be in exile, unable to worship at all. After this exile, they will return to the Lord their God and David their king—likely a Messianic reference.

Similarly, although there are many passages in the Major Prophets which talk about Israel's return from exile, Jeremiah 30:3 is representative: "For behold, days are coming, declares the Lord, when I will restore the fortunes of my people, Israel and Judah, says the Lord, and I will bring them back to the land that I gave to their fathers, and they shall take possession of it." The theme of Israel's restoration is the dominant theme of Jeremiah 30–33.[12] Clearly, the prophets and their audience looked forward to the time when God would bring national Israel back from their exile.

The Old and New Testament Expectation of a Kingdom of God

Closely connected to the previous prophetic theme of restoration and blessing is the theme of a future kingdom for Israel. The Old Testament

10 Cf. Vlach, *He Will Reign Forever*, 104–105. Vlach gives a short list containing Jeremiah 16:15; 29:14; 30:3; 31:10; Ezekiel 11:17; 20:34; 36:24; 38:8; Amos 9:14. These passages simply use the concept and vocabulary of "restoration," however, the theme of restoration and gathering the people back into the land extends to many other passages.

11 Goeman, "Implications of the Kingdom in Acts 3:19–21," 82.

12 Kaiser Jr., *Walking the Ancient Paths*, 339.

speaks extensively about a future kingdom for Israel.[13] As we saw in Hosea 3:4–5, the prophet foretold a time when the nation Israel would turn to David, "their king." Ezekiel 37:22 also notes the kingly theme, "And I will make them one nation in the land, on the mountains of Israel. And one king shall be king over them all, and they shall be no longer two nations, and no longer divided into two kingdoms." Similarly, Isaiah 2:2–4 speaks of a time that will occur "in the latter days," when the nations will come to Jerusalem to hear the word of the Lord. Isaiah specifies that the Lord will rule from Jerusalem during this time and judge the nations.

Some have tried to argue that the church has fulfilled the prophecy of Isaiah 2. Referring to this passage, Reformed paedobaptist Kenneth Gentry, writes, "Isaiah says that Christ's church will be established in 'the top of the mountains,' indicating she will be 'permanently fixed, rendered permanently visible.'"[14] Gentry argues that the reference to Judah and Jerusalem in Isaiah 2 represents the whole people of God, similar to Jeremiah 31:31.[15] However, this kind of interpretation seems forced and lacking contextual support. Judah and Jerusalem clearly refer to Israel, both ethnically and geographically. The passage also talks about much more than personal salvation. It talks about a geopolitical kingdom that exists during a time of international peace.[16]

Zechariah 12–14 also has important kingdom implications. Zechariah prophesies that God will give Jerusalem a spirit of repentance (12:10), which matches with the message earlier in Deuteronomy 30:6, where God promises to circumcise Israel's heart. The prophet Zechariah outlines the timing of this repentance two chapters later. Zechariah 14 prophesies that Jerusalem will be surrounded and fall to enemy armies (vv. 1–2), but the Lord will return and save Jerusalem and institute His kingdom (vv. 3–4). It is at that moment when "living waters shall flow out from Jerusalem" (v. 8) and "the LORD will be king over all the earth" (v. 9).

As the details of Zechariah 14 unfold, we read that other nations will be required to visit Jerusalem and observe the Feast of Booths (v. 16). However, some nations will not obey, so God will judge them (vv. 17–19). The

13 William D. Barrick, "The Kingdom of God in the Old Testament," *The Master's Seminary Journal* 23, no. 2 (Fall 2012): 173–92.

14 Kenneth L. Gentry, "Postmillennialism," in *Three Views on the Millennium and Beyond*, ed. Darrell L. Bock (Grand Rapids: Zondervan, 1999), 37.

15 Ibid., 36.

16 For a full discussion of this passage, see Vlach, *He Will Reign Forever*, 151–54.

presence of disobedient nations during the kingdom shows that Zechariah 14 is speaking of a time other than the eternal state.[17]

These Old Testament prophecies are just a select few of the vast number of Old Testament texts that speak of a future kingdom for Israel. The follow-up question is whether this kingdom expectation continues into the intertestamental and New Testament period. I have written on this issue in the past, and the prevailing expectation of the Jewish people leading up to the time of Christ and the apostles was that national repentance would lead to an Israelite kingdom.[18] So, if the Old Testament and intertestamental expectation was of a kingdom for Israel, does the New Testament do anything to qualify those expectations?

Far from it. The disciples identify with the common Jewish expectation of a coming restoration of the Israelite kingdom. The disciples demonstrate this by asking Jesus about the kingdom after His resurrection, "Lord, will you at this time restore the kingdom to Israel?" (Acts 1:6b). It is significant that the apostles asked this question after being instructed about the kingdom of God for forty days (Acts 1:3b). It is unlikely that after forty days of intense instruction with the resurrected Lord that they would miss the basic reality of *what* the kingdom of God is. Their question relates to the *when*, not the *what* of the kingdom.[19] The *what* had been clearly defined and understood.

Jesus does not correct the disciples' expectation of a kingdom. Instead, He tells the disciples that it is not for them "to know the times or the seasons" (1:7). As the apostolic ministry continues through the book of Acts, Peter again appeals to the Jewish understanding of the kingdom in Acts 3.[20]

After Peter and John heal a man who was lame from birth, the Jewish populace thronged around them to hear what these miracle-workers had to say. In Acts 3:19–21, Peter calls his Jewish brothers and sisters to repent, "so that times of refreshing may come from the presence of the Lord, and that he may send the Christ appointed for you" (v. 20). The phrase "times of refreshing" has clear parallels in Second Temple Jewish literature regarding the expectations of the eschatological age and the future kingdom

17 Ibid., 243–44.

18 Goeman, "Implications of the Kingdom in Acts 3:19–21," 84–87.

19 Vlach, *He Will Reign Forever*, 402–03.

20 For a full discussion of the implications of Acts 3, see Goeman, "Implications of the Kingdom in Acts 3:19–21," 75–93.

of Israel.[21] This reference to the kingdom makes sense given the Messianic context of Peter's message.[22]

Continuing his message, Peter says the Messiah will be in heaven, "until the time for restoring all things about which God spoke by the mouth of his holy prophets long ago" (v. 21). There are a couple important observations about this verse. First, Peter points to the prophets as the foundation for the kingdom expectations. As we saw, even in brief, it is clear that the prophets envisioned a glorious future kingdom for Israel. Second, Peter describes this time period as the "time for restoring" (χρόνων ἀποκαταστάσεως). The word for restoring (ἀποκαταστάσεως), is the cognate noun to the verb used in Acts 1:6 when the disciples asked Jesus if He was to restore the kingdom at that time. The word for restoration in Acts 3:21 is not used anywhere else in Scripture, which shows a strong and intentional connection to the verbal cognate in Acts 1:6. Thus, we see that Peter ties together the kingdom theme of Acts 1:6 and 3:21, urging the Jews to repent so that the kingdom restoration might take place.[23]

Apostolic Expectation of Israel's Restoration

As we have seen, the book of Acts continues the Old Testament expectation of a future restoration and kingdom for Israel. This apostolic certainty of Israel's restoration is perhaps nowhere more clearly expressed than in Romans 11:25–26a.[24] Paul writes, "Lest you be wise in your own sight, I do not want you to be unaware of this mystery, brothers: a partial hardening has come upon Israel, until the fullness of the Gentiles has come in. And in this way all Israel will be saved ..."

Paul notes that God has hardened Israel, as a nation, until the fullness of the Gentiles comes in. When the fullness of the Gentiles does come in, the nation will then experience wholesale repentance, returning to God and experiencing His divine blessing again.[25] Importantly, seeing a future Jewish conversion is not a dispensational-only interpretation. For example,

21 4 Ezra 7:75, 91, 95; 11:46; 13:26–29; 2 Baruch 73–74; 1 Enoch 45.5; 51.4; 96.3.

22 Goeman, "Implications of the Kingdom in Acts 3:19–21," 77.

23 Ibid., 79; Vlach, *He Will Reign Forever*, 417.

24 For a robust debate on the various views on Israel and the church in Romans 9–11, see Andrew Naselli and Jared Compton, eds., *Three Views on Israel and the Church: Perspectives on Romans 9–11* (Grand Rapids: Kregel Academic, 2019). My own perspective would line up most clearly with Michael J. Vlach, "A Non-Typological Future-Mass-Conversion View," in *Three Views on Israel and the Church: Perspectives on Romans 9–11*, ed. Andrew Naselli and Jared Compton (Grand Rapids: Kregel Academic, 2019), 21–76.

25 Moo, *The Epistle to the Romans*, 732–33.

notable Reformed paedobaptist scholar James Montgomery Boice[26] notes the following on Romans 11:

> During my student days I was told that the future explanation was a dispensational view only and that no Reformed theologians held to it. Having studied these views carefully, I find instead that the majority of the great commentators on Romans, including Reformed commentators, recognize that the passage is speaking of a future day of Jewish conversion.[27]

Similarly, Charles Hodge, another Reformed paedobaptist, argues at length for seeing this passage as applying to national Israel in the future.[28] In his magisterial Romans commentary, he writes, "The words, *all Israel*, in the next verse, cannot … be understood of the *spiritual* Israel; because the word is just before used in a different sense, 'blindness in part has happened unto Israel.' This blindness is to continue until a certain time, when it is to be removed, and then all Israel is to be saved."[29]

Those who acknowledge that this passage speaks to a future salvation for national Israel are not obligated to believe in a future kingdom for Israel.[30] It is possible to view this as a generic prophecy of many ethnic Israelites being saved. However, the mass conversion and restoration of Israel in Romans 11 fits flawlessly with the kingdom promises of the Old Testament prophets. Therefore, the burden of proof is on the interpreter who wants to separate the kingdom promises of salvation and restoration in the Old Testament from Romans 11.

Summary

In both the Old and New Testaments, the Bible refers to the nation of Israel as a special entity that has a unique role in God's plan. The Old Testament prophesies a future time when God will restore the nation of

---

26 Boice himself was a bit of an anomaly when it came to systems. He was a Reformed paedobaptist, but also premillennial and pretribulational, believing strongly in a future for Israel.

27 James Montgomery Boice, *Romans: God and History (Romans 9–11)*, vol. 3 (Grand Rapids: Baker Books, 1991), 1362.

28 Charles Hodge, *A Commentary on the Epistle to the Romans* (Philadelphia, PA: Alfred Martien, 1873), 585–87.

29 Ibid., 586. Emphasis in original.

30 In addition to Hodge, cf. James M. Hamilton Jr. and Fred G. Zaspel, "A Typological Future-Mass-Conversion View," in *Three Views on Israel and the Church: Perspectives on Romans 9–11*, ed. Andrew Naselli and Jared Compton (Grand Rapids: Kregel Academic, 2019), 97–140.

Israel to their land, and they will experience a restored kingdom. The New Testament does not correct this belief. Instead, the apostles assume the Old Testament promises concerning Israel.[31] If the people of Israel have a distinct role in the plan of God, then Israel and the church are to be viewed as distinct entities, although both form the people of God.[32]

If Israel and the church are not the same, there are significant implications for baptism. Namely, the requirements for being an Israelite are distinct from the requirements for being a member of the church. The biblical distinction between national Israel and the church should bring pause to the argument often used, which assumes the same standards of membership for the covenant community of Old Testament Israel and the new covenant community of Jews *and* Gentiles—the church.

An Argument for the Continuity of Covenant Community

The above argument relies on surveying biblical theology and analyzing the scriptural descriptions and prophecies concerning Israel. When we look at the Old Testament prophecies and New Testament reliance on those prophecies, there is a compelling case for a distinction between the church and Israel. If there is a distinction between the church and Israel, then one must prove continuity in the entrance requirements. One cannot simply assume that the standard for entrance is the same for both the nation of Israel and the church.

Proving that the entrance requirements are the same between Israel and the church is problematic for the Reformed paedobaptist. As noted earlier, there is no command to practice paedobaptism, nor is it even mentioned in the New Testament. Thus, to attempt a positive argument for continuity between Israel and the church, Reformed paedobaptists emphasize the similarity between the covenant communities. Specifically, Reformed paedobaptists argue that Israel and the church are the same regarding covenant membership. Just as Israel had unbelievers and believers in the community, the church also has believers and unbelievers. In other words, the covenant community looks the same for Israel and the church.

31 Ironically, the very argument that Reformed paedobaptists use most often (i.e., assume continuity unless the New Testament corrects our understanding) is ignored when discussing Israel's expectation of a kingdom.

32 For example, see Vlach, *He Will Reign Forever*, 161. Vlach argues that the people of God include both Gentiles and Jews, while the Jews retain a special plan in God's kingdom. Perhaps an analogy could be made in looking at the makeup of the church as male and female. Although Paul unequivocally states that in Christ there is no male or female (Gal 3:28), this does not negate the distinct roles that each play in God's program (cf. 1 Tim 2:12).

Since both Old Testament and New Testament communities include unbelievers, Reformed paedobaptists consider this to be evidence that the covenant community is the same in both Old and New Testaments.

This argument relies on the belief that the new covenant is an extension of the Abrahamic covenant, and the church is an extension of Israel. Hence, there is an expectation within the one covenant of grace that the people of God will similarly consist of believers and unbelievers. In formulating this argument, Reformed paedobaptists often distinguish between those who are elect and those who are members of the new covenant.[33]

In contrast, as explained in the last chapter, Baptists appeal to passages that show the new covenant has significant differences which distinguish it from life in the Old Testament. A primary example is Jeremiah 31:34, which shows that each member of the new covenant is regenerate. Ezekiel 37:27 also teaches that the Spirit of God will indwell each member of the new covenant. So, for the Baptist, there is no difference between those elected to salvation and new covenant members. They are the same—which is a contrast to Israel's existence under the old covenant.

Consequently, for the Reformed paedobaptist, one of the best ways to argue for continuity and similarity between Israel and the church is to show that there are new covenant members who are not regenerate. Strawbridge summarizes the argument as follows: "However, if it can be proved that there are people under new covenant obligations (i.e., 'in the covenant') who become apostates, then the claim that only regenerate people are in the new covenant will be shown to be false. And if this is false, then so is the view of baptism that is based upon it."[34] According to Strawbridge, if there are passages that show new covenant members can break the covenant, then this proves that non-regenerate individuals can be a part of the covenant, just like it was with the old covenant and the people of Israel.

33 Niell, "The Newness of the New Covenant," 133; Booth, "Covenant Transition," 198. Wilson notes, "There is a difference between being *elect*, and being a *covenant member*. The elect cannot be removed from God's sovereign decree; professing Christians can be removed from among God's people, and they frequently are. When they are removed, their unregenerate status is revealed. They are not regenerate, and never were. But they were really in the covenant, a fact that now applies to them to their sorrow" (Wilson, *To a Thousand Generations*, 90). Emphasis in original.

34 Gregg Strawbridge, "The Polemics of Anabaptism from the Reformation Onward," in *The Case for Covenantal Infant Baptism*, ed. Gregg Strawbridge (Phillipsburg, NJ: P&R Publishing, 2003), 280.

The Warning Passages in Hebrews

Out of all the passages used as evidence for those who break the new covenant, Reformed paedobaptists most often cite the warning passages of Hebrews. New Testament scholars typically recognize five warning passages in the book of Hebrews.[35] These passages are heavily debated, and a full discussion is beyond the scope of this book. However, we must evaluate whether these passages teach a distinction between new covenant members and the elect.

Perhaps the most cited of these warning passages is Hebrews 10:26–31. Gregg Strawbridge describes this passage as being decisive in his journey to paedobaptism,[36] and I have observed this trend in others as well. The text states:

> For if we go on sinning deliberately after receiving the knowledge of the truth, there no longer remains a sacrifice for sins, but a fearful expectation of judgment, and a fury of fire that will consume the adversaries. Anyone who has set aside the law of Moses dies without mercy on the evidence of two or three witnesses. How much worse punishment, do you think, will be deserved by the one who has trampled underfoot the Son of God, and has profaned the blood of the covenant by which he was sanctified, and has outraged the Spirit of grace? For we know him who said, "Vengeance is mine; I will repay." And again, "The Lord will judge his people." It is a fearful thing to fall into the hands of the living God.

Reformed paedobaptists believe these verses speak of individuals who are members of the new covenant but end up breaking the covenant. Commenting on verses 29–31, Strawbridge summarizes the argument:

> The writer argues that some individuals who have been "sanctified" (*hagiazō*, "set apart" or "consecrated") in "His people" (the visible people of God) may commit apostasy. Of course, these individuals were never regenerate.... They did not lose their

35 Herbert W. Bateman, "Introducing the Warning Passages in Hebrews: A Contextual Orientation," in *Four Views on the Warning Passages in Hebrews*, ed. Herbert W. Bateman (Grand Rapids: Kregel Academic, 2007), 27. These passages are defined by Bateman as Hebrews 2:1–4; 3:7–4:13; 5:11–6:12; 10:19–39; and 12:14–29. However, he acknowledges other scholars that view the passages more narrowly as 2:1–4; 4:12–13; 6:4–8; 10:26–31; 12:25–29. I am more inclined to view the passages in the latter manner.

36 Gregg Strawbridge, "Introduction," in *The Case for Covenantal Infant Baptism*, ed. Gregg Strawbridge (Phillipsburg, NJ: P&R Publishing, 2003), 4.

salvation, but they did become covenant *breakers*. To do this, they must have been recognized covenant *members*.[37]

This is certainly a possible interpretation of this warning passage. However, some significant considerations make this interpretation unlikely. First, the language of Hebrews does not distinguish between those who are saved and those who are a part of the covenant. For example, in the warning passages the author often addresses the entire church and includes himself in the address.

- "Therefore we must pay much closer attention to what we have heard, lest we drift away from it" (Heb 2:1)
- "Let us therefore strive to enter that rest" (Heb 4:11)
- "Therefore let us leave the elementary doctrine of Christ and go on to maturity, not laying again a foundation of repentance from dead works and of faith toward God" (Heb 6:1)
- "For if we go on sinning deliberately after receiving the knowledge of the truth, there no longer remains a sacrifice for sins" (Heb 10:26)
- "See that you do not refuse him who is speaking. For if they did not escape when they refused him who warned them on earth, much less will we escape if we reject him who warns from heaven" (Heb 12:25)

As the above references illustrate, not only does the author view the church holistically and corporately, but he also uses terms that describe believers (i.e., those who are saved). Notice the descriptions of these individuals in Hebrews 6. They have "been enlightened" (6:4a), they "have tasted the heavenly gift" (6:4b), "shared in the Holy Spirit" (6:4c), and "have tasted the goodness of the word of God and the powers of the age to come" (6:5). These descriptions use the language we would expect of genuine believers.[38]

We can say the same about the warning passage of Hebrews 10:26–31. These individuals have received the "knowledge of the truth" (26a),

37 Strawbridge, "The Polemics of Anabaptism from the Reformation Onward," 281–82. Emphasis in original.

38 Schreiner writes, "When the text says that the readers have been enlightened, been made partakers (sharers) of the Holy Spirit, have come to the knowledge of the truth, and have been sanctified, the intention is to say that they are Christians" (Thomas R. Schreiner, "Perseverance and Assurance: A Survey and a Proposal," *The Southern Baptist Journal of Theology* 2, no. 1 [Spring 1998]: 50).

a description indicative of those regenerated (cf. 1 Cor 2:14). They have also been sanctified (29b),[39] a word that has already been used twice in Hebrews 10 to refer to believers who have been perfected by Christ's sacrifice (10:10, 14). As Waymeyer notes, "The problem for the paedobaptist is that the verb 'to sanctify' (*hagiazo*) is used consistently throughout the book of Hebrews to refer to the setting apart of the genuine believer at the point of conversion as one who has been forgiven and perfected forever by the sacrifice of Christ (2:11 [2x]; 10:10, 14; 13:12)."[40]

As we can see, one is hard pressed to distinguish between believers and new covenant members in these passages. The Hebrew warning passages seem to describe genuine believers. The exegetical evidence is very weighty. But, if these passages refer to genuine believers, how do the warning passages in Hebrews reconcile with the doctrine of the perseverance of the saints? Grudem puts forward one possibility by arguing that these passages are "tests of genuineness," or, a retrospective analysis of the Christian life.[41] In other words, one proves the genuineness of his faith by *not* falling away, because those genuinely saved never fall away. Although Grudem's argument is possible, I ultimately lean toward the analysis of Schreiner and Caneday.[42] They argue that the warning passages in Hebrews are genuine warnings that God uses as a means to motivate true believers to persevere in the faith. The "if" of these warning passages never becomes a reality for the true believer because the Holy Spirit uses texts like these as part of the sovereign means by which saints persevere in the faith.

But, regardless of how one reconciles the Hebrews warning passages with God's sovereign perseverance of the saints, the nonnegotiable point is that Hebrews does not recognize a difference between believers and new covenant members. By inventing a distinction between a new covenant member and a believer, Reformed paedobaptists create a category for the

39 It should be noted that there are strong arguments for seeing the "one sanctified" as Christ here. However, for the sake of argument, I will assume the one sanctified here is the apostate, and thus bolster the paedobaptist position. See the discussions by White, "The Newness of the New Covenant (Part 2)," 370–74; Waymeyer, *A Biblical Critique of Infant Baptism*, 124–25.

40 Waymeyer, *A Biblical Critique of Infant Baptism*, 125.

41 Wayne A. Grudem, "Perseverance of the Saints: A Case Study of Hebrews 6:4–6 and the Other Warning Passages in Hebrews," in *The Grace of God, The Bondage of the Will: Biblical and Practical Perspectives on Calvinism, Volume One*, ed. Thomas R. Schreiner and Bruce A. Ware (Grand Rapids: Baker, 1995), 133–182.

42 Thomas R. Schreiner and Ardel B. Caneday, *The Race Set before Us: A Biblical Theology of Perseverance & Assurance* (Downers Grove, IL: IVP Academic, 2001); Schreiner, "Perseverance and Assurance," 32–62.

sake of their theological position. This distinction between a new covenant member and a believer is not consistent with how the Bible talks about covenants, the new covenant community, or, as we will see, the broader language of apostasy in the New Testament.

The New Testament Theme of Apostasy

The New Testament theme of apostasy is another reason we should see no difference between a new covenant member and one who is truly saved. Throughout the New Testament, Scripture describes apostates in the same terms as believers. For example, some individuals, like Hymenaeus and Alexander, have made "shipwreck of their faith" (1 Tim 1:19–20). Similarly, Hymenaeus and Philetus have destroyed the faith of some (2 Tim 2:18). If faith is the means of salvation and the mark of believers (cf. Eph 2:8–9; 1 Pet 1:5, etc.), then it is noteworthy that the Bible describes apostates in language of faith, which typically marks a genuine believer.

Similarly, John talks about individuals who believe in Jesus (John 2:23–25; 6:60–71; 8:31–59), but it becomes apparent that their belief was not genuine faith.[43] However, it is only apparent after the fact, because these individuals look like Christians until they show they are not. John explains it this way: "They went out from us, but they were not of us; for if they had been of us, they would have continued with us. But they went out, that it might become plain that they all are not of us" (1 John 2:19). In other words, it is only clear after the fact that they are not of us. There are often no descriptive differences or characteristics that might indicate a believer is not genuine. It only becomes apparent when someone abandons the faith.

Not only do the apostles talk about individuals who appear to be believers, but Jesus also mentions this. Jesus notes that there would be those who confess Him as Lord, and yet never truly have a relationship with Him (Matt 7:21–23). In the parable of the soils, He says there will be individuals who embrace the message of the Gospel, and yet fall away because of tribulation or persecution (Matt 13:20–21).

Most of these apostasy texts speak of individuals who appear as genuine believers until they fall away. These individuals abandon their faith and confession, not the new covenant. They abandon the faith because they were never genuine members of the covenant to begin with. In the words of White:

---

43 Schreiner, "Perseverance and Assurance," 47–48.

> Apostasy, then, is viewed as apostasy from a profession of faith, not from membership in the New Covenant. The visible church contains true covenant members and false: but *since the New Covenant is inherently soteriological in nature*, and is made in the blood of Christ himself, its members cannot apostatize anymore than Christ can lose his sheep (John 10:27–30) or fail to do the Father's will (John 6:38–39). Apostasy, then, is not from the New Covenant, but from false profession of faith in Christ, which may include membership in the visible church.[44]

In contrast to the above assessment, the Reformed paedobaptist creates an extra category to explain the phenomenon of apostasy. Because the Reformed paedobaptist presupposes that there are genuine new covenant members who are not believers, he assumes what he is trying to prove. But just because an interpretation is possible does not mean it is likely, or that it matches best with the full testimony of Scripture. The New Testament discussion of apostasy knows nothing of a special category of covenant breakers. In the New Testament language, one is either a part of the church or not. In the language of John, those who fall away show evidence that they were never a genuine member to begin with (1 John 2:19). As Waymeyer observes:

> *What the paedobaptist needs to demonstrate—and yet has* failed *to demonstrate—is that people who profess faith in Christ and yet later abandon that profession were members of the New Covenant prior to their apostasy.* Paedobaptists often list passages that describe apostasy or caution against it and then simply assume that they prove the New Covenant can be broken. In contrast, the Bible teaches that the one who abandons the faith is demonstrating that he was never truly part of the church or the New Covenant.[45]

In summary, Reformed paedobaptists want to argue from apostasy passages for a category of new covenant members who do not participate in the very core components of the new covenant: regeneration and the forgiveness of sins (Jer 31:34). They point to passages such as Hebrews 10:26–31, which are supposed to describe unbelieving new covenant members who abandon the covenant. However, the descriptions used in Hebrews 10:26–31 (as well as in other apostasy passages) are descriptions of believers. There are no descriptive differences between believers and new

44 White, "The Newness of the New Covenant (Part 2)," 359. Emphasis added.

45 Waymeyer, *A Biblical Critique of Infant Baptism*, 119. Emphasis in original.

covenant members. This is an invented category that is assumed in order to argue for a similarity between the old and new covenants.

Conclusion

This chapter has challenged the view of Reformed paedobaptists, that the people of God are essentially the same in the Old and New Testaments. Scripture speaks of national Israel as distinct from the New Testament church. The distinction between the church and Israel does not wipe out the possibility of infant baptism. However, it certainly raises the need to prove that the entrance requirements of the church are the same as the entrance requirements of national Israel. That is not something that can simply be assumed.

In order to make a positive presentation of a link between the old covenant community and new covenant community, Reformed paedobaptists often argue that the new covenant members can break the covenant, just like members of the old covenant. To support this idea, they look to apostasy or warning passages to show that there are unbelieving new covenant members who break the covenant, showing they are not a part of the elect.

However, by examining the New Testament teaching on apostasy, we can see that the New Testament uses the language of believers for apostates. Furthermore, the New Testament retroactively identifies apostates as those who were never a part of God's people. There is no exegetical reason to use a special category that identifies a new covenant member who is not a believer. Yet, this argument is a presuppositional necessity for Reformed paedobaptists because they consider unsaved infants to be full covenant members. However, the New Testament has no category or language for a new covenant member who is not also a genuine believer.

Chapter 5

Has Baptism Replaced Circumcision?

As we have discussed, Reformed paedobaptists rely on covenant theology to argue for infant baptism. The centerpiece of the entire argument is that there is one covenant of grace and a unified people of God without distinction from Old to New Testament. In the preceding two chapters, I pointed to some serious problems with these foundational aspects of the Reformed argument. However, the task is not done. Reformed paedobaptists use two supporting arguments to demonstrate that the covenant of grace is the same in both the Old and New Testaments. The two supporting arguments are the relationship between baptism and circumcision, and the example of household baptisms in the New Testament.

The most critical supporting argument for the Reformed paedobaptist position is the argument that baptism has replaced circumcision as the sign of the covenant of grace. This is the primary concept that Reformed paedobaptists rely on as positive support for infant baptism. John Calvin summarizes the typical Reformed argument when he writes:

> Now we can see without difficulty the similarity and difference of these two signs. The promise (in which we have shown the power of the signs to consist) is the same in both, namely, that of God's fatherly favor, of forgiveness of sins, and of eternal life. Then the thing represented is the same, namely, regeneration. In both there is one foundation upon which the fulfillment of these things rests. Therefore, there is no difference in the inner mystery, by which the whole force and character of the sacraments are to be weighed. *What dissimilarity remains lies in the outward ceremony, which is a very slight factor*, since the most weighty part depends upon the promise and the thing signified. We therefore conclude that, apart from the difference in the visible ceremony, whatever belongs to circumcision pertains likewise to baptism.... By this *it*

> *appears incontrovertible that baptism has taken the place of circumcision to fulfill the same office among us.*[1]

Similarly, Zacharias Ursinus, who represented the generation after Calvin, notes in his *Commentary on the Heidelberg Catechism*, "Baptism occupies the place of circumcision in the New Testament, and has the same use that circumcision had in the Old Testament."[2]

Modern proponents of Reformed paedobaptism have used the same argumentation. For example, I again refer to Warfield's succinct defense of Reformed paedobaptism:

> The argument in a nutshell is simply this: God established His church in the days of Abraham and put children into it. They must remain there until He puts them out. He has nowhere put them out. They are still then members of His Church and as such entitled to its ordinances. Among these ordinances is baptism, which *standing in similar place* in the New Dispensation to circumcision in the Old, is like it to be given to children.[3]

In the same way, Pierre Marcel notes that there is "a difference between the sacraments as regards outward appearance, but they are identical as regards their internal and spiritual significance."[4] Elsewhere Marcel writes, "The New Testament establishes no *essential* difference between circumcision and baptism; such differences as there are are only formal. Baptism has taken the place of circumcision."[5] A page later he writes that circumcision and baptism "are identical as regards the promise and the thing represented, and as regards content, reason, motive, usage, and efficacy."[6]

Likewise, Mark Ross states, "Those who subscribe to covenantal infant baptism maintain that baptism has now replaced circumcision as the mark of covenant membership, and that baptism's meaning and application are essentially the same as circumcision's in the Old Testament period."[7] Robertson agrees when he writes, "In the fullest possible sense, baptism under

1 John Calvin, *Institutes of the Christian Religion*, 1327. Emphasis added.

2 Ursinus, *The Commentary of Zacharias Ursinus on the Heidelberg Catechism*, 367.

3 Warfield, "The Polemics of Infant Baptism," 408. Emphasis added.

4 Pierre Marcel, *The Biblical Doctrine of Infant Baptism: Sacrament of the Covenant of Grace*, trans. Philip Edgcumbe Hughes (London: James Clarke & Co. Ltd., 1953), 90.

5 Ibid., 210. Emphasis in original.

6 Ibid., 211.

7 Ross, "Baptism and Circumcision as Signs and Seals," 97.

the new covenant accomplishes all that was represented in circumcision under the old."[8]

Booth connects circumcision and baptism so closely that he assumes any argument against infant baptism is also an argument against infant circumcision. He writes, "This clear connection between the two covenant signs of circumcision and baptism creates a difficult problem for opponents of infant baptism, for *any argument against infant baptism is necessarily an argument against infant circumcision.*"[9]

As the above citations indicate, there is remarkable unity among Reformed paedobaptists on this point. The idea that baptism has replaced circumcision is so central to the Reformed system, covenant theologians wrote it into the Reformed confessions. For example, the Belgic Confession[10] asserts, "Having abolished circumcision, which was done with blood, he established in its place the sacrament of baptism.... Moreover, what circumcision was to the Jews, that baptism is for our children" (34).

It is helpful to spell out why the connection between circumcision and baptism is so essential to the Reformed paedobaptist argument. Under the old covenant, infants were granted immediate entrance into the covenant community through circumcision. Therefore, unless there is some explicit scriptural guidance to change that pattern, we should grant infants immediate entrance into the covenant under the new administration (i.e., baptism into the church). If we can show that circumcision and baptism are the same, then this is strong support for the idea of one covenant and one covenant community. Thus, the link between baptism and circumcision is *the* crucial piece of evidence for the Reformed paedobaptist position.[11]

The connection between baptism and circumcision is an excellent discussion point to test one's theology. Both circumcision and baptism have significant descriptions in Scripture. Therefore, we have sufficient material from which to draw comparisons or contrasts. By observing the detailed narratives and descriptions of baptism and circumcision, one should be able to discern whether there are any essential differences between the

8 O. Palmer Robertson, *The Christ of the Covenants* (Phillipsburg, NJ: P&R Publishing, 1980), 166.

9 Booth, *Children of the Promise*, 109. Emphasis in original.

10 The Belgic Confession was written in 1561 and adopted in 1571.

11 Ross states it this way: "If no direct proof of the sort discussed above can be given for the paedobaptist position, what kind of evidence can be given? I would maintain that the case fundamentally rests on establishing two principal contentions: first, that baptism and circumcision have essentially the same meaning; and second, that the covenant community is similarly constituted in the Old and New Testaments (specifically, that children are members of the covenant community in both)" (Ross, "Baptism and Circumcision as Signs and Seals," 100).

two. Ultimately, one should be able to evaluate the Reformed paedobaptist claim that baptism has replaced circumcision.

A Brief Overview of Circumcision[12]

Although we know about circumcision primarily through the Old Testament description, it was not a unique custom known only to Israel. Jeremiah 9:25–26 provides a list of nations that seem to have practiced circumcision.[13] Besides Judah, this list specifies Egypt, Edom, the sons of Ammon, and Moab. Out of all the nations listed, Abraham[14] appears to have had the most significant interactions with Egypt. He spent time in Egypt during a severe famine in Canaan (Gen 12:10–20) and at least 23 years with Hagar, an Egyptian maidservant (Gen 16:1–3; 17:25).[15] In the time after Abraham, Israel spent over 400 years in Egypt where they developed as a nation and continued to practice the rite of circumcision, apparently unaltered (cf. Exod 4:24–26; 12:44, 48; Lev 12:3; Josh 5:2–9). Although Scripture is silent on the issue, it seems reasonable that when God instituted the sign of circumcision with Abraham, he interpreted circumcision in light of his familiarity with Egypt.

Egyptian circumcision differed from Israelite circumcision in a variety of ways.[16] First, Egyptian circumcision involved only a slight incision in the foreskin, rather than a removal of the entire foreskin as practiced by Israel. Second, the Egyptians performed circumcision on males 6–14 years old, rather than on male infants eight days old. Third, the evidence seems to indicate that circumcision was obligatory for only the rulers and priests

12 I'm grateful for the work of ThM student, Hunter Hays, "The Meaning and Significance of Circumcision" (ThM Thesis, Shepherds Theological Seminary, 2022). He helped bolster this section on circumcision by his observations and comments.

13 Peter C. Craigie, *Jeremiah 1–25*, Word Biblical Commentary 26 (Dallas, TX: Word, 1991), 153; William Lee Holladay, *Jeremiah 1: A Commentary on the Book of the Prophet Jeremiah, Chapters 1–25*, Hermeneia (Philadelphia, PA: Fortress Press, 1986), 319. Alternatively, this text could simply be saying that the circumcised (Judah) will be punished with the uncircumcised nations, who are then listed in verse 26. This is the translation followed by the KJV, "I will punish all *them which are* circumcised with the uncircumcised." I think it makes more sense to follow the translation of the ESV, "I will punish all those who are circumcised merely in the flesh."

14 Although Abraham is not so named until Genesis 17, for the sake of the reader I will refer to him as Abraham throughout.

15 We arrive at 23 years by taking the 10 years from Genesis 16:1-3 and adding the 13 years in Genesis 17:25.

16 John D. Meade, "The Meaning of Circumcision in Israel: A Proposal for a Transfer of Rite from Egypt to Israel," *Southern Baptist Journal of Theology* 20, no. 1 (2016): 35–54.

of Egypt, but in Israel it was required for every male Israelite (Gen 17:10). After presenting and evaluating the Egyptian evidence, Meade concludes, "Egyptian circumcision functioned as *a specific, voluntary, and initiatory rite to identify and affiliate the subject with the deity and to signify devotion to the same deity*."[17]

Given the above information, I believe we can reasonably establish the purpose of Egyptian circumcision. Since Egyptian circumcision focused primarily on the royal and priestly class, it seems correct to understand Egyptian circumcision as some sort of divine dedication of royalty or priests. If Israel was aware of the dedicatory implications of the Egyptian rite of circumcision for the royal and priestly class, then it would be natural to associate the sign of circumcision with the role of being a kingdom of priests. The title "kingdom of priests" is exactly how God labels Israel in Exodus 19:6.[18] If this understanding is correct, circumcision would at least be marking Israel out for a special role as a kingdom of priests. But it is unlikely that this nuance exhausts the full meaning of circumcision for the ancient Israelites.

In addition to the likely Ancient Near Eastern background of Egyptian circumcision, Scripture itself provides a helpful description that allows us to discern the meaning and significance of circumcision. Genesis 17 is the initial mention of circumcision in the Bible, and the context of the sign of circumcision is God's promise of an eternal covenant (Gen 17:7, 13, 19). Importantly, Genesis 17 was not the initiation of the covenant. God had already initiated and instituted His covenant with Abraham previously (cf. Gen 12:1–3, 7; 13:14–17; 15:7–21). As part of the covenant, God had promised Abraham blessing, descendants, land, nations, and kings. Circumcision was a sign that was tied to these promises of the Abrahamic covenant.[19]

---

17 Ibid., 45. Emphasis in original.

18 John D. Meade, "Circumcision of Flesh to Circumcision of Heart: The Typology of the Sign of the Abrahamic Covenant," in *Progressive Covenantalism: Charting a Course between Dispensational and Covenant Theologies*, ed. Stephen J. Wellum and Brent E. Parker (Nashville, TN: B & H Academic, 2016), 131.

19 In contrast, the Reformed paedobaptist will often only discuss the spiritual blessings and ignore the physical promises of the Abrahamic covenant. For example, Helopoulos writes, "When it comes to the sacrament of circumcision, it is important for us to note that it served not primarily as a sign of family, racial, or national identity—although it did distinguish the Jews from the people of other nations—but rather as a sign and seal of the most extravagant spiritual blessings that God bestows upon man" (Jason Helopoulos, *Covenantal Baptism*, Blessings of the Faith [Phillipsburg, NJ: P&R Publishing, 2021], 30).

A sign in the Old Testament can function in three different ways.[20] First, a *proof sign* endeavors to prove a proposition through extraordinary display. An example of this would be Isaiah 38, where God promises Hezekiah that He will add 15 years to his life (in response to his repentance), as well as deliver Jerusalem from the king of Assyria. To prove that this prophecy would occur, the prophet Isaiah says God will give a sign, specifically, the sundial will turn back ten steps (vv. 7–8). Second, *a symbol sign* represents something through association or similarity. An example of this is when Ezekiel sets up a model of Jerusalem under siege using a brick and an iron griddle, which is called "a sign for the house of Israel" (Ezek 4:1–3). Finally, there can also be a *cognition sign*, the purpose of which is to bring to remembrance something in the mind of an observer. One can further subdivide a cognition sign into two categories: identity signs, which mark something as having a specific identity or function, and mnemonic signs, which bring to mind something already known. An example of an identity sign would be the banners of Numbers 2:2, which each tribe would fly to identify the encampments. Although the ESV translates this word as "banners," the Hebrew word simply means signs. An example of a mnemonic sign is Exodus 13:9, where the eating of unleavened bread is a sign which reminds Israel of the Exodus experience and how God brought them out of Egypt.

In light of the above categories, how is the sign of circumcision functioning within the Abrahamic covenant? To answer this question, some scholars point to similarities in Genesis 9:8–17, where the rainbow functions as a mnemonic sign to remind God of His covenant between the creation and Creator.[21] The rainbow reminds God that He will never again destroy the world by flood (vv. 15–16). If the sign of circumcision is like the sign of the rainbow, then the sign of circumcision could be a reminder to God to be faithful to His covenant with Abraham to make his descendants as numerous as the stars in the sky (Gen 15:5).[22]

20 This paragraph relies on Michael V. Fox, "The Sign of the Covenant: Circumcision in the Light of the Priestly ʾôt Etiologies," *Revue Biblique* 81 (1974): 562–69.

21 DeRouchie notes the following, "Only these 'signs' in the Hebrew Bible are linked directly to בְּרִית ('covenant'), and each of these covenants 'signs' is denoted by the verb נתן ('to give, confirm, make') and qualified by the phrase 'between me and you' (cf. Gen 9:12, 13; 17:2, 10, 11; Ezek 20:12 with Exod 16:29). Because the rainbow (cf. Gen 9:15–16) and the Sabbath (Exod 31:13–15) explicitly function to *remind* the covenant parties of their obligations, circumcision very likely performs the same role" (Jason S. DeRouchie, "Circumcision in the Hebrew Bible and Targums: Theology, Rhetoric, and the Handling of Metaphor," *Bulletin for Biblical Research* 14, no. 2 [2004]: 185).

22 Fox, "The Sign of the Covenant," 595.

However, although there are a few parallels with the Noahic covenant, Genesis 17 does not indicate that the sign of the covenant is to remind God of anything.[23] Thus, it is conjecture to say that the sign of circumcision is to remind God of something. Moreover, in contrast to the Noahic covenant, there are significant obligations placed upon Abraham to walk blamelessly (v. 2). As such, although it is possible that the sign of the covenant reminds God of His promises, it seems more in line with the context of Genesis 17 and the command to be blameless that the sign would remind Abraham and his descendants of the need to live holy and righteous lives before God as His chosen people in light of His promises.[24] This emphasis would seem to coincide with the Egyptian concept of circumcision being a mark of dedication and commitment to a deity.

Within the context of Genesis 17, circumcision as a mark of dedication and commitment to God makes sense. However, there are later texts where this idea of dedication and commitment to God do not seem to be the best understanding of circumcision. When we look further into the Old Testament, we regularly see the idea of uncircumcision being used as a figurative depiction of ineffective body parts. The best example of this is probably Exodus 6:12 where Moses wonders how Pharaoh would listen to him, because he was of "uncircumcised lips." This description most likely parallels Moses's previous complaint in Exodus 4:10, where Moses claimed he was "slow of speech and of tongue."[25] Hence, the significance of the phrase "uncircumcised lips" most likely refers to a lack of ability.[26]

That uncircumcision refers to inability seems supported by how Scripture writers use the language of uncircumcision to refer to other body parts as well. For example, Jeremiah 6:10 says that the people of Israel had ears that were uncircumcised, and therefore "they cannot listen." The picture is one of having skin over the ears, and therefore the ears are incapable

23 Gordon J. Wenham, *Genesis 16–50*, Word Biblical Commentary 2 (Waco, TX: Word, 1998), 24.

24 Ibid.

25 Nahum M. Sarna, *Exodus*, JPS Torah Commentary (Philadelphia: Jewish Publications Society, 1991), 33.

26 However, some have interpreted the phrase as an inherent unfitness or unsuitability to be God's spokesperson. See T. Desmond Alexander, *Exodus*, Apollos Old Testament Commentary 2 (Downers Grove, IL: InterVarsity Press, 2017), 129. This understanding of Exodus 6:12 might fit better with the Egyptian belief that circumcision was about dedication and commitment, however, I think inability remains a prominent meaning for the metaphor of uncircumcision.

of hearing.[27] Like Exodus 6, this illustration of uncircumcision seems to indicate inability. Similarly, elsewhere Scripture refers to an uncircumcised heart as a metaphor for a dull, insensitive heart (cf. Deut 10:16; 30:6; Jer 4:4; 9:25). Leviticus 26:41 notes that the solution to an uncircumcised heart is humility and turning from iniquity.[28] All of these examples seem to be consistent with the idea that language of uncircumcision emphasizes the inability to function as one ought to.[29]

In summary, circumcision likely was a visible reminder to Israel of their special, holy status before God. They were to function as a kingdom of priests to the watching nations. Additionally, circumcision was a reminder of God's promises to Abraham—namely, a multitude of descendants, nations, kings, land, and blessing. Due to the prevalence of circumcision in Israelite society, uncircumcision became a ready illustration of dysfunction and inability. Prophets regularly referred to mouths, ears, and hearts as uncircumcised in order to describe a failure to function properly.

In the next section, I will provide additional details on circumcision while comparing circumcision and baptism. I will seek to show that there are significant areas of difference between the two. As such, I will contend it is incorrect for Calvin (or any paedobaptist) to say, "whatever belongs to circumcision pertains likewise to baptism."[30]

Differences between Circumcision and Baptism

As noted above, the Reformed defense of paedobaptism repeatedly links circumcision and baptism. This argument is crucial to the Reformed paedobaptist. Relating circumcision and baptism is the primary way they can

27 Holladay, *Jeremiah 1: A Commentary on the Book of the Prophet Jeremiah, Chapters 1–25*, 214.

28 Jacob Milgrom, *Leviticus 23–27: A New Translation with Introduction and Commentary*, Anchor Yale Bible 3B (New York: Doubleday, 2001), 2332–33.

29 However, scholars have noted that these examples could be construed as examples of the need for dedication or consecration. For example, Sarna writes, "From early times, the terms for uncircumcision and circumcision came to be used figuratively. A mind blocked to God's commandments has been described as "an uncircumcised heart" (Lev. 26:41; Jer. 9:25; Ezek. 44:7, 9), a heart that required "circumcising" (Deut. 10:16; 30:6; Jer. 4:4); one unreceptive to God's word as having "an uncircumcised ear" (Jer. 6:10); one impeded in his speech as having "uncircumcised lips" (Exod. 6:12, 30). All these metaphors prove conclusively that circumcision in Israel was no mere formal outward ritual but was invested with a spiritual aspect that betokened dedication and commitment to God" (Nahum M. Sarna, *Genesis*, JPS Torah Commentary [Philadelphia: Jewish Publications Society, 1989], 387).

30 John Calvin, *Institutes of the Christian Religion*, 1327.

bring infants near baptism. If circumcision and baptism are unrelated, then the main biblical evidence for infant baptism has received a fatal blow.

Although Reformed arguments emphasize the apparent similarities between baptism and circumcision, they give little attention to the significant differences between the two. There are at least seven significant differences between circumcision and baptism. These differences demonstrate that it is incorrect to say everything applicable to circumcision also applies to baptism. Even more so, these differences should challenge the idea that baptism and circumcision are related.

Circumcision was a Male-only Rite

The first major difference between circumcision and baptism is that circumcision was a male-only sign, whereas baptism does not distinguish between male and female. Under the Abrahamic covenant, "Every male among you shall be circumcised" (Gen 17:10b). However, under the new covenant, every disciple, male or female, is baptized (cf. Acts 8:12). Reformed paedobaptists often downplay this point of difference by appealing to covenant expansion and inclusion. For example, referring to this issue, Helopoulos writes, "The new covenant establishes a more inclusive, free, and gracious era, and we should expect to see its sacrament of initiation become more inclusive, not less."[31]

However, this reasoning runs into two problems. First, as the rest of the examination of circumcision and baptism makes clear, baptism is *more* restrictive than circumcision. Circumcision was acceptable for anyone who was Jewish (adults or children), no questions asked. In contrast, we reserve baptism *only* for those who make professions of faith. Even paedobaptists require a profession of faith by adults before baptism. Thus, the standard for baptism is more restrictive than circumcision. Second, women enjoyed full covenant participation under Moses without circumcision, so it is incorrect to argue their inclusion in baptism somehow finally brings them into full participation in the covenant community.

We can illustrate this point by discussing the Passover. Circumcision was required for every male who wanted to participate in the Passover, even for the non-Jew. If any non-Israelite male wanted to observe the Passover, he needed to be circumcised (Exod 12:48). However, although the Passover stipulations dictate "no uncircumcised person shall eat of it" (v. 48), women could eat of the Passover with full participation.[32] So, al-

31 Helopoulos, *Covenantal Baptism*, 106.

32 According to the Mishnah, they were not allowed to eat of it if they were in an unclean state from menstruation or childbirth (*m. Pesachim* 9:4).

though women could fully participate in the covenant, the sign of circumcision belonged only to the males.

A further problem with the Reformed paedobaptist explanation is the problem of continuity, the primary principle upon which Reformed paedobaptists rely. They argue that if there was to be any kind of departure from Old Testament practice, then we would expect to see that departure clearly laid out in the New Testament.[33] Yet, there is no mandate in the New Testament to baptize baby girls, nor is there any description of it happening! There is narrative description of baptizing women who have made a profession of faith, but no indication anywhere that we should expect a male-only covenant sign to transition from male infants to male *and* female infants. It is a major inconsistency in the argument, and it seems that adherents to paedobaptism rely on the argument of continuity only when convenient.

Lastly, Reformed paedobaptists are unable to give a good theological reason why the covenant sign would apply to only males under the old covenant but expand to include females in the new covenant.[34] It is difficult to suggest an explanation since covenant paedobaptists are forced to argue that the covenant of grace is the *same* in the old covenant (see chapter three). So why would there be a sudden difference in the expression of that sign? An argument of more inclusion is unsatisfactory, especially if the Reformed paedobaptist considers the covenant of grace to be the same in its essence.

Circumcision Was Observed on the Eighth Day After Birth

A rather significant contrast between circumcision and baptism is the question of timing. God commanded Abraham and his descendants to circumcise their male children on the eighth day after birth (Gen 17:12). However, there is no indication in the New Testament about a specific day on which we should perform baptisms. In fact, at the time of Cyprian of Carthage (200–258 AD), there was a significant debate about when an

33 Ross, "Baptism and Circumcision as Signs and Seals," 110.

34 But see the reasons listed by Brownson, who notes, "We could point to the movement away from bloody sacrifice to spiritual sacrifice. We could note the abolition of the ceremonial law in the New Covenant. We might point to Jesus' attempts to express the deeper intent of the law, rather than merely its external demands. We could point to the full inclusion of women in the church (Gal. 3:28), and the need for a covenant sign that included them (which circumcision could not do). All these factors doubtless played a part. But at bottom, a large portion of the answer must also be that circumcision was so closely identified with Jewish ethnicity that to continue to circumcise believers would have distorted the missional movement of the gospel beyond Israel to the 'ends of the earth'" (Brownson, *The Promise of Baptism*, 141).

infant should be baptized.[35] This kind of debate seems unlikely if infant baptism was already being practiced as an apostolic mandate handed down to replace circumcision. Although circumcision was linked with the eighth day after birth, the New Testament links the timing of baptism to the exercise of faith.

Circumcision was a Physical Sign

Although this point may seem minor, it is significant that circumcision was a physical mark that always remained with a Jewish male. The removal of the foreskin was always visible and recognizable to both Jew and Gentile. Historically, some Jews tried to remove the evidence of circumcision to fit in with the Gentiles (1 Macc 1:15; *Antiquities* 12.241).[36]

In contrast, baptism carries with it no visible mark or physical reminder. This is potentially problematic for the paedobaptist. There have been examples in paedobaptist churches where an individual can't remember whether he was baptized as an infant, and since there is no way of telling, the church grants him another baptism. In Roman Catholicism, these are called conditional baptisms.

Like the previous section, covenant paedobaptists argue that transitioning from a physical to a non-physical expression of the sign is consistent with progressive revelation. However, one must ask why was it necessary to change from a physical to a non-physical sign if circumcision and baptism signify the same thing? The Mosaic Law already included many acts and practices of washing and sprinkling. If we understand baptism and circumcision to be equivalent, it seems odd that God would not simply have instituted baptism from the start. It seems difficult to argue that baptism, being a non-physical sign, is a better sign of the covenant than circumcision, which is physically observable and impossible to forget.

Circumcision Marked a National Identity

The physical nature of circumcision relates to the fact that circumcision was the mark of a physical, national identity. Those who were physically descended from Abraham were circumcised to show their affiliation with him (Gen 17:10). This mandate applied to the later nation of Israel as well. Similarly, non-Israelites who wanted to embrace the national identity of

35 Jewett, *Infant Baptism and the Covenant of Grace*, 18.

36 Josephus notes in *Antiquities* 12.241 that the Jews hid their circumcision so they could appear to be Greeks.

Israel were commanded to undergo circumcision to demonstrate their affiliation with the nation (cf. Exod 12:48–49).

In contrast, baptism belongs to all nations and all peoples who express faith in Christ. One who is baptized can simultaneously be a citizen of any nation (not just Israel). This is a significant difference between baptism and circumcision, yet Reformed paedobaptists often downplay the national identity of circumcision. But this point deserves to be explored in more detail.

On the one hand, New Testament baptism is described clearly in Galatians 3:26–27. Paul writes that those in the church have exercised faith and been baptized (vv. 26–27). Furthermore, verse 28 separates this baptism from national or personal identity. Paul specifies, "There is neither Jew nor Greek, there is neither slave nor free, there is no male and female, for you are all one in Christ Jesus." Baptism is for all those who have faith in Christ, regardless of their national identity. National distinctions are secondary to membership in the church.

In contrast to how baptism is described in the New Testament, circumcision is viewed in the Old Testament as the hallmark of Jewish identity and a marker of a multigenerational covenant with Abraham and his descendants.[37] Abraham was told at the outset that every male associated with him must be circumcised (Gen 17:10). Circumcision marked every male who was associated with Abraham, because he was the start of the nation of Israel. This unique situation is why even those who would go out and form other nations were circumcised. This included Ishmael (Gen 17:23) and Abraham's other sons by his wife, Keturah (Gen 25:1–6), all of whom were not recipients of the covenant. Abraham circumcised these individuals because of their direct relationship with Abraham, yet they were sent out to start other nations, which was also a fulfillment of God's promise to Abraham, that he would be the father of a multitude of nations (cf. Gen 17:4).

Later generations of Abraham's descendants were expected to follow this same pattern because they were descended from his genealogical line. Circumcision was not dependent upon one's own faith or genealogical descent from parents who exercised faith. Circumcision was primarily related to one's national identity. *All* offspring of Abraham were to be circumcised regardless of their spiritual condition or that of their parents.[38]

37 Kenneth A. Mathews, *Genesis 11:27–50:26*, New American Commentary 1B (Nashville, TN: Broadman & Holman, 2005), 202.

38 Gavin Ortlund, "Why Not Grandchildren? An Argument against Reformed Paedobaptism," *Themelios* 45, no. 2 (2020): 337.

Another evidence of circumcision being linked with national identity is the study of Passover regulation. As previously noted, any uncircumcised males were prohibited from participating in the Passover (Exod 12:43–49). This prohibition specifically targets foreigners because it would be assumed that Israelites were circumcised.[39] Thus, in Exodus 12:43–49, the instruction targets the foreigner who wants to fully participate in the nation's celebration of Passover. The clear implication is that by undergoing circumcision the foreigner joined himself to the nation of Israel and was able to fully participate in Passover observance. Physical circumcision was intrinsically related to being identified with the nation of Israel.

A notable point is that Israelites were not kicked out of the nation for failing to exercise faith. In fact, there is no indication anywhere that unbelievers who circumcised their children were in the wrong. The next section further confirms that circumcision primarily functioned as a national identity marker for the nation of Israel and not as a function of belief.

Circumcision was Knowingly Practiced on Unbelieving Adults

Most reformed paedobaptists would cringe at the thought of baptizing an adult unbeliever who does not make a profession of faith. I am not aware of any such practice in a Reformed church. And if baptism and circumcision are essentially equal, as paedobaptists claim, one would expect the same principle in circumcision. However, in strong contrast to the Baptist *and* paedobaptist practice of baptism, there are multiple examples in Scripture of adults who are circumcised without reference to a profession of faith. These examples demonstrate that circumcision was performed on adults who were not genuine believers.

The first example of this would be Genesis 17 itself, where God instructs Abraham to circumcise *every* male (v. 10). Abraham followed this exhaustive mandate, circumcising those born in his house *and* those he had

---

39 It should be noted that the book of Jubilees viewed a Jew not being circumcised as one of the most revolting acts of treachery. Jubilees, which is dated by most scholars to the second century BC, says this: "I am now telling you that the Israelites will prove false to this ordinance. They will not circumcise their sons in accord with this entire law because they will leave some of the flesh of their circumcision when they circumcise their sons. All the people of Belial will leave their sons uncircumcised just as they were born. Then there will be great anger from the Lord against the Israelites because they abandoned his covenant, departed from his word, provoked, and blasphemed in that they did not perform the ordinance of this sign. For they have made themselves like the nations so as to be removed and uprooted from the earth. They will no longer have forgiveness or pardon so that they should be pardoned and forgiven for every sin, for (their) violation of this eternal (ordinance)" (15:33–34). Translation from James C. VanderKam, *Jubilees: A Commentary on the Book of Jubilees, Chapters 1–50*, vol. 1, Hermeneia (Minneapolis, MN: Fortress Press, 2018), 507.

purchased (vv. 23, 27). We know from earlier in Genesis that this would have included at least 318 men who were born in his house (Gen 14:14), plus other foreigners he had purchased. It is not conceivable that Abraham would have interviewed all those men and asked them for professions of faith before circumcising them.[40] In fact, that would have gone against the command of Yahweh. The command was simply to circumcise them all—faith was not a requirement.

We should also observe that Abraham circumcised Ishmael, although Scripture is explicit that Ishmael was outside of God's promise (Gen 16:11–12; 21:10–13; Gal 4:21–31). Not only is there no indication that Ishmael ever exercised faith in Yahweh, but Scripture unambiguously describes him as *not* being a child of the promise! Importantly, Abraham was told even *before* circumcision that Ishmael was not a part of the covenant (Gen 17:18–21).

Many paedobaptists would argue that whatever the meaning of circumcision, it would also have to apply to Ishmael.[41] I would agree, and so I would argue there are irreconcilable differences between Ishmael's circumcision and the New Testament definition of baptism. Of greatest significance is the fact that Ishmael never exercised faith yet was circumcised at thirteen (Gen 17:25). Ishmael's example is difficult for the Reformed paedobaptist who argues that we baptize infants to communicate that they belong to the covenant. Such is certainly not the case with Ishmael's circumcision. Since Abraham knew Ishmael was not a part of the covenant, Ishmael must have been circumcised for a different reason than his own inclusion in the covenant.[42]

In Joshua 5:2–8 we glean more insight into circumcision and its application to unbelievers. The people of Israel were preparing to conquer the land of Canaan, but there was a problem. The current generation that had just emerged from wandering in the wilderness had not been circumcised (Josh 5:7).[43] This lack of circumcision is probably evidence of the

40 Jewett, *Infant Baptism and the Covenant of Grace*, 98.

41 Ross, "Baptism and Circumcision as Signs and Seals," 92.

42 As noted in the previous section, I would argue that Ishmael and the sons of Keturah (Gen 25:1–6) were circumcised because of the unique importance of Abraham as the progenitor of the covenant. Ishmael and Abraham's later sons were circumcised due to their familial association with Abraham in obedience to Genesis 17, even though they were not themselves recipients of the promise. Importantly, Abraham knew they would not be recipients of the promise ahead of time.

43 There is an interpretive issue in this passage about what it means that Israel was circumcised a "second time" (Josh 5:2). This could mean that Israel had been circumcised according to the Egyptian method, and now was being circumcised according to the Abrahamic

continued disobedience of the hard-hearted generation that God had brought out of Egypt. The generation that came out of Egypt was circumcised (Josh 5:5), but they either refused to circumcise their children after being disallowed entry into the land of Canaan, or they were unable to perform circumcisions while wandering in the wilderness. Regardless, almost the entire nation was uncircumcised.

There are a couple of essential observations to make about this text. First, the generation coming out of Egypt was a wicked generation set on rebellion against God (cf. Exod 14:10–14; 16:2–3; 17:2–7; Num 14:26–30). Ezekiel 20:8 says that this generation continued worshipping the idols of Egypt even after they left Egypt. Significantly, even though most of those who came out of Egypt were engaged in wickedness, there was never any suggestion that their circumcision was not a valid mark of their relationship to Abraham.

Second, we see in Joshua 5 that Israel circumcised an entire *adult* generation in one day (Josh 5:9). There is no indication that there was any profession of faith by any of those who were circumcised. It would certainly be a logistical nightmare for Joshua and the leaders to interview even half of the adult males and listen to their profession of faith before circumcision.[44] To fully recognize the significance of this narrative and the difference between circumcision and baptism, all we need to do is substitute baptism for circumcision in this story. If we try to imagine this story taking place in a modern context, it is simply not possible. No true church would indiscriminately dispense baptism to adults without verifying their profession of faith.

It is worth emphasizing at this point that the above examples show that circumcision of the children of unbelievers was legitimate. In contrast to the typical Reformed paedobaptist practice of a child needing at least one believing parent to be baptized,[45] these narratives demonstrate that the spiritual condition of one's parents did not influence the mandate of Genesis 17 to circumcise *every* male. The generation of Israelites that wandered in the wilderness was idolatrous and unfaithful to God, yet God commanded each male Israelite to be circumcised—and so they were. Each

---

method before entrance into the land of Canaan. Or "a second time" could refer to the current generation replacing the previous wilderness generation that died in the wilderness. The second option seems preferable.

44 Numbers 26:51 records 601,730 males, 20 years and older who made up the army of Israel. These men would have needed to be circumcised, as well as any children 19 years old and younger, possibly another 200,000 or so.

45 Cf. Westminster Confession, Article 28.4.

Israelite's right to circumcision was unrelated to a profession of faith or the parent's status as a believer.

Circumcision was a Sign of National Promises

Another difference between circumcision and baptism is that circumcision was a specific reminder of national promises given to Israel. As noted above, baptism has no exclusivity to any nation—it has broad application to all nations. Additionally, in all the New Testament texts which explain the significance of baptism, there is no reference to national promises. This is a significant contrast to circumcision, where the promises to Abraham are foundational to the explanation of circumcision.

We see this in Genesis 17, which is not the initiation of the covenant, but is a further explanation of the covenant that God instituted with Abraham earlier (cf. Gen 12:1–3; 13:14–17; esp. 15:7–21).[46] Prior to Genesis 17, there was already a promise of blessing to Abraham (12:2), as well as blessing for those who blessed Abraham and cursing for those who mistreated him (12:3). God also promised Abraham a plurality of descendants,[47] who would make up a great nation (12:2; 15:5). Last, but certainly not least, God also promised Abraham a specific land allotment (12:1, 7; 13:14–17; 15:7, 18–21). In sum, many a Bible college or seminary student has learned to recite the tri-fold promise of the Abrahamic covenant: blessing, land, and offspring.

Importantly, Genesis 17 changes none of these previous promises, but only repeats and expands them. Expanding the idea of a plurality of descendants, God promises Abraham that he will be the father of a multitude of nations (vv. 4–6). The reference to nations (plural) is important. Minimally, in addition to the Israelites, the Ishmaelites, Edomites, and Midianites are also descended from Abraham.[48] Besides the promise of multiple

---

46 A few scholars see multiple covenants given to Abraham, e.g., T. Desmond Alexander, *From Eden to the New Jerusalem: An Introduction to Biblical Theology* (Grand Rapids: Kregel Publications, 2008), 175–82; T. Desmond Alexander, "Genesis 22 and the Covenant of Circumcision," *Journal for the Study of the Old Testament* 25 (1983): 17–22. However, it is much more consistent with biblical revelation (cf. Ps 105:8–9) to view Genesis 17 and 22 as further expansions of the one Abrahamic covenant. For defense of this, see Jeffrey J. Niehaus, "God's Covenant with Abraham," *Journal of the Evangelical Theological Society* 56, no. 2 (2013): 249–71; Peter J. Gentry and Stephen J. Wellum, *Kingdom through Covenant: A Biblical-Theological Understanding of the Covenants* (Wheaton, IL: Crossway, 2012), 275–80; Keith Essex, "The Abrahamic Covenant," *The Master's Seminary Journal* 10, no. 2 (Fall 1999): 191–212.

47 As a side note, this may be the best explanation for why the sign of circumcision was given to males only. It is through the male line that generations were continued and propagated.

48 Sarna, *Genesis*, 124.

nations coming from Abraham, God also promises him that kings (plural) will come from Abraham (v. 6). Genesis 17 thus solidifies the promise given to Abraham in the preceding chapters. God would give Abraham a plurality of descendants, which Genesis 17 specifies to include the idea of nations and kings.

Genesis 17 also continues the land promise. God tells Abraham, "And I will give to you and to your offspring after you the land of your sojournings, all the land of Canaan, for an everlasting possession, and I will be their God" (v. 8). This promise is unchanged from previous chapters. God unequivocally promises that the land of Canaan belongs not just to Abraham, but to his descendants, "for an everlasting possession."

Most important for our purposes is the fact that circumcision is specifically called the "sign of the covenant" (Gen 17:11). Circumcision was to point to the promises of the covenant that God made with Abraham. As Wellum puts it, "What promises were signified by circumcision? *All* the promises tied to the Abrahamic covenant, which included not only salvific promises but also national ones, particularly the land promise (e.g., Gen 12:7; 15:12–21; 17:8)."[49] These promises *and* the sign of these promises applied to Abraham and to all his descendants. It was a perpetual sign that was to exist, "throughout their generations" (v. 9).

In contrast to the clear link between the national promises to Abraham and his descendants (Israel), baptism signifies no national promises.[50] This is an undervalued point that is often ignored by Reformed paedobaptists. God did not give baptism as a sign linking someone to the promise of land or the growth of a great nation. Reformed paedobaptists should give this distinction between baptism and circumcision greater consideration.

Circumcision was Unrelated to the Exercise of Faith

Perhaps the most significant difference between circumcision and baptism relates to faith. As already demonstrated in chapter one, both the New Testament and early church sources view faith as integral to baptism. It was not until Ulrich Zwingli that there was a serious alternative of any significance. Because of Zwingli, some covenant theologians separated faith from baptism. However, as I showed in chapter one, it is just not possible to do that. Both Roman Catholic and Lutheran paedobaptists would agree that faith is essential to baptism. It is only those in the Reformed paedobaptist camp that downplay the relationship between faith and baptism.

49 Wellum, "Baptism and the Relationship between the Covenants," 155. Emphasis in original.

50 Waymeyer, *A Biblical Critique of Infant Baptism*, 52.

Because of the presumed link between baptism and circumcision, Reformed paedobaptists will often appeal to circumcision as evidence that faith is not required for baptism. For example, noted Reformed theologian and paedobaptist R.C. Sproul writes:

> The most common argument against infant baptism is that it signifies things that flow from faith, and since infants are not capable of expressing or embracing faith, they should not receive the sign. But if that argument were correct, it would nullify the legitimacy of circumcision in the Old Testament. If we reject infant baptism on the basis of the principle that a sign that involves faith must never be given until after faith is present, we also negate the legitimacy of circumcision in the Old Testament.[51]

Sproul is engaging in circular reasoning here. He assumes that baptism and circumcision are the same, so what applies to one must apply to the other. But as we have already seen, there are some significant differences between baptism and circumcision. I argue that those differences demonstrate that baptism and circumcision are not equal. In contrast to baptism, there is no indication that faith was a prerequisite for circumcision.

We find proof that faith is not essential to circumcision by looking at passages that apply to foreign circumcisions. Texts that refer to foreigners becoming circumcised are devoid of any language of faith. For example, in Genesis 34:14–24, Jacob's sons tell the men of Shechem that they need to be circumcised to intermarry with Israel's women, but there is no mention of faith or commitment to Yahweh. Although Genesis 34 deals with deceit and treachery, there is no reason to question the standard that Jacob's sons gave to Shechem. As another example, in Exodus 12:43–49, we read that a stranger could partake of the Passover meal if he circumcised himself and all his males (v. 48). The simple requirement of Exodus 12 is that a foreigner needs to be circumcised to participate in the meal. There is no reference to further commitment to Yahweh or to faith. Although one could make a reasonable case that commitment to Yahweh is assumed, this is a drastic difference from the New Testament picture of baptism. For how much the New Testament associates faith with baptism, it is even more noteworthy that the exact opposite is the case for circumcision. Not once is faith linked with circumcision in the Old Testament. The best we can argue is that it is assumed. However, faith is explicitly and repeatedly linked with baptism in the New Testament.

51 Sproul, *What Is Baptism?*, 63.

Many Reformed paedobaptists would challenge the above point by arguing that circumcision and baptism both relate to faith in the same way. To prove this point, they appeal to Romans 4:11, "[Abraham] received the sign of circumcision as a seal of the righteousness that he had by faith while he was still uncircumcised." Does this verse show that faith is linked with circumcision in the same way as baptism?

The pertinent issue in Romans 4:11 is the meaning of circumcision as a "seal of the righteousness that he had by faith." Historically, some Reformed paedobaptists have interpreted this passage as evidence that circumcision was related to Abraham's faith. For example, John Murray notes, "For if circumcision signified faith, the faith must be conceived of as existing prior to the signification given and, in a way still more apparent, a seal or authentication presupposes the existence of the thing sealed and the seal does not add to the content of the thing sealed."[52]

For Murray, circumcision signified the genuine faith of Abraham. Similarly, Boice, another Reformed paedobaptist, says, "After Abraham had believed God and God had imparted righteousness to him, God gave the seal of circumcision to validate what had happened. In the same way, baptism is a seal that the person being baptized has been identified with Jesus Christ as his disciple."[53] For both Murray and Boice, circumcision was a seal of the faith that Abraham already possessed. This understanding is similar to the traditional Baptist interpretation of this passage.[54] But this interpretation causes some problems of consistency in Reformed paedobaptist circles.

If we understand circumcision in the way proposed by Murray and Boice (not to mention most Baptists), then one implication of that text is that faith must precede circumcision. And if faith is necessary for circumcision, why is faith not referenced with circumcision anywhere else?[55] This dilemma has prompted a much more popular interpretation of Romans 4:11 in Reformed paedobaptist circles.

---

52 John Murray, *The Epistle to the Romans*, New International Commentary on the New Testament (Grand Rapids: Eerdmans, 1968), 137.

53 James Montgomery Boice, *Romans: Justification by Faith (Romans 1–4)*, vol. 1 (Grand Rapids: Baker Books, 1991), 458.

54 Jewett, *Infant Baptism and the Covenant of Grace*, 86.

55 Ross states, "But if we understand circumcision in the manner proposed by Murray, Boice, Piper, and a host of others, it is difficult to explain why the covenant sign of circumcision was applied to Abraham's seed without reference to the faith of the recipients, or to the inward spiritual change supposedly signified and sealed by circumcision" (Ross, "Baptism and Circumcision as Signs and Seals," 91). Ross goes on to list Ishmael and Esau as examples of those circumcised, but who clearly did not have faith.

The most popular Reformed paedobaptist interpretation of Romans 4:11 is as a divine promise of justification by faith. In this view, the promise of circumcision in Romans 4:11 is the same promise that baptism represents in the New Testament. Ross presents this view when he writes:

> Circumcision is not a guarantee that Abraham has faith, nor even that Abraham has righteousness. What circumcision guarantees is the word of God's promise: *that righteousness will be given on the basis of faith*. In other words, circumcision is the authenticating mark that certifies the truth of God's promise, that he will give righteousness to the one who has faith. What is certified is not so much a truth about Abraham, or any other circumcised person, but a truth about God. In particular, circumcision certifies the truth of God's word in the gospel, namely, that all who believe will be accounted righteous.[56]

Thus, according to Ross and other Reformed paedobaptists, Romans 4:11 is not talking about an objective reality, but a conditional possibility that is available to anyone. In the words of paedobaptist David Gibson, "Circumcision is sign and seal that God justifies the wicked (Rom. 4:5)."[57] Ross further explains:

> On this understanding of circumcision as a sign and seal, there are no problems of meaning in giving circumcision to those not known to have faith, nor to those who later show themselves to have no faith. Since the sign and seal of circumcision is not a guarantee of either the faith or the righteousness of the one circumcised, the discovery that a circumcised person is an unbeliever does not invalidate the circumcision as an authenticating mark. God's promise is not invalidated by the unbelief of his covenant children. His word stands: those who believe will be accounted righteous.[58]

Reformed paedobaptists like Ross consider circumcision to be a reminder of God's promise that He will justify on the basis of faith. There is no necessary precondition of faith before circumcision. Circumcision is a sign that *if* one believes, he will be justified. Reformed paedobaptists then apply this same interpretation to infant baptism. When an infant is bap-

---

56 Ibid., 94. Emphasis in original.

57 David Gibson, "Sacramental Supersessionism Revisited: A Response to Martin Salter on the Relationship between Circumcision and Baptism," *Themelios* 37, no. 2 (2012): 196.

58 Ross, "Baptism and Circumcision as Signs and Seals," 94–95.

tized, it is not a display of a present reality, but a reminder that God will provide justification to any who respond in faith. This interpretation is the most common position embraced by Reformed paedobaptists today, and it has a few significant problems.[59]

The first problem is viewing circumcision as a guarantee. According to the Reformed paedobaptist interpretation, circumcision (and baptism in its place) is a seal because it refers to God's guarantee that He will grant righteousness to anyone who has faith. However, a problem with this thinking is that there is no difference between the circumcised Jew and uncircumcised pagan. Both have that same promise! The pagan also has God's guarantee that if he turns to God in faith, he will be justified. Circumcising (and at later times baptizing) a child, "does not communicate anything that is objectively true about the 'covenant child' which is not also true of every other child born into this world."[60]

An additional, and more significant problem is that Reformed paedobaptists ignore the immediate context of Romans 4:11–12. Paul is not arguing generically about circumcision, but about Abraham's circumcision specifically. Paul has intentionally chosen Abraham for his argument, because Abraham was revered by the Jews.[61] An examination of the text shows that Abraham clearly had genuine faith before circumcision. The text says it this way:

> He received the sign of circumcision as a seal of the righteousness that he had by faith while he was still uncircumcised. The purpose was to make him the father of all who believe without being circumcised, so that righteousness would be counted to them as well, and to make him the father of the circumcised who are not merely circumcised but who also walk in the footsteps of the faith that our father Abraham had before he was circumcised.

59 For a thorough discussion of the problems and issues, see the excellent work by Matt Waymeyer, "Romans 4:11 and the Case for Infant Baptism," *The Master's Seminary Journal* 29, no. 2 (Fall 2018): 233–55.

60 Ibid., 238.

61 "But why has Paul singled out Abraham as the reference point for this expansion? One reason is undoubtedly polemical. Abraham was revered by the Jews as their 'father' and his life and character were held up as models of God's ways with his people and of true piety. 'Abraham was perfect in all his deeds with the Lord, and well-pleasing in righteousness all the days of his life' (Jub. 23:10); Abraham 'did not sin against thee' (Pr. Man. 8); 'no one has been found like him in glory' (Sir. 44:19). In keeping with the nomistic focus of first-century Judaism, Abraham was held up particularly as a model of obedience to God. His righteousness and mediation of the promise were linked to this obedience, it even being argued that he had obeyed the law perfectly before it had been given" (Moo, *The Epistle to the Romans*, 278).

The phrase, "a seal of the righteousness that he had by faith while he was still uncircumcised," communicates clearly that Abraham had faith prior to circumcision. This was not a potential faith, but an objective reality. As Waymeyer notes, "At the time of Abraham's circumcision, righteousness was not his *potential* possession—it was his *actual* possession, and circumcision served to confirm this reality."[62]

The usage of the term "seal" (σφραγίς) itself also argues that the faith Abraham had was a present reality. A seal signifies something that "confirms or authenticates" something else.[63] Concerning this verse in Romans 4, one of the most prominent New Testament lexicons notes, "He (Abraham) received the sign of circumcision as something that confirms the righteousness through faith that was already present."[64] We see a similar usage of the idea of "seal" in 1 Corinthians 9:2, where the Corinthian believers are called "the seal of [Paul's] apostleship." Commenting on 1 Corinthians 9:2, Waymeyer correctly notes, "Paul's point in this verse is that the very existence of the Corinthians' faith in Christ authenticated the fact that he was a true apostle, and in this way they themselves were the confirmation of his apostleship."[65]

The meaning of seal in 1 Corinthians 9:2 is also the most natural meaning for Romans 4:11. Abraham's circumcision was a confirmation of his righteousness—a condition that came through faith. As Waymeyer summarizes, "According to Romans 4:11, then, Abraham's circumcision did not seal his *need* for righteousness; it confirmed *the presence of a righteousness he already possessed.*"[66]

Reformed paedobaptists are hesitant to embrace this straightforward interpretation because it would mean that Abraham's circumcision was unique. Ross argues:

> Surely, whatever meaning circumcision had for Abraham, it had also for Ishmael and for every other male in Abraham's household circumcised on the same day as Abraham (Gen. 17:23). This must be the starting point in our understanding of circumcision,

62 Ibid., 240. Emphasis in original.

63 William Arndt, Frederick W. Danker, Walter Bauer, and F. Wilbur Gingrich, *A Greek-English Lexicon of the New Testament and Other Early Christian Literature* (Chicago: University of Chicago Press, 2000), 980.

64 Ibid.

65 Waymeyer, "Romans 4:11 and the Case for Infant Baptism," 240.

66 Ibid., 241.

> baptism, or any other sacrament: there is one meaning for all who rightly receive the sign.[67]

Ross's presupposition, that each circumcision must have the same meaning, goes against the stated purpose of Romans 4. In the words of Romans 4, Abraham's unique experience was "to make him the father of all who believe without being circumcised [i.e., Gentiles] … and to make him the father of the circumcised who are not merely circumcised but who also walk in the footsteps of the faith that our father Abraham had before he was circumcised [i.e., Jewish believers]." In other words, Abraham uniquely could identify as the father of faith for both Jew and Gentile *because* his faith was prior to circumcision. Waymeyer summarizes:

> In this way, circumcision signified in Abraham what it did not (and could not) signify in any other Jew who was circumcised. For not only was circumcision a divine seal which certified Abraham's present state of justification, but it also equipped him to serve in the unique role as spiritual father of both Jewish and Gentile believers. In contrast, the circumcision of male infants throughout the history of Israel was neither a seal of the righteousness of their faith (Rom. 4:11a) nor the means of enabling them to fulfill this unique purpose that could only be fulfilled by Abraham (Rom. 4:11b–12). For this reason, there is "a crucial disanalogy" between the circumcision of Abraham and the circumcision of his physical descendants, for circumcision served as a seal of righteousness by faith for Abraham *alone* and was never intended to have this meaning for the other members of the covenant. Only by ignoring this distinction can the paedobaptist insist that circumcision was "a seal of the righteousness of the faith" for all who were circumcised and therefore the Old Testament counterpart to water baptism.[68]

This straightforward interpretation of Romans 4:11–12 is not unique to Baptists. As we saw from the quotes of Murray and Boice, there are other Reformed paedobaptists who take this interpretation as well. And it is much more consistent with Romans 4 to do so. Abraham's circumcision was a unique experience that qualified him to be the father of all who would exercise faith. Romans 4:11 does not say circumcision is a *promise* of justification of faith, but a *seal* of a faith that already existed in Abraham.

67 Ross, "Baptism and Circumcision as Signs and Seals," 92.

68 Waymeyer, "Romans 4:11 and the Case for Infant Baptism," 243–44.

Therefore, we cannot use Romans 4:11 as a generic template that applies to everyone who was circumcised in the Old Testament. This also means that no text in Scripture relates the generic rite of circumcision with faith. Circumcision is unrelated to faith. However, as we saw in the first chapter, baptism is consistently related to the exercise of faith—a phenomenon that boldly contrasts itself with circumcision.

What Does Circumcision Mean and How Does It Relate to Baptism?

We can now summarize the meaning of circumcision and discuss how it does (or does not) relate to baptism. As shown above, circumcision is tied to the Abrahamic covenant and represents both the physical and spiritual promises of that covenant. These promises include blessing, land, and a plurality of descendants. In comparing what we know about circumcision from ancient Egypt, I have proposed that Israelite circumcision primarily symbolized consecration and dedication to Yahweh. Thus, Israel dedicated each male to Yahweh as a royal priest through circumcision. Circumcision belonged to each male in Israel because of God's promise of increased offspring, which occurs through the male line.

Reformed paedobaptists may not reject this summary, but in attempting to link circumcision and baptism, they must argue that circumcision represents more than the above. For example, Ross argues that the meanings of baptism *and* circumcision "can be summarized in two terms of two fundamental concepts: cleansing and consecration."[69] As already noted above, the idea of consecration matches well with the ancient Egyptian concept of circumcision and the biblical descriptions. However, the concept of cleansing does not readily find a parallel in passages on circumcision.

Ross appeals to Romans 4:11 as evidence that circumcision has to do with forgiveness of sins (and thus metaphorical cleansing).[70] However, not only is there no language of cleansing in Romans 4:11, but the text is an appeal to Abraham's unique experience as the father of faith for both the circumcised *and* uncircumcised. In other words, the application of Romans 4:11 would apply equally to the uncircumcised, not just the circumcised. Ross also appeals to Deuteronomy 30:6, where God promises He will circumcise the heart of the people of Israel. Yet again, there is no mention of

69 Ross, "Baptism and Circumcision as Signs and Seals," 100.

70 Ibid., 101.

the language of cleansing, and Ross is assuming the point he is trying to make. The argument that circumcision relates to cleansing remains unpersuasive, having no evidence to back it up.

Nevertheless, the signs of circumcision and baptism remain linked for the Reformed paedobaptist. If baptism has replaced circumcision, the Reformed paedobaptist needs to explain why the sign of entrance into the covenant has changed. The typical explanation is that circumcision was the bloody sign of sacrifice before Christ's death on the cross, but baptism is a fitting sign of entrance *after* Christ's death, since His blood has already been shed. Chapell explains:

> The bloody sign of circumcision that prefigured the shedding of Christ's blood no longer remains appropriate after the Lamb of God has shed his blood once for all in order to remove our sin (cf. Heb. 10:10; 1 Peter 1:18). Therefore, New Testament believers receive a new sign of the covenant that indicates what Christ has accomplished for them. Baptism with water is the sign of washing away our sin (cf. Acts 22:16; 1 Cor. 6:11; Heb. 9:14).[71]

Chapell gives a reason why there was a transition in covenantal sign. However, there is little evidence for this interpretation. If blood is such a major part of the symbolism of circumcision, one wonders why the Bible *never* mentions this connection in the Old or New Testament. In fact, although the Bible mentions circumcision or uncircumcision 86 times in 64 verses,[72] only twice is there any reference to blood at all (Ezek 44:7; Exod 4:25). Neither of these references to blood relates to the symbolism of circumcision.

In Ezekiel 44:7, God chastens Israel for admitting uncircumcised foreigners to the sanctuary while offering food, fat, and blood to Yahweh. This passage has nothing to do with blood pertaining to circumcision, only with the blood of sacrifice. The only other passage which mentions blood alongside circumcision is the enigmatic passage of Exodus 4:25–26, where either Moses's life or his son's life is in danger because the son was not circumcised.[73] After Zipporah circumcises their son, she touches his feet and

71 Bryan Chapell, "A Pastoral Overview of Infant Baptism," in *The Case for Covenantal Infant Baptism*, ed. Gregg Strawbridge (Phillipsburg, NJ: P&R Publishing, 2003), 16.

72 Word usage statistics provided by Logos Bible Software 9. The search included all occurrences of verbs ערל, מול, and מלל. Non-verbs ערלה, ערל, and מולה were also included.

73 The difficulties in Exodus 4:25–26 are significant. Only pronouns are used, and Moses's name is never mentioned. Although a very difficult passage, I understand the passage to be saying that Moses's son, Gershom, was in danger of being killed by God for not being cir-

says, "Surely you are a bridegroom of blood to me" (v. 25). The translation "bridegroom of blood" (חֲתַן־דָּמִים) is probably better translated, "blood relative."[74] Although it is possible that the blood in this passage has to do with circumcision, even so, it would be the only place in the Bible where blood is mentioned in the context of circumcision. If the blood of circumcision is such a vital part of the typology of circumcision, one would think it would receive more attention. However, passages which focus on the importance of circumcision make no such mention of blood (e.g., Gen 17).

The strongest connection between circumcision and baptism is that Scripture describes both as entrances into a covenant community. This is undoubtedly a strong and real connection between the two. However, recognizing both circumcision and baptism as rites of entrance highlights the differences between the two. As Waymeyer states:

> In the Old Testament, the means of entrance into the nation of Israel was *involuntary, physical, and external*—one became a Jew by being born of Jewish parents. In the New Testament church, however, the means of entrance is *voluntary, spiritual, and internal*—one becomes a member of the church by exercising faith in Christ and being born again.[75]

Although I will address New Testament baptism fully in chapter seven, here it is enough to acknowledge that the Old Testament describes circumcision in ways that differ significantly from baptism. Thus, the Reformed paedobaptist assertion that baptism stands in the same place as circumcision is incorrect. Yet, the Reformed paedobaptist will point to Colossians 2:11–12 as an example of baptism being equated with circumcision. It is to this crucial text we now turn our attention.

Colossians 2:11–12 and the Circumcision without Hands

> In him also you were circumcised with a circumcision made without hands, by putting off the body of the flesh, by the circumcision of Christ, having been buried with him in baptism, in

---

cumcised. Zipporah then circumcised the son, touched his feet (possibly with the foreskin), and called him a "bridegroom of blood," probably meaning he was confirmed as her covenantal family member. For a defense of this view, see Duane A. Garrett, *A Commentary on Exodus*, Kregel Exegetical Library (Grand Rapids: Kregel Academic, 2014), 225–31; Douglas Stuart, *Exodus*, New American Commentary 2 (Nashville, TN: Broadman & Holman, 2006), 152–56.

74 Garrett, *A Commentary on Exodus*, 228–30; Stuart, *Exodus*, 154.

75 Waymeyer, *A Biblical Critique of Infant Baptism*, 79. Emphasis in original.

> which you were also raised with him through faith in the powerful working of God, who raised him from the dead (Col 2:11–12).

This is the most consistently referenced passage by paedobaptists when trying to support the link between circumcision and baptism. Without Colossians 2:11–12, the connection between circumcision and baptism is entirely based on inference.[76] Hence, this passage is essential for Reformed paedobaptists, because it alone might provide a biblical connection between circumcision and baptism.

Unsurprisingly, every Reformed paedobaptist makes an appeal to this passage as a clear biblical statement of baptism replacing circumcision. For example, Chapell writes about this text, "These words remind us that salvation comes through faith, and also that *the rite of circumcision that once signified the benefits of Abraham's covenant has been replaced by baptism.*"[77] Herman Hoeksema, another paedobaptist, says of this passage, "A more direct proof that circumcision and baptism are essentially the same in meaning … could not be given."[78]

Perhaps the words of John Calvin summarize the Reformed view of Colossians 2:11–12 best: "What do these words mean, except that the fulfillment and truth of baptism are also the truth and fulfillment of circumcision, since they signify one and the same thing? For he is striving to demonstrate that baptism is for the Christians what circumcision previously was for the Jews."[79] But is it true that Paul's aim in this passage is to show the believers of Colossae that "baptism is the same thing to Christians that circumcision formerly was to the Jews?"

The Context of Colossians 2:11–12

These two verses do not occur in a vacuum. New Testament scholars have argued that Colossians 2:11–12 is part of an overall argument that ranges from 2:8–23.[80] In this section, Paul directly confronts the problems that

---

76 Jack Cotrell, *Baptism: A Biblical Study* (Joplin, MO: College Press Publishing, 1989), 136.

77 Chapell, "A Pastoral Overview of Infant Baptism," 17. Emphasis in original.

78 Herman Hoeksema, *The Biblical Ground for the Baptism of Infants* (Grand Rapids: First Protestant Reformed Church, 1998), 16. This pamphlet is available online: https://www.prca.org/resources/publications/pamphlets/item/612-the-biblical-ground-for-the-baptism-of-infants.

79 John Calvin, *Institutes of the Christian Religion*, 1333.

80 David W. Pao, *Colossians and Philemon*, Zondervan Exegetical Commentary on the New Testament (Grand Rapids: Zondervan, 2012), 149; Martin Salter, "Does Baptism Replace

the believers at Colossae were facing. In the first part (2:8–15), Paul draws attention to what Christ has already accomplished. Then, in 2:16–23, Paul challenges the behavior and practices of the false teachers.[81] It is difficult to say with certainty what exactly the false teachers were espousing in Colossae, but as Porter notes, "It seems to have been related to competition from some form or forms of religious belief—quite possibly with ties to Judaism or some other group with tendencies toward, or interest in, mysteries—which threatened to substitute such religious practices for belief and worship of Christ."[82]

Scholars have put forward the following evidence to argue that the false teaching related somehow to Judaism.[83]

1. Mention of festivals, food, purity, and Sabbaths (2:16–21) are all distinctively Jewish elements.
2. Circumcision appears three times (2:11, 13; 3:11), suggesting it was a contentious issue in Colossae.
3. Worship of angels (θρησκείᾳ τῶν ἀγγέλων) in 2:18, particularly if angels (τῶν ἀγγέλων) is taken as a subjective genitive, has a strong Jewish background.
4. The Lycus valley, it is argued, had substantial Jewish minorities.

Although one should not be dogmatic about this, many New Testament scholars would agree that the evidence "appears to favor a syncretism with Jewish elements providing the controlling framework."[84] Therefore, concerning Colossians 2:11–12, Salter writes, "Paul's purpose is not to discuss baptism or circumcision *per se*, but rather to include them within the section highlighting the fullness already possessed in Christ through all he has accomplished."[85] Although his purpose is not directly tied to circumcision or baptism *per se*, his theological point is certainly clear enough. And what he says may have implications to whether baptism replaces circumcision.

Circumcision? An Examination of the Relationship between Circumcision and Baptism in Colossians 2:11–12," *Themelios* 35, no. 1 (2010): 16–17.

81 Pao, *Colossians and Philemon*, 149.

82 Stanley E. Porter, *The Apostle Paul: His Life, Thought, and Letters* (Grand Rapids: Eerdmans, 2016), 370.

83 Salter, "Does Baptism Replace Circumcision?," 17.

84 Pao, *Colossians and Philemon*, 31.

85 Salter, "Does Baptism Replace Circumcision?," 17.

The Meaning of "Circumcision Made without Hands"

Of primary importance is the fact that Paul is not talking about physical circumcision in Colossians 2:11–12. Although Reformed paedobaptists appeal to this text as evidence that baptism has replaced circumcision, physical circumcision is not present here. Paul uses the modifier "made without hands" to make sure that the readers know he is talking about a spiritual circumcision that God does, not man. As O'Brien notes:

> When Paul at Colossians 2:11 speaks of a circumcision "not made with hands" (ἀχειροποίητος) he sets in antithesis Jewish circumcision (which was done by the hand of man) with the work of God which the readers had experienced. God himself had decisively effected the change from the old life to the new (a point that is further underscored by the passive verbs used in the paragraph to signify the divine activity … the subject of which is God), a theme which the apostle emphatically struck at chapter 1:21, 22.[86]

As noted earlier in this chapter, because of the prevalence of circumcision, it became an apt metaphor used with the mouth, ears, and heart. The metaphor likely pictured the inability and dysfunction of a body part (cf. Exod 6:12, 30). Although Reformed paedobaptists will usually acknowledge that Colossians 2:11–12 is talking about spiritual circumcision, they will argue that physical circumcision always typified spiritual circumcision. Because baptism is described in Colossians 2 as symbolizing *spiritual* circumcision, Reformed paedobaptists see baptism as the replacement of *physical* circumcision, which was the prior symbol of spiritual circumcision.

That physical circumcision was always typological and pointed to spiritual circumcision is a point often assumed by Reformed paedobaptists. However, I would challenge this idea, because there is no explicit connection between physical circumcision and spiritual circumcision in the Old or New Testament (unless Colossians 2:11–12 is that evidence).[87]

---

86 Peter T. O'Brien, *Colossians, Philemon*, Word Biblical Commentary 44 (Dallas, TX: Word, 1982), 116.

87 A potential link between physical and spiritual circumcision could be found in Jeremiah 9:25–26. Jeremiah writes, "Behold, the days are coming, declares the LORD, when I will punish all those who are circumcised merely in the flesh—Egypt, Judah, Edom, the sons of Ammon, Moab, and all who dwell in the desert who cut the corners of their hair, for all these nations are uncircumcised, and all the house of Israel are uncircumcised in heart." However, this text could also easily be understood as using circumcision as an illustration. Israel was circumcised, but it did nothing to shield them from God's judgment because their heart was un-

Waymeyer summarizes the problem of connecting physical circumcision and spiritual circumcision as follows:

> First, when the Lord originally commanded circumcision as the sign of the covenant in Genesis 17:10–14, there was no hint that the rite had anything to do with the spiritual circumcision of one's heart. The physical circumcision of the male reproductive organ was simply presented as a sign which very appropriately symbolized promises involving the physical seed of Abraham. Second, the concept of circumcision was not used metaphorically to refer to spiritual circumcision until 700 years later (Deut 10:16; 30:6). Therefore, as far as we know from the biblical record, the nation of Israel administered circumcision for 700 years without the slightest indication from God that the sign of the covenant might have anything to do with a "circumcised heart." And third, it simply makes good sense that the biblical writers would take a well-known physical act and use it as a metaphor for a spiritual reality without intending to communicate anything about the inherent significance of the physical act itself.[88]

Waymeyer's position is consistent with how the prophets regularly speak. Prophets commonly use metaphor, especially with body parts. Compare, for example, the Old Testament's metaphorical description of a heart that is sick (Isa 1:5; Jer 8:18; 17:9; Ps 69:21; Prov 13:12; Lam 5:17). The prevalence of this metaphor rivals, or even surpasses the frequency of the uncircumcised heart metaphor. Yet, few would say that physical sickness is always supposed to remind us that we are spiritually sick (although that might preach well).

Perhaps one of the best illustrations of prophetic imagery with body parts is Isaiah 6:10. In this passage, God commands Isaiah to deliver His message. In so doing, he will fatten the heart of the people, he will make their ears heavy, and paste their eyes shut. Here we have three descriptions of physical impairment and inability to understand spiritual truths. Yet, these are not typological. Rather, they are illustrative and metaphorical. The same is likely the case for circumcision. An uncircumcised heart pictured a vital organ that was covered and unable to function correctly. It was insensitive to the things of God. On the other hand, a circumcised heart was sensitive to the things of God and would obey His commands. In

---

responsive to God. The physical circumcision provided a ready picture to understand the true problem of the heart which was unable to respond in obedience.

88 Waymeyer, *A Biblical Critique of Infant Baptism*, 66–67. Cf. Cotrell, *Baptism: A Biblical Study*, 136–38.

the words of Beasley-Murray, "The prophetic call for heart circumcision is a pictorial application of the rite, not an exposition of its meaning."[89]

To summarize, physical circumcision has a distinct meaning (which we have already discussed). Because of the prevalence of circumcision in Israelite society, it becomes a natural metaphor for the prophets to incorporate. However, there is a lack of evidence that physical circumcision was intended to remind Israel that a spiritual circumcision must take place. It remains most likely that Paul uses the metaphor of circumcision in a similar way to the prophets of the Old Testament—not intending to exposit the meaning of *physical* circumcision, but using a ready and accessible metaphor to emphasize God's work, not man's. We turn now to examine the details of Paul's argument, and how baptism relates to spiritual circumcision in Colossians 2.

The Relationship between Baptism and Circumcision in Colossians 2:11–12

Although I have proposed that an Old Testament Israelite would not have viewed physical circumcision as a type that pointed to spiritual circumcision, circumcision did indeed become a well-known spiritual metaphor in prophetic literature (cf. Deut 10:16; Jer 4:4; 6:10; Ezek 44:7; Hab 2:16). The New Testament continued this prophetic metaphor of spiritual circumcision (cf. Acts 7:51; Col 2:11–12). Addressing how Paul uses the metaphor of spiritual circumcision in Colossians 2:11–12 is our primary concern in this section.

In order to address how Paul is using spiritual circumcision and how it relates to baptism, we must answer two questions related to the text of Colossians 2:11–12. First, what does "the body of flesh" refer to? Second, what does the "circumcision of Christ" signify?

There are three options for what "body of flesh" could mean.[90] First, it could be a reference to man's sinful nature. Paul often refers to the flesh meaning a moral dimension or component (e.g., Col 2:18; Rom 8:5–7; Eph 2:3, etc.). If that is the nuance here in Colossians 2:11, this could match with Romans 6:6, which refers to a body of sin. Although the phrase is different in Romans 6, it could fit in concept. Second, the phrase could refer to human frailty that is subject to suffering and death. Conceptually this could match with Romans 7:24, which uses the phrase "body of death" to refer to the broken and corrupted body burdened by living in a fallen

89 Beasley-Murray, *Baptism in the New Testament*, 158.

90 Salter, "Does Baptism Replace Circumcision?," 22–23.

world. Few interpreters have found this second view convincing. Third, the phrase "body of flesh" could be a reference to Christ's physical body being stripped away as a metaphor of his death. This would fit with Colossians 1:22, where the same phrase, "body of flesh," is a reference to the death of Christ.

The meaning of the "body of flesh" relates to what the "circumcision of Christ" signifies. The "circumcision of Christ" could refer to either: (1) the circumcision that Christ gives (scholars often understand this to mean baptism), or (2) the circumcision which Christ experienced (i.e., His death). Either meaning would make sense in context, but perhaps it is slightly preferable to view the "circumcision of Christ" as a reference to His death.[91]

Table 5.1. Meaning of Colossians 2:11

"Body of Flesh"	"Circumcision of Christ"	Summary
Of Believers	For Believers	The "circumcision not made with hands" has removed the sinful/fleshly body (old nature) from believers through a circumcision that Christ has given to them (i.e., baptism?).
Of Christ	To Christ	The "circumcision not made with hands" has been granted to believers through Christ's putting off the flesh and His circumcision (both a reference to his death).

Those who argue that this text applies to believers point out, "Paul has been talking about what happened *in* and *to* the Colossians, not *for* them; what Christ did for them comes in 2:13b–14."[92] However, the connection of the phrase "body of flesh" with Colossians 1:22 and the death of Christ seems persuasive. Moreover, the context of Colossians 2 seems to be about the believer's identity in Christ. So a description about what Christ underwent on the cross would be entirely appropriate.[93] In the words of

91 Schreiner, "Baptism in the Epistles," 76; James D. G. Dunn, *The Epistles to the Colossians and to Philemon*, New international Greek Testament Commentary (Grand Rapids: Eerdmans, 1996), 157–58; O'Brien, *Colossians, Philemon*, 117; Beasley-Murray, *Baptism in the New Testament*, 152–53.

92 Salter, "Does Baptism Replace Circumcision?," 24.

93 Beasley-Murray, *Baptism in the New Testament*, 153.

Schreiner, "At his death, so to speak, God cut off Christ's bodily life, just as the foreskin is removed in circumcision. The only circumcision believers need, then, is the circumcision they receive by virtue of their incorporation into Christ's death on the cross."[94]

In sum, Colossians 2:11 is saying one of two things. The "circumcision not made with hands" is either (1) the removal of the old nature through baptism, or (2) it is what is granted to believers through Christ's death. Although I lean significantly toward the second option, both are possible. Regardless, neither implies that baptism has replaced physical circumcision. Colossians 2:11 focuses on spiritual regeneration, which comes through the work of Christ.

The next verse, Colossians 2:12, connects to the previous verse grammatically.[95] The initial phrase of verse 12 ("having been buried with him in baptism") connects to the main verb of verse 11 ("you were circumcised"). In other words, verse 12 grammatically explains *how* the circumcision "made without hands" occurs. Whereas the previous verse seemed to focus on Christ's sacrifice on the cross, now the incorporation of believers into Christ is emphasized. In a culminating sense, Colossians 2:12 describes the believer's relationship to Christ's death and burial ("having been buried with him in baptism"). But it also describes more!

Not only does verse 12 show that baptism is the symbol of the believer's union with Christ's death, but the verse goes on to say that baptism is also a symbol of the believer's union with Christ's resurrection.[96] Paul writes, "in which [i.e., baptism] you were also raised with him." In other words, Colossians 2:12 explicitly depicts baptism as the symbol of the believer's burial *and* resurrection with Christ. In this way, Colossians 2:11–12 details the same picture of baptism found in Romans 6.[97] In both texts, Paul describes baptism as a symbol of the believer's identification with Christ's burial and resurrection. Thus, Paul's argument in Colossians 2:11–

---

94 Schreiner, "Baptism in the Epistles," 76.

95 Pao, *Colossians and Philemon*, 166.

96 Some commentators understand the phrase, "in which you were also raised with him," to be a reference to Christ (see Pao, *Colossians and Philemon*, 167–68; Dunn, *The Epistles to the Colossians and to Philemon*, 160–61). If that were the case, the phrase would be translated, "in whom [i.e., Christ] you were also raised with him." However, the proximity of the pronoun to the word "baptism" inclines many commentators and translations to understand it correctly as a reference to physical baptism (see Salter, "Does Baptism Replace Circumcision?," 25; Schreiner, "Baptism in the Epistles," 77; Beasley-Murray, *Baptism in the New Testament*, 153–54).

97 Beasley-Murray, *Baptism in the New Testament*, 152.

12 seems rather straightforward. Spiritual circumcision occurs through the believer's baptism into Christ's death and resurrection.

Before moving on from Colossians 2:11–12, I must repeat the point from chapter one. In this passage Paul describes the entire baptismal process as happening "through faith." In the words of Salter, "Baptism incorporates the believer, by faith, into the death, burial, and resurrection of Christ."[98] In other words, faith is essential to the Christian baptismal experience. The baptismal experience signifies a believer's identity with Christ through His death, burial, and resurrection—and it all is through faith.

Colossians 2:11–12 says nothing about baptism replacing circumcision. If it did, then this would be the ideal place for Paul to say such a thing. Although Colossians 2:12 provides a connection between baptism and circumcision, Paul does not connect baptism with *physical* circumcision, but with a "circumcision made without hands."[99] Paul, like the prophets before him, uses the picture of circumcision metaphorically.

Even if we assume that baptism has replaced circumcision, which is an unsupported assumption, Reformed paedobaptists still need to account for the details of the text. Colossians 2:11–12 teaches that baptism symbolizes the burial and resurrection of Christ, and that entire process is through faith. These details represent a significant departure from the symbolism of physical circumcision in the Old Testament. Thus, it is incorrect to say that Old Testament circumcision symbolizes the same realities as baptism in Colossians 2. If the symbolism of physical circumcision and baptism are so radically different, then one cannot say with Calvin, "there is no difference in the inner mystery."[100] The Reformed paedobaptist cannot assume that because children were circumcised in the Old Testament, they should be baptized today. The connection between baptism and circumcision is an assumption which lacks biblical support.

History of the Analogy between Circumcision and Baptism

Although the evidence between circumcision and baptism is lacking, it is undeniable that many throughout church history have assumed this connection. Thus, I think it would be helpful to briefly discuss the history of

98 Salter, "Does Baptism Replace Circumcision?," 28.

99. Given the nature of Paul's opponents and their teaching in Colossians, it is possible that the rhetorical effect of Paul's argument here would have resulted in a downplaying of physical circumcision, which was often relied upon by the Judaizers. But the effect would have been significantly strengthened if Paul had equated physical circumcision and baptism.

100 John Calvin, *Institutes of the Christian Religion*, 1327.

the analogy between circumcision and baptism. There have been a variety of studies that help shed light on this issue.[101]

In 1990, Hunt published a historical survey entitled, "Colossians 2:11–12, The Circumcision/Baptism Analogy, and Infant Baptism." In this study he examines a variety of patristic sources which talk about infant baptism. He selects the baptismal texts of Tertullian, Origen, Cyprian, Gregory Nazianzen, and Augustine. In his judgment, according to the evidence we have access to, infant baptism was not implemented based on an analogy between circumcision and baptism. He explains, "Placing the evidence of Tertullian, Origen and Cyprian side by side, it is clear that the analogy between circumcision and baptism did not give rise to the practice of infant baptism. It was not used as an argument for infant baptism until after the practice was clearly established on other grounds."[102] Hunt suggests that the analogy between circumcision and baptism was first introduced in Italy or North Africa, "sometime in the second quarter of the third century."[103]

At the end of his analysis of these primary baptismal texts, Hunt concludes:

> The patristic evidence does not suggest that the analogy between circumcision and baptism gave rise to the practice of infant baptism, nor that Colossians 2:11–12 were initially understood to imply infant baptism. It suggests rather that this analogy was not used as an argument for infant baptism until after the practice has arisen on other grounds. The silence of the NT concerning an explicit prohibition of infant baptism is outweighed by the silence of the early centuries in which there is no mention of the analogy between circumcision and baptism in the early references to infant baptism.
>
> Colossians 2:11–12 was understood in the light of the analogy with circumcision in the patristic period. To the present writer, the earlier patristic understanding of circumcision as a figure for our response to the gospel, which is expressed in baptism, is closer to Paul's meaning in these verses than the later patristic under-

101 Two excellent examinations of the history of the early church and the connection between circumcision and baptism are as follows: Everett Ferguson, "Spiritual Circumcision in Early Christianity," in *The Early Church at Work and Worship, Volume 2: Catechesis, Baptism, Eschatology, and Martyrdom* (London: James Clarke & Co. Ltd., 2014), 144–54; J. P. T. Hunt, "Colossians 2:11–12, The Circumcision/Baptism Analogy, and Infant Baptism," *Tyndale Bulletin* 41, no. 2 (1990): 227–44.

102 Hunt, "Colossians 2:11–12," 232.

103 Ibid.

> standing of circumcision as a type of the outward rite of baptism itself. However, post-patristic exegesis of Colossians 2:11–12, and the use of these verses in connection with infant baptism, have been dominated by the later patristic understanding of this analogy.[104]

Everett Ferguson, who has studied baptism in the early church extensively,[105] has conducted another important historical study on this issue. In his study, published in 2014, he proposes that the association between circumcision and baptism is a secondary development that came about because of the primary association of circumcision with the seal of the Holy Spirit.[106]

In summarizing his study, Ferguson notes:

> It may be recalled that those passages which make circumcision in some sense the equivalent of baptism begin to appear later than those which identify circumcision with the Spirit. In the early writers the counterpart of circumcision is not baptism but what happens in baptism. The progression of thought would be as follows: (1) the Spirit as the seal of the new covenant on the analogy of circumcision as the seal of the Mosaic covenant, (2) the Spirit given in baptism, an extension natural enough and perhaps present from the beginning but reinforced by the association of both the covenant and baptism with the death of Christ, which inaugurated the new covenant, (3) baptism as the counterpart of circumcision.[107]

According to both Hunt and Ferguson, the earliest church writings did not equate circumcision and baptism. The practice of infant baptism developed apart from an appeal to that analogy. Over time, however, the connection between baptism and circumcision became prevalent, most likely because of the connection that writers made between circumcision and the Holy Spirit. In any case, the connection between circumcision and baptism has become an essential centerpiece to the Reformed paedobaptist argument for infant baptism.[108]

104 Ibid., 244.

105 See his notable tome of 900 pages, Ferguson, *Baptism in the Early Church*, 199–816.

106 Ferguson, "Spiritual Circumcision in Early Christianity," 150.

107 Ibid., 154.

108 In the words of Ross, "I would maintain that the case [for infant baptism] fundamentally rests on establishing two principal contentions: first, that baptism and circumcision have essentially the same meaning; and second, that the covenant community is similarly

Inconsistencies in the Reformed Paedobaptist Practice of Baptism

My contention in this chapter has been that baptism and circumcision are not the same, nor do they symbolize the same realities. This assertion is in strong contrast to the covenantal argument for infant baptism. Reformed paedobaptists incorrectly view circumcision and baptism as being the same in substance and meaning, having little (if any) discontinuity between the two. At this point, I think it is helpful to note that, even if we grant the continuity between baptism and circumcision, the Reformed paedobaptist argument is inconsistent with how it applies the link between circumcision and baptism.[109]

As we have noted, Reformed paedobaptists view baptism as standing in the same place as circumcision and having the same role. To quote Zacharias Ursinus again, "Baptism occupies the place of circumcision in the New Testament, and has the same use that circumcision had in the Old Testament."[110] The typical Reformed paedobaptist argument is that if baptism occupies the place of circumcision, and circumcision applied to children, so too should baptism apply to children. In other words, the Old Testament context and significance of circumcision continue to apply to the New Testament sign since there is no indication in the New Testament that this practice has been altered.

However, we have already noted the Reformed paedobaptist's inconsistency on the continuity issue. For example, there is no New Testament justification for baptizing baby girls when only baby boys were circumcised. Additionally, paedobaptists do not appropriately address why baptism is not applied on the eighth day after birth.

But there is another, more serious, inconsistency between the application of circumcision and baptism. That difference is that infant baptism is only given to infants who have at least one believing parent.[111] As the Westminster Confession states, "Not only those that do actually profess faith in and obedience unto Christ, but also the infants of one or both believing parents, are to be baptized" (28.4). The key idea in the Westminster

---

constituted in the Old and New Testaments" (Ross, "Baptism and Circumcision as Signs and Seals," 100).

109 This section of the chapter is heavily influenced by Ortlund, "Why Not Grandchildren? An Argument against Reformed Paedobaptism," 333–46. Ortlund points to many inconsistencies in the Reformed paedobaptist position.

110 Ursinus, *The Commentary of Zacharias Ursinus on the Heidelberg Catechism*, 367.

111 Brownson, *The Promise of Baptism*, 190–93.

Confession is that the infant must have one or both believing parents to be eligible for baptism.

However, as discussed earlier, Genesis 17 ties the circumcision rite to an intergenerational mandate. Every Israelite had to be circumcised based on his physical, albeit removed, relationship to Abraham. This then begs the question, why limit infant baptism to the children of believers? What textual basis is there to do such a thing? If circumcision was given based on family ties, why couldn't a grandchild or great-grandchild be baptized on that same basis?

Historically, this happened in many paedobaptist churches. An intergenerational view of infant baptism was much more prevalent in history than in modern times. There have been many Reformed paedobaptists who held this position. One of the clearest representatives of this position is Samuel Rutherford, who notes:

> I prove that the proposition "I will be thy God and the God of thy seed" extends the covenant to the seed of the faithful to many generations downward until it please the Lord to translate his Son's Kingdom and remove the candlestick from a people. Neither can the meaning be: "I will be thy God and the God of thy seed, except the nearest parents of thy seed be unbelievers," for that is contrary to the Scriptures above cited [Genesis 17 and Joshua 5].[112]

As Rutherford points out, it is inconsistent with Genesis 17 and Joshua 5 to say that parents must be believers for their infants to be baptized. If circumcision and baptism are essentially equal, what license do Reformed paedobaptists have to change the standard of inclusion? Although many Reformed churches limit baptism to infants who have believing parents, that is certainly not the practice we see with circumcision in the Old Testament, nor is it consistent with many of the key figures of Reformed paedobaptism.[113] Where in the Bible does that standard change into the modern practice of Reformed paedobaptists?

Not only do most Reformed paedobaptists inconsistently apply infant baptism, but they also display a rather significant inconsistency in disallow-

---

112 Samuel Rutherford, "On the Baptism of the Children of Adherents," in *A Peaceable and Temperate Plea for Paul's Presbytery in Scotland* (London: John Bartlet, 1642), 4.

113 As a sample of those who believed infant baptism should not be restricted to those infants with believing parents, Ortlund lists John Calvin, John Knox, the Italian Reformer Girolamo Zanchi (1516–1590), the Swiss French Reformer William Bucanus, Richard Hooker, Samuel Rutherford, and Cotton Mather (Ortlund, "Why Not Grandchildren? An Argument against Reformed Paedobaptism," 342–46).

ing paedocommunion (i.e., the belief that children can participate in the Lord's Table before a profession of faith). In the Old Testament, those who were circumcised could participate in the Passover meal (Exod 12:43–49). The details of Exodus 12 would seem to indicate that children were present and participating in the Passover experience. Jewett notes that the Passover instructions themselves *require* household celebration.[114] Advocates of paedocommunion are quick to point out that "every single passage in the entire Bible that mentions or discusses children speaks of them as included in whatever religious event is under consideration."[115]

Ironically, those who hold to the minority position of paedocommunion argue for paedocommunion using the same arguments that Reformed paedobaptists use against Baptists.[116] Primarily, they say that children have always been full covenant members of the community. Thus, children are to be allowed full covenant participation. The New Testament nowhere says that children should suddenly be disallowed from the full covenant participation they experienced under the old covenant. Thus, they are entitled to participate in the covenant meal, the Lord's Supper.

The words that famed theologian B. B. Warfield used to defend paedobaptism could likewise defend paedocommunion. He states, "God established His church in the days of Abraham and put children into it. They must remain there until He puts them out. He has nowhere put them out. They are still then members of His Church and as such entitled to its ordinances."[117] In this way, the same arguments for paedobaptism would equally fit with paedocommunion.

An outsider cannot fail to observe the inconsistency with which most Reformed paedobaptists reject the continuity between the old covenant Passover meal and the new covenant Lord's Supper. To use the argument that paedobaptists use, would we expect the new covenant, in all its glories and blessings, to be less inclusive than the old covenant?

To avoid this obvious implication, some Reformed paedobaptists reject the identification of the Lord's Supper with the Passover.[118] It is, how-

114 Jewett, *Infant Baptism and the Covenant of Grace*, 204.

115 James B. Jordan, "Children and the Religious Meals of the Old Creation," in *The Case for Covenant Communion*, ed. Gregg Strawbridge (Monroe, LA: Athanasius Press, 2006), 50.

116 Gregg Strawbridge, ed., *The Case for Covenant Communion* (Monroe, LA: Athanasius Press, 2006).

117 Warfield, "The Polemics of Infant Baptism," 9:408.

118 Estelle explicitly notes, "The Lord's Supper is not to be identified with the Passover meal" (Bryan D. Estelle, "Passover and the Lord's Supper: Continuity or Discontinuity?," in

ever, almost beyond doubt that the Last Supper was indeed a Passover meal.[119] This, of course, does not prove that they are the same. But one does wonder why Reformed paedobaptists are so inconsistent on this issue, refusing to draw a line from the Old to New Testament. As Jewett notes:

> In order to appreciate the issue that confronts the Paedobaptist here, we must remember that the argument from infant circumcision to infant baptism, so pivotal in the whole debate, is but a detailed application of the more basic theological principle of continuity in redemptive revelation. Paedobaptists, then, should not appeal to a parallel between circumcision and baptism which they refuse to acknowledge between the Passover and the Lord's Supper. In fact, as far as the evidence of Scripture is concerned, the parallelism between the covenant meals of Passover and Eucharist is even more overt than that between the initiatory rites of circumcision and baptism.[120]

To further confound the issue, Reformed paedobaptists have regularly acknowledged that participation in the Lord's Supper is an expression of faith. For example, the Belgic Confession says it this way: "When we eat the sacrament with our mouths we also do as certainly receive by faith (which is the hand and mouth of our soul) the true body and blood of Christ, our only Saviour, in our souls for the support of our spiritual lives" (35). Similarly, the Westminster Confession says, "Worthy receivers outwardly partaking of the visible elements in this sacrament do then also inwardly by faith really and indeed, yet not carnally and corporeally, but spiritually, receive and feed upon Christ crucified ..." (29.7).

The necessity of faith is one of the main reasons covenantal paedobaptists say a child cannot participate in communion. For example, Beeke writes, "Children of the covenant, though heirs of the promise and included in the body of the church, do not possess in infancy or childhood the faith with the requisite knowledge and powers of judgment to answer

---

Children and the Lord's Supper, ed. Guy Waters and Ligon Duncan [Ross-shire, UK: Christian Focus Publications, 2011], 32).

119 For an excellent summary of the comparisons and similarities between the two descriptions, see Leon Morris, *The Gospel According to John*, New International Commentary on the New Testament (Grand Rapids: Eerdmans, 1995), 684–96. The early church also seemed to connect the Lord's Supper and Passover. The mid-second century apocryphal text, *Epistle of the Apostles* (*Epistula Apostolorum*) 15, states, "And you therefore celebrate the remembrance of my death, which is the Passover" (J. K. Elliot, *The Apocryphal New Testament: A Collection of Apocryphal Christian Literature in an English Translation* [Oxford: Clarendon Press, 1993], 565).

120 Jewett, *Infant Baptism and the Covenant of Grace*, 202.

the demand of the Apostle Paul for self-examination and spiritual discernment."[121]

One cannot help but appreciate that the appeal to faith that many paedobaptists make against paedocommunion is the same argument that Baptists make against paedobaptism. Although the connection between the Lord's Supper and Passover is even stronger than the connection between baptism and circumcision, most covenantal paedobaptists will withhold full covenantal involvement from a child because of the child's inability to exercise faith. If the New Testament is clear enough that faith is a prerequisite for participating in the Lord's Supper, then the New Testament is even *more clear* that faith is a prerequisite to participating in baptism.

Conclusion

The Reformed paedobaptist relies heavily on the connection between circumcision and baptism. Although we will explore a full definition and explanation of baptism in chapter seven, this chapter has brought to light the numerous differences between baptism and circumcision. While baptism and circumcision are both viewed as initiatory rites, that is where the similarity ends. Circumcision was a male-only sign that signified the promises of the Abrahamic covenant and a special national identity. Circumcision was also given to unbelieving adults and unbelieving children who were outside the promise of God. This contrasts strongly with baptism, which even paedobaptists acknowledge should not be given to adults who do not profess faith in Christ.

Despite the significant dissimilarities between baptism and circumcision, many paedobaptists appeal to Colossians 2:11–12 as a proof text. Although this text links the idea of baptism and circumcision, it is clear from the context that it is not referring to physical circumcision, but a spiritual circumcision, which was a common metaphor in use among the prophets. Additionally, a brief examination of the historical work by Hunt and Ferguson revealed that the connection between baptism and circumcision was not readily apparent until the third century.

This chapter concluded with a brief look at the inconsistencies in the Reformed paedobaptist approach. If Reformed paedobaptists really did view infant baptism as analogous to circumcision, why only baptize an infant if his father or mother is a believer? Why deny that same child full

121 Joel R. Beeke, "'Only for His Believers': Paedocommunion and the Witness of the Reformed Liturgies," in *Children and the Lord's Supper*, ed. Guy Waters and Ligon Duncan (Ross-shire, UK: Christian Focus Publications, 2011), 178.

covenant participation through communion? These issues demonstrate that the Reformed paedobaptist is being driven by something other than a consistent exegesis of the relevant biblical texts.

Comparing baptism and circumcision shows significant problems with the paedobaptist system. Although Reformed paedobaptists claim that the Old Testament should be followed unless the New Testament implements a change, they do not consistently follow this foundational principle.

Chapter 6

Household Baptisms and the Covenantal View of Families

THIS CHAPTER IS ESPECIALLY significant to the discussion of paedobaptism because many of the arguments used in this chapter also apply to the Catholic, Lutheran, and Methodist positions on infant baptism. Historically, all paedobaptist supporters have appealed to the so-called household baptism texts in the New Testament as evidence that entire households (including infants) were baptized. Thus, in this chapter, I will address those general arguments alongside the more specific Reformed arguments of the Reformed paedobaptist.

Challenging General Paedobaptist Arguments about Household Texts

All paedobaptists acknowledge that there is no explicit mention in the New Testament of infant baptism. However, the paedobaptist remains undeterred by this fact. To be fair, although it is noteworthy that there is no mention of infant baptism, this does not prove that infants were not baptized. But, given the lack of explicit New Testament mention, almost all paedobaptists have relied on two primary arguments that are interconnected. Although not all paedobaptists use these arguments, paedobaptists have historically used them to argue for infant baptism in the New Testament.

Argument 1: When an Entire Household is Mentioned, no Individuals are Excluded

In some of the baptism narratives we read that an individual and "all his family" (Acts 16:33) or "his entire household" (Acts 18:8) were baptized. Paedobaptists will often claim that in baptism texts, anytime a variation of the wording "all his household" or "his entire household" occurs, "no single member of the household was excluded from baptism."[1] If no single household member is excluded in these passages, that would mean that if infants were present in the family, they would also have been baptized.

Paedobaptists appeal to Genesis 17 as support for this idea. In Genesis 17:23, "every male" of the household was circumcised, a statement which includes infants of eight days and older (cf. Gen 17:12).[2] Importantly, paedobaptists claim it is not just the link between baptism and circumcision at play in Genesis 17, but the concept of family solidarity as well. Therefore, any New Testament reference to "his entire household" or "all his family" must refer to *all* the family members without exception, just like in Genesis 17 (although there it is only males). Assuming the exhaustive nature of the word "all" or "entire," many paedobaptists argue that infants would have been baptized in these household baptism texts.

We should note that while paedobaptists universally argue an entire household includes children, some paedobaptists argue that slaves were not included.[3] This concession seems to be made because, according to the paedobaptist, slaves would have had to make a profession of faith prior to baptism. Thus, although some paedobaptists are willing to include slaves in household baptisms, many are not, because of the need of a profession of faith.

We can bring two significant counterpoints to the above argumentation. First, we must include household slaves in the household formula. The paedobaptist appeal to Genesis 17 undermines the idea that household slaves would have been excluded from the household formula. Genesis 17:12–13 specifies that foreign slaves were to be circumcised. Thus, it is inconsistent to say children would be included, but not slaves, when the Old Testament paradigm is to include both.

However, it is difficult to see every slave professing faith in Christ at the same time their master does. Many of these households had a significant number of slaves.[4] Are we to suppose that in each case, every slave professed Christ immediately along with the master of the house? Alter-

1 Joachim Jeremias, *Infant Baptism in the First Four Centuries*, trans. David Cairns (London: SCM Press, 1960), 19–20.

2 Jonathan M. Watt, "The Oikos Formula," in *The Case for Covenantal Infant Baptism*, ed. Gregg Strawbridge (Phillipsburg, NJ: P&R Publishing, 2003), 80–81.

3 Ibid., 80; Jeremias, *Infant Baptism in the First Four Centuries*, 19–21. Contra Booth, who correctly includes slaves when "household" is referenced (*Children of the Promise*, 126).

4 Historians estimate 16–20% of the entire population were slaves. Bartchy writes, "In the urban areas as well, the number and quality of slaves one owned were critical factors in determining the owner's reputation and social status; more than one senatorial household included more than four hundred slaves" (S. Scott Bartchy, "Slaves and Slavery in the Roman World,"

natively, a paedobaptist could argue that the master forced the slaves to be baptized without a profession of faith. One can see the obvious problems with that! Therefore, it is understandable why paedobaptists often exclude household slaves from the household formula, even though the Old Testament paradigm certainly included slaves as part of the household.

A second challenge to the household formula is the specific examples where Scripture talks about the whole household, but certain family members are intentionally excluded. The classic example of this is 1 Samuel 1:21–22.[5] The Greek version of this text uses the same language as the New Testament examples in Acts. The story reveals, "The man Elkanah and *all his house* went up to offer to the LORD the yearly sacrifice and to pay his vow" (v. 21, emphasis added).

Although the Greek of Samuel uses the same household formula as Acts in verse 21, verse 22 quickly reveals that Hannah stayed behind. The reason Hannah didn't go up with Elkanah was that she was caring for an infant child. Although the text does not say the child stayed with Hannah, we obviously should *not* include the child as part of "all his house" that went up to offer the yearly sacrifice. This is an obvious example of the household formula being used when at least two individuals (and probably more) were not included. We see that there are verifiable examples in Scripture that exclude individuals from this supposed household formula. Therefore, one cannot argue, as some paedobaptist advocates often do, that the mention of the entire household *always* means *every member* of the household without exception.

Argument 2: When a Household is Mentioned, Infants are Present

This argument connects to the previous one. The first argument assumes that no one is excluded when an entire household is mentioned. However, this has no application to the subject of infant baptism if there are no infants present. Thus, this second argument emphasizes that when Scripture speaks of households, infants are present.

Honest biblical interpreters are usually hesitant to see infants where they are not mentioned, and rightfully so. Thus, most paedobaptist interpreters will only argue this point cumulatively. They will note that, with the many mentions of households getting baptized, would it be fair to say

in *The World of the New Testament: Cultural, Social, and Historical Contexts*, ed. Joel B. Green and Lee Martin McDonald [Grand Rapids: Baker Academic, 2013], 170–71).

5 Waymeyer, *A Biblical Critique of Infant Baptism*, 15; Jewett, *Infant Baptism and the Covenant of Grace*, 52.

none of them had infants? Or, to state it another way, could all of those household references exist and not one infant be present in *any* of them?

This may initially seem like a compelling argument. But the claim itself assumes we should even ask the question. The reality is that the so-called "household formula" is used throughout Scripture without reference to children. When we read about households elsewhere, we do not think to ask if it also applies to infants.

For example, in John 4:53, we read of a father who had a child healed by Jesus. The text states that "he himself believed, and all his household." Does any exegete ask whether infants are included in this statement? I suppose some Lutheran paedobaptists would be adamant to say that infants are capable of belief, but Reformed paedobaptists would not go that route.

In another example, Cornelius is described as "a devout man who feared God with all his household" (Acts 10:2). Again, are we justified in asking whether infants were included in the household formula? Infants cannot fear God.

Perhaps the best illustration of this principle is Titus 1:11, where the same Greek phrase as Acts 18:8 is used. In Titus 1:11, we read that false teachers were "upsetting whole families." Would any rational interpreter ask whether infants were being deceived by false teachers? The point is obvious. It is not the intention of this so-called "household formula" to include or exclude infants. In the words of Jewett:

> When we read that Jesus healed the nobleman's son and his *whole* house believed (John 4:53); that Cornelius was a man who feared God with *all* his house (Acts 10:2); or that certain unruly persons subvert *whole* houses with their teaching (Titus 1:11), who will quibble about infants? We all know infants cannot "believe in the Lord," "fear God," nor be "subverted" in their minds by heretics; therefore, we read such texts without so much as thinking to ask if there were infants in these houses. Why then insist, when we read that "he and all his were baptized" or that "she was baptized and her household," that these homes were or were not blessed with infants, according to our theological proclivities?[6]

The typical paedobaptist will argue that with all the references to household baptisms, one should expect an infant to be present in at least a handful of cases. However, as we have seen in this section, the so-called "household formula" is used with reference to other situations where including infants makes no sense. I propose that we treat these baptism texts

6 Jewett, *Infant Baptism and the Covenant of Grace*, 51.

fairly, like we treat the other mentions of households. We should recognize that the biblical authors are making a holistic point about acceptance or rejection, not intending us to ask about the status of infants.

God's Covenantal and Corporate Dealings with the Household

To the credit of many Reformed paedobaptists, they often view the previous two arguments as being weak attempts to force an interpretation on texts that are not intended to address the specific issues demanded of them. Thus, Reformed paedobaptists often move beyond the above arguments and appeal to the idea that God's covenant is with families, not just individuals. In the Reformed paedobaptist view, God deals corporately with the family or household in both the Old and New Testaments. Booth notes it this way:

> The family or household, as a social unit, looms large on the pages of Scripture. God's covenantal dealings are always manifest in terms of their effects upon the family, both negatively and positively.... Since children were members of the Abrahamic covenant, we must assume that they continue to be members of the new covenant (there being no command in the New Testament to exclude them). God has consistently dealt with households in every age and has embraced children along with their parents.[7]

Doug Wilson makes a similar point when he writes:

> The point being made here is *not* that these are narratives of infant baptisms. The point is that they are narratives of *household* or *family* baptisms (1 Cor 1:16). The gospel is for the *generations* of the earth. One of the most precious doctrines of Scripture for believing parents is the teaching of *covenantal succession* from one generation to the next (Ps. 102:28)... This corporate mindset, alien to the modern individualist, is simply taken for granted in Scripture.[8]

Similarly, drawing attention to the corporate solidarity between parents and children, Hodge writes, "In the sight of God parents and children are one. The former are the authorized representatives of the latter; they act for them; they contract obligations in their name. In all cases, therefore,

7 Booth, *Children of the Promise*, 125.

8 Wilson, *To a Thousand Generations*, 18–19.

where parents enter into covenant with God, they bring their children with them."[9]

Gentry gives voice to a similar sentiment, "There is *nothing* in the New Testament that undermines and invalidates the Old Testament covenantal principle of family solidarity. In fact, everything confirms its continuing validity. Thus, a covenantal understanding of baptism leads inexorably to infant baptism."[10]

Explaining how baptism and family solidarity go together, Watt notes, "From patriarchs to patres-familias, the master of the family spoke for those who were his. When he was baptized, so were they."[11]

Behind each of the above quotations are the foundational principles of covenant paedobaptist presuppositions. First, Reformed paedobaptists are assuming the existence of the covenant of grace, which stays the same from the Old to New Testament and is essentially the same as the Abrahamic covenant. Second, they assume there is only one people of God, and God deals with the families of the church in the same way he dealt with the families of Israel. Therefore, God's promises to the physical descendants of Abraham are now spiritually applied to all the families of the church. As such, this argument is simply an outworking of the Reformed paedobaptist theology, which we have already critiqued in previous chapters. Nevertheless, in what follows, I will note additional arguments against the specific covenantal view of family structures that Reformed paedobaptists use.

Scripture Specifies Women and Children When They Are Included in the Narrative

Reformed paedobaptists argue the Bible does not mention children in baptism narratives because the ancient cultures would assume the whole household was involved, including children. I agree with the point that the ancient cultures in Scripture were much more family-centered than our individualistic Western society. However, just because the family was a central component of ancient life does not mean that we can ignore the fact Scripture *does* often include both women and children in narratives.

There are significant examples in both the Old and New Testaments where women and children are featured prominently (cf. Josh 8:35; 1 Sam 22:19; Jer 40:7; 2 Chron 20:13; Matt 14:21; 15:38; Acts 21:5). According to the paedobaptist model, mention of women and children is unnecessary

9 Hodge, *Systematic Theology*, 3:555.

10 Kenneth L. Gentry, *The Greatness of the Great Commission* (Tyler, TX: Institute for Christian Economics, 1990), 87.

11 Watt, "The Oikos Formula," 84.

since we could assume they follow the corporate head of the household. But Scripture regularly talks about women and children as key actors independent of their households.

A notable example of this is Acts 8:12, where the historian Luke notes, "But when they believed Philip as he preached good news about the kingdom of God and the name of Jesus Christ, they were baptized, both men and women." Luke mentions that both men and women were baptized. Is it reasonable that children were baptized without being noted by the thorough historian? This proposition becomes less likely when we note that Luke has no problems talking about children when they are involved in the narratives (cf. Acts 21:5).[12]

The simple but essential point is that Scripture frequently mentions women and children when they are active participants in narratives. It is one thing to appeal to a social construct of family and corporate solidarity. It is quite another thing to admit that Scripture regularly talks about women and children, but never once in the regular mentions of baptism talks about children being baptized. When one sees how often the Bible talks about children, the silence surrounding infant baptism is quite deafening.

The New Testament Highlights Family Division because of the Gospel

If God has a covenantal saving purpose for families and not just for individuals, we would expect the message of family unity in salvation to be clear in the New Testament. However, the New Testament describes family division as the norm. Jesus regularly taught the disciples to expect that following Jesus would bring family division. Jesus said, "Do not think that I have come to bring peace to the earth. I have not come to bring peace, but a sword. For I have come to set a man against his father, and a daughter against her mother, and a daughter-in-law against her mother-in-law. And a person's enemies will be those of his own household" (Matt 10:34–36).

Commenting on this text, Osborne paints the grim picture given by Christ, "The sword of Matt 10:34 will penetrate even families and violently cause the closest relationships to be severed. When the kingdom truths enter society, choices will be made, resulting even in family members turning against those who choose Christ, betraying them to their deaths (10:21)."[13]

Matthew 10 is not just an out-of-the-ordinary message from Jesus. He also states a similar message in Luke 12:51–53:

---

12 Jewett notes, "At least one should not suppose that the Baptist is tyrannized by his system when he raises such a question" (Jewett, *Infant Baptism and the Covenant of Grace*, 53).

13 Grant R. Osborne, *Matthew*, Zondervan Exegetical Commentary on the New Testament 1 (Grand Rapids: Zondervan, 2010), 404–405.

> Do you think that I have come to give peace on earth? No, I tell you, but rather division. For from now on in one house there will be five divided, three against two and two against three. They will be divided, father against son and son against father, mother against daughter and daughter against mother, mother-in-law against her daughter-in-law and daughter-in-law against mother-in-law.

This kind of message would have been very insulting to a family-centered society. In fact, to the early church, this message would have been a necessary affirmation that what they were doing was in line with God's will—even though families were being broken apart. As Green notes in his commentary on Luke:

> This message potentially serves an important apologetic function in community definition. Within a culture wherein kinship ties played so crucial a socio-religious role, a message such as this one might well be suspect. How could a ministry the effects of which include the dissolution of family ties be sanctioned by God? Jesus posits just such divisions not only as a legitimate consequence of his mission but as confirmation that he is carrying out a divine charge.[14]

Reformed paedobaptists have difficulty interpreting the above passages in a way that matches their presuppositions. Many ignore these passages. For example, one of the most prominent books defending covenantal infant baptism, *The Case for Covenantal Infant Baptism*, does not include a single reference to Luke 12:51–53 in any of its fifteen chapters.[15] Others, such as James Brownson, attempt to interpret these passages as a reference to being *willing* to give up one's family and not allow them to misplace our allegiance to Jesus. In Brownson's words, "Like every other aspect of our lives, it is only when we relinquish our families and take up our cross that we can receive them back again, not as a natural right, but as a gift from God."[16]

---

14 Joel B. Green, *The Gospel of Luke*, New International Commentary on the New Testament (Grand Rapids: Eerdmans, 1997), 509.

15 Gregg Strawbridge, ed., *The Case for Covenantal Infant Baptism* (Phillipsburg, NJ: P&R Publishing, 2003).

16 Brownson notes, "It is clear that God's covenant with Israel in the Old Testament was not only with individuals, but with families" (Brownson, *The Promise of Baptism*, 127). However, the idea that God covenants with families is perhaps a bit simplistic. There are many

However, Jesus was not speaking metaphorically or only about a willingness to give up family. Jesus was talking about real life. We see this in Mark 13:12, another text completely ignored by covenantal paedobaptists. In Mark 13:12, Jesus describes the future that His followers can expect, "And brother will deliver brother over to death, and the father his child, and children will rise against parents and have them put to death." Mark 13 is speaking prophetically about the future. It doesn't matter whether you place Mark 13 in 70 AD or in the future tribulation period. Regardless, Jesus unambiguously states that the gospel will cause real division in families. Christians can expect to see families not just torn apart by the gospel, but even delivering one another over to death because of it.

The rest of the New Testament shows that what Jesus said would happen, did happen. In the church at Corinth, Paul recognizes that new believers regularly experience situations where a spouse may leave a marriage rather than believe in Christ. In such cases, Paul instructs believers to let their unbelieving spouse leave (1 Cor 7:15).[17] However, if the spouse wants to stay, the marriage is still to be honored, despite the continued unbelief of the spouse (1 Cor 7:13–14). Not only does Paul note the common occurrence of this situation, but the fact that he mentions unbelieving husbands *and* wives shows the idea of corporate headship of a family did not work out as neatly as Reformed paedobaptists often argue.

Peter addresses a similar situation in 1 Peter 3. In writing to the dispersed churches, Peter envisions the common situation of wives having to submit to an unbelieving husband (1 Pet 3:1–2). Apparently, there were many situations in the first century church where families were not unified in their faith. This is not surprising and matches with what Jesus said would happen. The problem is for the Reformed paedobaptist who argues that the promise of salvation extends to families and not just individuals.

The Old Testament Also Does Not Describe Family Salvation

The Reformed paedobaptist also argues that in the Old Testament, God makes covenants with families and not individuals.[18] The implication is that, because the same covenant of grace is operating in both the Old and

---

examples of members of the family being left out of the covenant because of God's choice. For example, God excluded Ishmael from the covenant. God also chose Jacob, but not Esau.

17 Beasley-Murray remarks, "The fact that the Corinthians were constrained to write to Paul about the matter shows that the problem was not ephemeral: the unconverted husbands and the unconverted wives were not relenting" (Beasley-Murray, *Baptism in the New Testament*, 319).

18 Brownson, *The Promise of Baptism*, 121.

New Testaments, God has a saving purpose not only for individuals but also for families in the New Testament as a continuation of the pattern found in the Old Testament. Thus, a critical component of this argument is the assumption that God saves families in the Old Testament.

However, no passage or promise guarantees that God will save the children of believers. In fact, a survey of Old Testament families quickly shows that, often, fathers and sons walk very different paths. The first human, Adam, was father to the first murderer, Cain. Noah, the recipient of the gracious Noahic covenant, was father to the disgraceful Ham. The great high priest of Israel, Aaron, fathered two profane sons, Nadab and Abihu. Another high priest of Israel, Eli, fathered worthless, wicked sons, Hophni and Phinehas. Even the bright and shining light of the judges, Samuel, fathered deviant sons, Joel and Abijah. David, a godly champion who trusted in Yahweh, fathered two power-hungry sons, Absalom and Adonijah, as well as a rapist, Amnon. Solomon, the wisest of all kings, fathered a foolish son, Rehoboam. Hezekiah, a righteous king who walked in the ways of David, fathered a disastrously idolatrous son, Manasseh. These examples show that even the godliest men of the Old Testament had unbelieving family members. Not only is there no promise in the Old Testament that God will save the children of believers, the narrative examples contradict such a claim.

There is certainly a sense in which each Israelite family was a part of the Abrahamic covenant because of their relationship to the twelve sons of Jacob. However, the Reformed paedobaptist tries to equate the physical promises of Israel's ancestry under the Abrahamic covenant with the salvation promises for the church under the new covenant. Not only is that methodology suspect, but it also ignores the biblical evidence as seen above. Both Old and New Testaments give an abundance of examples and teachings that confirm that salvation relates to the individual decision of putting one's faith in the Lord. There is no promise from God that says He will save a child because He is the son or daughter of a believer.[19]

---

19 The writing of paedobaptists is confusing on this point. Paedobaptists universally acknowledge that God is not obligated to save children of believers. However, at the same time, paedobaptists say that there is a promise that God has made to save the family. For example, Brownson notes, "This means, of course, this New Covenant promise is no more to be presumed upon than the Old Covenant promise was. It is still possible for children to spurn the promise and to fail to respond in faith. Households may struggle with divisions within them, as they groan in awaiting the fullness of God's redemption. Yet the promise remains, and is not eclipsed in the movement from the Old Covenant to the New" (Brownson, *The Promise of Baptism*, 127). This confusion seems inherent to the system itself, all to avoid saying God has not fulfilled His promise.

Specific Household Passages Used by Paedobaptists

We have seen that there are some significant problems with some of the common arguments and lines of reasoning that paedobaptists use. The use of so-called "household formulas" does not mean there were infants who were baptized, nor is there indication that God promises to save families corporately. I will now move on to a detailed examination of the common baptism texts appealed to by paedobaptists. Not only is there no indication or evidence of infant baptism in any of these passages, but a thorough assessment of these texts supports the idea that only those who put their faith in Christ received baptism.

Peter's Call to Baptism (Acts 2:38–39)

> And Peter said to them, "Repent and be baptized every one of you in the name of Jesus Christ for the forgiveness of your sins, and you will receive the gift of the Holy Spirit. For the promise is for you and for your children and for all who are far off, everyone whom the Lord our God calls to himself."

This is one of the most cited passages used by Reformed paedobaptists because they view it as a line of continuation between the Old and New Testaments. Beeke and Lanning note, "Significantly, these words of Peter declare that certain things had not changed and would not change in the new era. The pattern of God's dealings with believers and their children, as old as creation itself, would continue as a constitutional principle of the visible church."[20]

Although Reformed paedobaptists often put these verses forward as evidence for God's consistent dealings with believers and their children (and thus indirect evidence for paedobaptism), an analysis of this passage shows otherwise. The primary question that we must ask of the passage is, what promise is given in Acts 2:39? Beeke and Lanning answer that question this way:

> First, it is clear that Peter speaks of "the promise" as rhetorical shorthand for the covenant of grace, which embodies the promise of salvation that he calls upon his hearers to embrace (see Acts 2:21). This promise is the same as the promises made to Abraham, to David, to Israel, and even to the Gentiles. It includes the prom-

20 Joel R. Beeke and Ray B. Lanning, "Unto You, and to Your Children," in *The Case for Covenantal Infant Baptism*, ed. Gregg Strawbridge (Phillipsburg, NJ: P&R Publishing, 2003), 49–50.

> ise of the Holy Spirit and forgiveness of sins referred to in the previous verse (Acts 2:38).[21]

So, according to Beeke and Lanning, the main referent of the promise in Acts 2:39 is the covenant of grace.[22] This aligns with the typical Reformed belief in one covenant and one covenant people. But I would contend that there is a more contextually sound answer to the question.

Rather than seeing the promise of Acts 2:39 as a reference to the covenant of grace, we can go back a few verses and see the same promise that Peter has already been discussing. In Acts 2:33, Peter describes Jesus, "Being therefore exalted at the right hand of God, and having received from the Father the promise of the Holy Spirit, he has poured out this that you yourselves are seeing and hearing."

Peter references the promise of the Holy Spirit in Acts 2:33 as an explanation for what the people were seeing on the day of Pentecost. The people were seeing Joel 2:28–32 on display (cf. Acts 2:17–21). This display included the pouring out of the Holy Spirit (Acts 2:17) and was in fulfillment of what Jesus had promised at the end of Luke (cf. Luke 24:49) and what He had confirmed again before his ascension in Acts 1:4.[23] It is not difficult to trace the mention of this promise in Luke and Acts. Luke tells us exactly what the promise of Acts 2:39 was—the promise of the Holy Spirit, not the covenant of grace.[24]

So, if the promise is the Holy Spirit, who then are the recipients of the promised Holy Spirit? The Reformed paedobaptists are quick to point out that the promise is to "your children." But there are three groups that are described in this verse: "you," "your children," and "those who are far off." The third group, "those who are far off," is either a reference to diaspora Jews,[25] or more likely, Gentiles.[26]

---

21 Ibid., 55.

22 Although Beeke and Lanning do include the promise of the Holy Spirit in their discussion, their emphasis is on the covenant of grace being the main referent of this phrase.

23 It is important to remember that Luke and Acts comprise one historical account made up of two volumes. The same author composed both in an effort to record the history of Jesus's ministry on earth, as well as His continued ministry through the apostles. Thus, the connection between Luke 24:49 and Acts 2 is quite strong.

24 David G. Peterson, *The Acts of the Apostles*, The Pillar New Testament Commentary (Grand Rapids: Eerdmans, 2009), 156.

25 Ibid.

26 "The allusion is probably to Isa 57:19, which Paul also employed with reference to God's inclusion of the Gentiles (Eph 2:14, 17)" (John B. Polhill, *Acts*, New American Commentary 26 [Nashville, TN: Broadman & Holman, 1992], 117).

What is most important for our discussion is how these groups are modified. There is a limiting phrase, "everyone whom the Lord our God calls to himself." It is not *all* of "you," *all* of "your children," and *all* of the Gentiles. In the Abrahamic covenant, descendants of the twelve tribes of Israel participated by birth. In contrast, entrance into the promise of the new covenant ministry of the Spirit is through God's divine election and enablement—only those who are called by God participate. As Waymeyer notes, "Therefore, in the very passage that paedobaptists hold up as an express indication of continuity, there is an express indication of *discontinuity*. After all, the promise is not for all of your children without exception (like the Abrahamic promise), but rather only for those whom the Lord calls to Himself in salvation."[27]

The Reformed paedobaptist wants to read Acts 2:39 as evidence of strong continuity between the Old and New Testaments. Beeke and Lanning summarize:

> Peter's words in Acts 2:39 are therefore a covenantal formula. "Unto you, and to your children" simply restates "between me and thee and thy seed after thee" (Gen. 17:7). These words assert the identity of the covenant of grace under all dispensations and the continuity of the covenant pattern in which promises made to believers are extended to their children.[28]

However, the modifying phrase, "everyone whom the Lord our God calls to himself," shows that this is not an exhaustive promise to everyone being addressed. The Greek phrase, translated here as "everyone," is translated by the NASB, "as many as." It is the same phrase that is used in Mark 6:56 where the evangelist writes, "And wherever he came, in villages, cities, or countryside, they laid the sick in the marketplaces and implored him that they might touch even the fringe of his garment. And as many as touched it were made well."

Out of all the sick that were present in the marketplaces, only "as many as touched [his garment]" were made well. Mark 6:56 provides an important grammatical parallel to Acts 2:39. Mark 6:56 says that only those who touched Jesus's garment were healed. In the same way, only those

---

27 Waymeyer goes on to note that most of the time when paedobaptists reference Acts 2:39 they leave off reference to the modifying clause "everyone whom the Lord our God calls to himself," because it is so detrimental to the paedobaptist position (Waymeyer, *A Biblical Critique of Infant Baptism*, 30).

28 Beeke and Lanning, "Unto You, and to Your Children," 56.

who are called by God receive the promise (Acts 2:39).[29] God had declared that the Abrahamic covenant was, "between me and you and your offspring after you," perpetually and without qualification. But in contrast to that promise, Acts 2:39 qualifies that only those whom God has called to salvation would be recipients of the promise of Joel 2 and the ministry of the Holy Spirit. Therefore, this passage cannot be used to support the idea that families are viewed corporately in the new covenant. And as such, we cannot use it as evidence for infant baptism.

Cornelius (Acts 10:1–2)

> At Caesarea there was a man named Cornelius, a centurion of what was known as the Italian Cohort, a devout man who feared God with all his household, gave alms generously to the people, and prayed continually to God.

This passage is the first of five primary examples that paedobaptists give of households being baptized. According to Beeke and Lanning, "In each case, the households are received into the visible church together with the heads of those households."[30] Although those who were baptized were accepted into the church, the real question is whether there is anything in these texts that indicates an exception to the rule that faith is the prerequisite to baptism.

In this present example, it is immediately apparent that Cornelius, although he was a Roman soldier, had a saving knowledge of the God of Israel. What is also important, as noted earlier, is that in addition to Cornelius, "all his household" also feared God. The point of this phrase is not to discern whether infants can fear the Lord or not. However, there needs to be fairness here from the paedobaptist. If one wishes to say that the whole household was baptized (including infants if there were any), then one would also need to acknowledge either (1) infants can fear God, or (2) everyone in the household was grown to the point of being able to fear God.

The details of the Cornelius narrative confirm the connection between faith and baptism. As the story unfolds, Peter presents the Lord's message to those in Cornelius's house. This message had a profound effect on the people, so that "the Holy Spirit fell on all who heard the word" (Acts 10:44). While Peter's Jewish companions were amazed that Gentiles could also receive the Holy Spirit, Peter states, "Can anyone withhold water for

---

29 Waymeyer, *A Biblical Critique of Infant Baptism*, 30.

30 Beeke and Lanning, "Unto You, and to Your Children," 52.

baptizing these people, who have received the Holy Spirit just as we have? And he commanded them to be baptized in the name of Jesus Christ" (vv. 47–48a). The story is clear. Those who were baptized were the same ones who had "received the Holy Spirit just as we have." And who is it that "received the Holy Spirit just as we have?" It was those who heard the word (v. 44) and embraced it.

Thus, we have Cornelius and his household hearing the word preached. They then believe in that word and the Holy Spirit comes upon them. Then Peter commands that all those who had received the Spirit were to be baptized. This text does not give any evidence of infant baptism. Neither does it provide evidence for a corporate family dynamic where Cornelius's acceptance of the word counts for his wife, children, or slaves. Rather, the text clearly states that the household feared God (v. 2), they all heard the word (v. 33, 44), they all received the Holy Spirit (v. 44, 47), and then they all were baptized (v. 48).[31] Rather than providing evidence for the paedobaptist position, this narrative provides evidence for the Baptist position laid out in chapter one—baptism is linked with the expression of faith.

Lydia's Household Baptism (Acts 16:13–15)

> And on the Sabbath day we went outside the gate to the riverside, where we supposed there was a place of prayer, and we sat down and spoke to the women who had come together. One who heard us was a woman named Lydia, from the city of Thyatira, a seller of purple goods, who was a worshiper of God. The Lord opened her heart to pay attention to what was said by Paul. And after she was baptized, and her household as well, she urged us, saying, "If you have judged me to be faithful to the Lord, come to my house and stay." And she prevailed upon us.

The second of the household baptism texts is Lydia's household baptism. In my mind, this text is the only household text which could conceivably make an argument for paedobaptism. However, this is not because of what it positively says, but only because of what it does *not* say.

This household baptism text says nothing about the household fearing God or exercising faith like the other household texts do. As Booth

31 Jewett notes, "Everything in the narrative commends the conclusion that those who were baptized were those who heard the word and received the Spirit in his charismatic endowment. It is perhaps for this reason that the case of Cornelius' house is seldom urged, sometimes not even mentioned in the literature defending infant baptism" (Jewett, *Infant Baptism and the Covenant of Grace*, 48).

notes, "Luke specifically indicates that Lydia responded to Paul. He tells us nothing about her family until he says that 'she and her household' were baptized."[32] What Booth observes is true. But then, Booth exemplifies a rather illogical approach by letting his paedobaptist presuppositions drive what he sees in the text. He writes, "The only conclusion we can draw about the baptism of the other members of Lydia's household is that they were baptized because they were members of the household of the believer Lydia."[33] One must ask if this is genuinely the *only* conclusion one can draw from this text.

Unfortunately, in this case the text does not say why the household of Lydia was baptized. Nevertheless, it is certainly premature and presuppositional to claim that the household was baptized because it was a household. The text is clear that Paul presented the gospel to all who were at the river. The text says nothing about Lydia going back to fetch anyone at her house, so it is entirely possible that those who made up her household were with her at the river, and they heard and responded to Paul's message.

It is also possible that Lydia was unmarried. Given the fact that she was traveling over 300 miles from her native Thyatira for business, and that she was comfortable inviting the apostles into *her* house, it is reasonable to assume she was an unmarried woman running a business.[34] In such a case, her household would likely not have included any children.

Regardless, this text is very scant on details and thus inconclusive. Although this text is quite condensed, it is only an issue because paedobaptists want to use the absence of evidence (specifically no mention of belief or faith) for evidence of absence. However, given this narrative's lack of detail, Baptists and paedobaptists alike should be careful not to read their presuppositions into the text.

Philippian Jailer (Acts 16:32–34)

> And they spoke the word of the Lord to him and to all who were in his house. And he took them the same hour of the night and washed their wounds; and he was baptized at once, he and all his family. Then he brought them up into his house and set food before them. And he rejoiced along with his entire household that he had believed in God.

32 Booth, *Children of the Promise*, 147.

33 Ibid.

34 Jewett, *Infant Baptism and the Covenant of Grace*, 49.

Reformed paedobaptists often use this third household baptism text as proof positive that when the head-of-household was converted, he represented the family. After all, in answer to the Philippian jailer's question, "What must I do to be saved?" Paul and Silas respond without ambiguity, "Believe in the Lord Jesus, and you will be saved, you and your household" (Acts 16:30–31). Paedobaptists often view this as evidence that Paul and Silas were referring to "the practice of including whole households in the covenant of grace."[35]

However, Paul uses salvation language here, not general inclusion in a covenant. The book of Acts regularly uses the language of "being saved" to communicate eternal salvation (cf. Acts 2:21, 47; 4:12; 11:14; 15:1, 11; 16:30, 31, etc.). To argue that Paul implies the Philippian jailer is the household leader and his decision will incorporate his family into the covenant community is based completely on presuppositions. The text is specifically talking about salvation. And since all my Reformed brothers and sisters would deny vicarious salvation—the Philippian jailer's belief cannot bring his family eternal life—then we are left with the conclusion that the rest of the context will tell us how salvation comes to the family. And such is the case.

Reading the context alleviates any doubts about what Paul and Silas were talking about. Acts 16:32 says, "And they spoke the word of the Lord to him and *to all who were in his house*" (emphasis added). Paul and Silas proclaimed the gospel message not just to the jailer, but to the whole household as well. Although the paedobaptist is quick to jump to the conclusion of verse 34, "he was baptized at once, he and all his family," there are surrounding details we must account for. The *entire* household listens to the word preached by Paul and Silas (v. 32). Also, it is the *entire* household that rejoices that the Philippian jailer had believed (v. 34).[36] It is inexplicable that the *entire* household would rejoice with the Philippian jailer unless they too had accepted the message of Paul and Silas.[37] There is no indication that anyone in this household was baptized who did not first hear the message of the gospel and respond with joy. The emphasis of the text is that the whole household was saved! Commenting on this passage, Jewett notes, "The universe of discourse is household salvation, not infant baptism."[38]

35 Booth, *Children of the Promise*, 144.

36 Beasley-Murray, *Baptism in the New Testament*, 315.

37 This principle is made clear in John 3:20, "For everyone who does wicked things hates the light and does not come to the light, lest his works should be exposed."

38 Jewett, *Infant Baptism and the Covenant of Grace*, 50.

Crispus (Acts 18:8)

> Crispus, the ruler of the synagogue, believed in the Lord, together with his entire household. And many of the Corinthians hearing Paul believed and were baptized.

Although this passage is often included in defense of the idea of infant baptism, even paedobaptists acknowledge that all of Crispus's household believed.[39] There are no details in this text that support infant baptism, though it is regularly appealed to as a part of the cumulative argument that households are treated together corporately.[40] However, the details of the text support the view proposed in chapter one—that those who exercise faith are baptized.

Stephanas in Corinth (1 Cor 1:14–16)

> I thank God that I baptized none of you except Crispus and Gaius, so that no one may say that you were baptized in my name. (I did baptize also the household of Stephanas. Beyond that, I do not know whether I baptized anyone else.)

This is the last of the household baptism texts. Usually, when paedobaptists appeal to this text, they mention it in isolation. However, 1 Corinthians 1 is not the only mention of the household of Stephanas. Paul also mentions this household in 1 Corinthians 16.

While true that Paul says he baptized the household of Stephanas, Paul *also* says, "the household of Stephanas were the first converts in Achaia, and that they have devoted themselves to the service of the saints" (1 Cor 16:15). Paedobaptists usually neglect this last mention because it uses the language of conversion and Christian service. Paul's description of the household in 1 Corinthians 16:15 is that of mature believers who all had converted to Christ and devoted themselves to His service. Like many of the other household texts, this description matches our expectation that baptism is the privilege of those who have converted by exercising faith in Christ.

Summarizing and Evaluating the Household Texts

Historically, paedobaptists have attempted to argue that it is unlikely that there are *no* infants in these households. However, as I have pointed out in

39 Watt, "The Oikos Formula," 80.

40 For example, see Beeke and Lanning, "Unto You, and to Your Children," 51–52.

this section, not only is faith specifically mentioned in many of the passages, but the descriptions of these households are consistent with the exercise of faith. In the case of Cornelius, the household fears God, listens to the word, and is filled with the Holy Spirit prior to baptism. The household of the Philippian jailer hears the word preached by Paul and Silas, and the family rejoices (an action incompatible with a rejection of Christ). In the most abbreviated of the household texts, the entire household of Crispus believes in Paul's message and then is baptized. In the only mention of a household baptism outside of Acts, Stephanas and his household are described as converts and avid servants of the Lord.

The above examples support the idea that baptism was given only to believers. The household narratives describe the recipients of baptism as manifesting faith, service, and joy in their new lives. The only possible exception to this is Lydia's household, where there is no further description of Lydia's household apart from the comment that her household was baptized. It seems inappropriate to build a case for infant baptism based on what a text does *not* say, especially since the narrator likely assumes the reader will fill in the blanks about faith and baptism being connected in all the other baptism narratives.

The words of Beasley-Murray are an appropriate summary of the household baptism texts in Acts. He writes, "Luke, in writing these narratives, does not have in view infant members of the families. His language cannot be pressed to extend to them. He has in mind ordinary believers and uses language applicable only to them. Abuse of it leads to the degradation of the Scripture."[41]

Because it is difficult to argue for the presence of infants in these passages, most Reformed paedobaptists emphasize the corporate household in these texts. For example, Booth notes, "The one clear fact emerging from these texts is that whenever the head of a family was baptized, so was his or her entire household. The Bible does not tell us that the household was baptized because each member of it believed and professed personal faith (although some may indeed have believed)."[42]

However, as noted above, the descriptions given in the household texts coincide with what we would expect if those in the household professed faith. To ignore the details of the household texts is irresponsible. In the words of Bruce Ware, a detailed examination of the household

41 Beasley-Murray, *Baptism in the New Testament*, 315.

42 Booth, *Children of the Promise*, 148–49.

texts teaches "that baptism follows the reception of the gospel and faith in Christ."[43]

Finally, the Reformed paedobaptist's overemphasis on household solidarity goes against the clear teaching of Scripture that the gospel will fracture families. Jesus was clear that family members will turn against one another because of the gospel (Matt 10:34–36; Mark 13:12; Luke 12:51–53). This was a significant problem in the early church, so Paul and Peter needed to address what to do when living with an unbelieving spouse (1 Cor 7:15; 1 Pet 3:1–2). If we are to buy into the Reformed argument, it would be a significant exception for a spouse or a child to disagree with the head of the household, yet what are we to make of the frequency of these kinds of texts? The evidence agrees with Beasley-Murray, who writes, "To say the least, it is plain that the early Church had experience of other kinds of conversions than those of whole households and to exaggerate the normality of the matter is to forget the situation out of which the Gospels came."[44]

Children in the Gospels

In addition to the above arguments of family solidarity, paedobaptists will point to the words of Jesus as evidence that children of believers are members of the kingdom. Three parallel accounts of Jesus's interaction with children are typically cited: Matthew 19:13–15, Mark 10:13–16, and Luke 18:15–17. Since Mark is the most comprehensive of these three, I will only examine that text.[45]

> And they were bringing children to him that he might touch them, and the disciples rebuked them. But when Jesus saw it, he was indignant and said to them, "Let the children come to me; do not hinder them, for to such belongs the kingdom of God. Truly, I say to you, whoever does not receive the kingdom of God like a child shall not enter it." And he took them in his arms and blessed them, laying his hands on them (Mark 10:13–16).

---

43 Bruce A. Ware, "Believers' Baptism View," in *Baptism: Three Views*, ed. David F. Wright (Downers Grove, IL: InterVarsity Press, 2009), 27.

44 Beasley-Murray, *Baptism in the New Testament*, 319.

45 My thinking on this section has been heavily influenced by Waymeyer, *A Biblical Critique of Infant Baptism*, 36–44.

For the Reformed paedobaptist, there is a link in this text between the children of believers and the kingdom of God. John Murray summarizes this argument as follows:

> If little children belong to the kingdom of God, if they belong to Christ, if they are to be received into the fellowship of believers, if they are to be reckoned as possessing the qualities and rights that constitute them members of the kingdom of God and of the church, is there any reason why they should not receive the sign of that membership?[46]

Murray and other paedobaptists allow certain presuppositions to influence their interpretation of this text. There are at least three presuppositions assumed by paedobaptists, and each of them is questionable. These presuppositions are as follows:

1. Those who brought their children to Jesus were genuine believers.
2. Receiving the children and blessing them indicates they were members of the kingdom of God.
3. The passage is primarily about the children's inclusion in the kingdom of God.

The first assumption is that the parents of these children were believers. In commenting on this passage, Wilson says, "The teaching of Scripture is very plain. Children of believers are members of Christ's kingdom. Little children and infants of believers are expressly included by Christ in the kingdom of *God*, in the kingdom of *heaven*."[47] This is an important point for the Reformed paedobaptist, because in infant baptism, only those with at least one believing parent are candidates. But what in the text justifies understanding these parents as believers? They are not even described in the text. As Waymeyer notes:

> The problem is that the passage itself does not say that these parents were believers. In light of the reality that most people among the multitudes who followed Jesus outwardly were *not* true believers, how can paedobaptists so confidently assume the faith of these individuals? Even the fact that these parents brought their children to Jesus cannot be cited as evidence of the parents'

46 Murray, *Christian Baptism*, 63.

47 Wilson, *To a Thousand Generations*, 16. Emphasis in original.

> salvation, for it was common practice for children to be brought to rabbis and elders to be blessed in this way.[48]

The second assumption is that Christ receiving the children and blessing them makes them members of the kingdom of God. However, we should note that the laying on of hands and blessing was a common occurrence in both Old and New Testaments. Carson writes, "Children in Jesus' day were often brought to rabbis and elders to be blessed, customarily by placing hands on them (cf. Gen 48:14; Num 27:18; Acts 6:6; 13:3; cf. Matt 9:18, 20; Mark 10:16)."[49] Thus, laying hands on children and blessing them is not in and of itself evidence of belonging to the kingdom.

Waymeyer once again illustrates the illogical nature of this paedobaptist assertion:

> Suppose that among the multitude in Mark 10 were ten sets of parents who wanted the blessing of Jesus for their children. Among these ten, suppose that seven of the sets of parents were faithful followers of Yahweh and believers in Messiah, two sets were Jewish but unfaithful and unbelieving, and the final set consisted of two heathen Gentiles who had a growing curiosity about this Jewish teacher. Would Jesus have stopped the action, pointed to the seven sets of parents and said: "Permit *their* children to come to me, but [now pointing to the others] not theirs, and *certainly* not theirs!"? This is what the paedobaptist view requires, and yet it seems a little hard to picture.[50]

Waymeyer's illustration reveals the fallacious assumption that when Jesus receives the children and blesses them, it is directly corresponding to the spiritual condition of the parents. Nowhere does the text say such a thing. We would never logically arrive at that conclusion unless we had a preconceived point to prove.

The third presupposition is that the passage is primarily concerned with teaching that children are a part of the kingdom of God. However, the text reads, "for to such belongs the kingdom of God," not, "to these be-

48 Waymeyer cites John 6:60–66 as an example of the fact that many of those who followed Jesus were not genuine believers (Waymeyer, *A Biblical Critique of Infant Baptism*, 37). Emphasis in original.

49 D. A. Carson, "Matthew," in *The Expositor's Bible Commentary: Matthew, Mark, Luke*, ed. Frank E. Gaebelein (Grand Rapids: Zondervan, 1984), 420.

50 Waymeyer, *A Biblical Critique of Infant Baptism*, 43.

longs the kingdom of God."[51] The different wording is significant because it puts the emphasis on the *kind* of individual, not on the *specific* individual.

Evidence of this distinction is found in Greek literature, as well as in the Greek translation of the Old Testament. In his record on Cyrus's philanthropic efforts to win the hearts of those he governed, the Greek historian, Xenophon, relates, "These and many other such things he contrived in order to have first place among those by whom he wanted to be loved" (Xen., *Cyrop.* 8.2.26).[52] The word translated "these" (ταῦτα) is the normal near demonstrative and refers to the acts specifically mentioned by Xenophon in his history. The phrase, "other such things" (τοιαῦτα), translates the same word we read in Mark 10:14, "*to such* [τοιούτων] belongs the kingdom of God." It seems clear in Xenophon that this word is putting the emphasis on kind of acts, not on the specific acts that are mentioned.

Similarly, in biblical literature, we find the wording of Mark 10:14 in the Greek translation of the Old Testament. Proverbs 29:29 [31:11 Eng] reads, "The heart of her husband is confident with her; *a woman such as this* will not be in want of good spoils" (LES, emphasis added). Or Jeremiah 28:19a [51:19 Eng], "Jacob's portion is not like that." The phrases "a woman such as this" (Prov 29:29) and "like that" (Jer 28:19) are translations of the same Greek pronoun found in Mark 10:14. Like Xenophon, these passages show that this wording emphasizes kind. In other words, in Mark 10:14 Jesus was not saying the kingdom belonged to these specific children per se, but it belonged to anyone (adult or child) who received the kingdom like a child.[53]

One only needs to read one verse more to be convinced that the above interpretation is the intended meaning of the passage. In Mark 10:15, Jesus summarizes the point of the passage, "Truly, I say to you, whoever does not receive the kingdom of God *like a child* shall not enter it" (emphasis added). The point of the passage is, if one wants to receive the kingdom of God, he must receive it with characteristics of a childlike faith.

Although many Reformed paedobaptists appeal to this text (or one of its synoptic parallels), it is difficult to view this passage as evidence for paedobaptism. I agree with the words of Reformed paedobaptist Bryan Chapell, who notes, "While such references accurately communicate the

---

51 The Greek word translated "to such" is τοιοῦτος.

52 ταῦτα μὲν δὴ καὶ τοιαῦτα πολλὰ ἐμηχανᾶτο πρὸς τὸ πρωτεύειν παρ' οἷς ἐβούλετο ἑαυτὸν φιλεῖσθαι. Translation is my own.

53 "In other words, Jesus did not mean that the kingdom of God belonged to these *children themselves*, but rather to *those (of any age) who received the kingdom like a child*" (Waymeyer, *A Biblical Critique of Infant Baptism*, 38). Emphasis in original.

compassion of God, I have found them unconvincing as the reason we should baptize infants."[54]

Children in the Pauline Epistles

Paedobaptists will occasionally appeal to Paul's commands for children to be obedient to their parents in Ephesians 6:1 and Colossians 3:20 as support for infant baptism. The argument assumes that the children referenced in these passages are a part of the covenant community, regardless of any profession of faith. The paedobaptist follows the now-familiar argument: since Paul views children as covenant members, then they ought not to be denied the covenant sign of baptism.

However, in both Ephesians 6:1 and Colossians 3:20, one would be hard-pressed to see these children as non-believers. Ephesians 6:1 is part of a structure that includes wives, husbands, and parents—all of whom we assume to be believers and manifesting the Spirit-filled living discussed in Ephesians 5:15–20.[55] If we trace Paul's thinking back even further, it is clear he is referring to believers throughout Ephesians (1:3–14; 2:1–10, etc.).[56]

Similarly, when Colossians 3:20 mentions children, there is no reason to assume they are unbelievers or that they have not demonstrated faith in their lives. Paul seems to assume the children will respond to his admonition for obedience, and it is reasonable to assume that Paul believed, like John, that only believers would listen to apostolic authority (cf. 1 John 4:6). After all, Paul's letter to the Colossians is addressed "to the saints and faithful brothers in Christ at Colossae" (Col 1:2).

Baptists do not disagree with the reality that there are young children who are a part of the church. There are many young boys and girls who have professed faith and have been baptized in church. Regardless, the real question is whether we should even mention these texts while debating infant baptism. In the words of Jewett, "it is hardly clear that the apostolic admonition to filial obedience implies the apostolic approval of infant baptism."[57]

---

54 Chapell, "A Pastoral Overview of Infant Baptism," 27.

55 Lincoln notes, "Following on from the exhortations to wives and husbands in 5:22–33, the next groups within the household to be addressed are children and parents. It should be remembered that the instructions given are to be seen both as part of the wise and Spirit-filled living that the writer had discussed in 5:15–20 and as coming under the umbrella of the exhortation to mutual submission that had introduced the household code in 5:21" (Andrew T. Lincoln, *Ephesians*, Word Biblical Commentary 42 [Dallas, TX: Word, 1990], 395).

56 Waymeyer, *A Biblical Critique of Infant Baptism*, 45.

57 Jewett, *Infant Baptism and the Covenant of Grace*, 54.

Although Ephesians 6 and Colossians 3 are regularly referenced by paedobaptist advocates, the most often cited passage from Paul is 1 Corinthians 7:14. Paedobaptists often appeal to this text to show that unsaved children are a part of the covenant people of God. First Corinthians 7:14 notes, "For the unbelieving husband is made holy because of his wife, and the unbelieving wife is made holy because of her husband. Otherwise your children would be unclean, but as it is, they are holy." According to Reformed paedobaptists, like Booth, this passage teaches that:

> The children of believers, while not automatically the recipients of saving grace, do come under the covenant of grace and thereby occupy a privileged position before God. They are set apart (i.e., "made holy") for a special redemptive purpose. Even in households where there is only one believing parent, the children occupy a distinctively privileged or consecrated position before the Lord ...[58]

Reformed paedobaptists often assume without question that this passage is referring to covenantal belonging. Doug Wilson says it this way, "The New Testament recognizes that children of believers are holy ones or saints. We are taught that children of at least one believing parent are holy ones. This does not guarantee that each child is personally holy, but rather teaches that they are *federally holy*, or, put another way, *covenantally holy*."[59]

Based on this assumption, Reformed paedobaptists teach that children should be baptized because they are holy and belong to the covenant.[60] Booth writes, "These 'holy, cleansed' children must receive the cleansing sign of baptism to mark them off from the 'unholy' or defiled children of unbelievers, just as circumcision performed this task in the Old Testament."[61] For the Reformed paedobaptist, children being related to a regenerate member of the new covenant automatically makes them a member of the new covenant.

However, the paedobaptist interpretation of this passage has some significant problems. The most significant of these is that 1 Corinthians 7:14 ascribes the same holy status to an unbelieving spouse. Even though the adult spouse is unsaved, the text describes both the unregenerate spouse

58 Booth, *Children of the Promise*, 133.

59 Wilson, *To a Thousand Generations*, 17. Emphasis in original.

60 Fesko, *Word, Water, and Spirit*, 350.

61 Booth, *Children of the Promise*, 134–35.

and the children as "holy."[62] Although Reformed paedobaptists push for the inclusion of children in the covenant based on their "holy" status in 1 Corinthians 7:14, they are strangely silent when talking about the same covenantal status for the unbelieving spouse. Although the unbelieving spouse has the same "holy" description—which is actually the main point of Paul's argument—the typical paedobaptist will not give the same privileges of covenant status to an unbelieving adult.[63] The Reformed paedobaptist will point to this text and say that children have special covenantal status and deserve baptism. However, they would not baptize an unsaved adult spouse. However, this text does not suggest that there is any meaningful difference between the unsaved spouse and the children. Paul views them the same way. It is only one's presuppositions that would lead to seeing a difference.[64]

In light of the context of 1 Corinthians 7, there are two potential understandings of the meaning of "holy" or "sanctified" in 1 Corinthians 7:14.[65] First, the text could be saying that the spouse and children are holy in the sense that they have been given special access to the gospel in ways that unbelievers do not have.[66] By constantly interacting with a saved husband/father or saved wife/mother, the unsaved spouse and children will be given opportunities to see the gospel's power in everyday life. They will also be exposed to teaching and instruction that they would never find in a non-Christian environment.

Although the above principle is undoubtedly true to a degree, scholars have proposed a second interpretation that may match better with the

---

62 The unbelieving spouse is described as holy using the verb (ἡγίασται), while the children are described as holy by the use of an adjective (ἅγιά). However, these two words are cognates, and no difference can be pressed in the context.

63 Fesko argues, "But while the unbelieving spouse might be sanctified, this does not automatically entitle the person to the sign of the covenant, because as an adult, he or she must make a profession of faith, as would be the case for slaves within a household" (Fesko, *Word, Water, and Spirit*, 350).

64 Jewett, *Infant Baptism and the Covenant of Grace*, 126; Waymeyer, *A Biblical Critique of Infant Baptism*, 32–34. Waymeyer notes, "Consequently, if Paul is not envisioning the same type of holiness in both cases, his logic is undermined" (Waymeyer, *A Biblical Critique of Infant Baptism*, 33).

65 For a survey of these options, see Mark Taylor, *1 Corinthians*, New American Commentary (Nashville, TN: Broadman & Holman, 2014), 174–75; Waymeyer, *A Biblical Critique of Infant Baptism*, 34–36.

66 Fee notes, "This does not mean that they have acquired salvation or holiness. But from Paul's perspective, as long as the marriage is maintained the potential for their realizing salvation remains" (Gordon D. Fee, *The First Epistle to the Corinthians*, New International Commentary on the New Testament [Grand Rapids: Eerdmans, 1987], 300).

context of 1 Corinthians 7. In this view, Paul is answering the question of the legitimacy of mixed marriages. This would be the most natural question faced by the Corinthians, especially since Paul had taught extensively about the need to be completely devoted to Christ. Thiselton explains this idea as follows:

> The key controlling principle lies in the recognition of the nature of the anxiety which Paul seeks to allay. The believer asks Paul with genuine concern: if I have left behind the old life and become a new creation in Christ, does not my relation with my unbelieving, unrepentant spouse and my entire home atmosphere threaten to pollute and to corrode my purity as one who belongs to Christ? Paul has argued readily enough that relations with a pagan prostitute tear apart the limbs of Christ (6:12–20). How can someone who has been purchased by Christ to belong to him (6:20), who is the Spirit's holy shrine (6:19), also "belong" to a spouse who does not "belong" to Christ?[67]

This viewpoint also has Old Testament precedent since the Law forbids Israel from marrying outside the nation (Exod 34:11–16; Deut 7:1–5; cf. Neh 13:23–30). In fact, perhaps the Corinthians would have been aware of Ezra 10:1–17, where part of Israel's repentance included putting away the foreign, unbelieving wives *and* children. The Corinthians were likely motivated to be holy and set apart for Christ. They wanted to know if they needed to separate themselves from unbelieving spouses and children, which was something that Israel had done in the Old Testament. Perhaps they were already aware of Paul's view, which he would include in another letter to them, "Do not be unequally yoked with unbelievers. For what partnership has righteousness with lawlessness? Or what fellowship has light with darkness?" (2 Cor 6:14).

If the above accurately depicts the context, it is most reasonable that the Corinthians asked Paul what they should do in mixed marriages. Paul's answer was, in the words of Taylor, "No such contamination exists in the marriage of the believer to the unbeliever. The union is lawful and holy according to God's established pattern for marriage."[68] In other words, an unbelieving spouse and children will not corrupt the Corinthian believers. Although God condemns entering an unequal relationship as a believer (cf. 2 Cor 6:14), God sanctions those relationships where they already ex-

67 Anthony C. Thiselton, *The First Epistle to the Corinthians*, The New International Greek Testament Commentary (Grand Rapids: Eerdmans, 2000), 528.

68 Taylor, *1 Corinthians*, 175.

ist. The Corinthians could continue in those mixed marriages with a clear conscience.

The paedobaptist stands on shaky ground by appealing to 1 Corinthians 7:14. Paedobaptists want to view the child's "holy" status as a covenantal bond, but they reject such a classification for the unsaved spouse. There is no textual warrant for such selectivity, nor can 1 Corinthians 7:14 provide any meaningful support for the paedobaptist position. As Beasley-Murray says, this text "yields no positive evidence concerning the Apostolic doctrine of baptism and it would be best omitted from the discussion concerning that doctrine."[69]

Conclusion

This chapter has examined the last major thread of the traditional paedobaptist argument. Some paedobaptists have used the household baptism texts to argue that infants were present in family baptisms. I have shown how that reasoning is inconsistent with the biblical evidence. Because of the difficulties of pressing such an argument, the more popular argument shies away from whether there were infants in those households (a point now said to be inconsequential). The crux of the argument, according to the Reformed paedobaptist, is that households are treated as complete households, following the actions of their corporate head.

However, there are some significant problems with the reasoning of the Reformed paedobaptist. First, even when households are mentioned, there is evidence that not every individual is included (cf. 1 Sam 1:21–22). Second, the assumption that families would follow the head-of-household figure is challenged by the explicit statements by Jesus, Paul, and Peter. The New Testament indicates that Christians should expect division and broken families because of Christ. Christ himself challenged the priority of the nuclear family when he said, "My mother and my brothers are those who hear the word of God and do it" (Luke 8:21). Similarly, Jesus told the disciples they could expect to lose physical family members but gain spiritual family members in the Messianic community (Matt 19:29).[70]

The Reformed paedobaptist appeals to a variety of texts to support the idea of family solidarity and covenantal baptism. The household texts in Acts and 1 Corinthians are primary, but many paedobaptists appeal to Gospel and epistolary texts that refer to children. Paedobaptists promote these texts as evidence of a special status granted to children in the new

69 Beasley-Murray, *Baptism in the New Testament*, 199.

70 Carson, "Matthew," 426.

covenant community. However, I am convinced that when one works through these texts with an honest assessment of the details, there is no support for infant baptism at all. Not only is there no evidence for infant baptism, but the evidence matches with what we read in the rest of Scripture. Namely, that those who are baptized have made a profession of faith.

Chapter 7
The Biblical Significance and Mode of Baptism

In the first chapter of this book, I presented evidence for the intrinsic link between faith and baptism. In the rest of the book, I have spent considerable time and effort evaluating the Reformed paedobaptist's attempt to explain why faith is not a prerequisite for baptism. Through this detailed assessment, we have observed the many problems with the Reformed paedobaptist position.

We now turn to what Waymeyer has called "the most compelling argument against the practice of infant baptism."[1] To make a final argument against infant baptism, I offer a positive, biblically defined discussion about the significance of baptism. I contend that when we examine the biblical picture of baptism, we realize infants can't participate until they grow old enough to exercise faith.

Therefore, to show the significance and meaning of baptism, this chapter will start by surveying the possible background of New Testament baptism. We will then look at how John's baptism helps inform our understanding of baptism. We will also spend significant effort examining the details and definitions that Scripture gives concerning baptism. We will then contrast this biblical definition of baptism with the Reformed paedobaptist understanding. Finally, we will conclude by discussing the mode of baptism and how that contributes to understanding the significance of baptism.

Historical Background of New Testament Baptism

A full discussion of the historical background of baptism is beyond the scope of this book. In any case, it would be difficult to improve on the

1 Waymeyer, *A Biblical Critique of Infant Baptism*, 85.

studies which have already been published.[2] In summary, there are typically four viable options that scholars put forward as the historical background for New Testament baptism.

1. Mystery Religion Adaptation
2. Qumran Ceremonial Cleansings
3. Proselyte Baptism
4. Jewish Purification and Washing Rituals

The two most probable options which form the basis for New Testament baptism are Jewish proselyte baptism or purification washings.[3] Many have argued proselyte baptism is best understood as the background for Christian baptism.[4] According to the Talmud, proselyte baptism was part of three obligations for Gentile converts to Judaism. Circumcision, immersion, and sacrifice were all required according to rabbinic literature (*b. Kerithoth* 8b–9a).[5] This view appeals to interpreters in part because proselyte baptism is similar to New Testament baptism in that it represents an initiatory rite of commitment.[6]

However, there are a few issues that make the connection between New Testament baptism and proselyte baptism difficult.[7] First, proselyte baptism focused on Gentile converts, but New Testament baptism was primarily for Jews (and later expanded to include Gentiles). Second, there is a chronological problem. The earliest mention of proselyte baptism dates

---

2 See the summaries put forward by Andreas J. Köstenberger, "Baptism in the Gospels," in *Believer's Baptism: Sign of the New Covenant in Christ*, ed. Thomas R. Schreiner and Shawn D. Wright, NAC Studies in Bible & Theology (Nashville, TN: B & H Academic, 2006), 11; Grant R. Osborne, "Baptism," in *Baker Encyclopedia of the Bible*, ed. W. A. Elwell, vol. 1 (Grand Rapids: Baker, 1988), 257–59. Also, see the extensive study by Ferguson, *Baptism in the Early Church*, 23–96.

3 For summaries and evaluations of the first two views, see the sources in the previous footnote.

4 For example, Waymeyer, *A Biblical Critique of Infant Baptism*, 89.

5 Ferguson notes, "The argument was that the Jewish fathers entered the covenant at Sinai by circumcision, immersion, and the sprinkling of blood. Circumcision was based on Josh. 5:5; the sprinkling of blood (necessary for entering the congregation and partaking of consecrated things) on Exod. 24:5, 8; and immersion on the principle that there is no sprinkling of blood without immersion (cf. Exod. 19:10). Making proselytes was still possible, even though there are 'no sacrifices today,' on the basis of Num. 15:14–15 ('There shall be for both you and for the resident alien a single statute, a perpetual statute throughout your generations')" (Ferguson, *Baptism in the Early Church*, 76).

6 Köstenberger, "Baptism in the Gospels," 12.

7 For a good summary of these issues, see Jewett, *Infant Baptism and the Covenant of Grace*, 63–68.

to the second century AD.[8] The practice may have been earlier, but Philo, Josephus, and *Joseph and Aseneth* do not mention it. Because these early and extensive Jewish sources do not mention the practice (even when talking about Gentile conversion), it raises questions whether proselyte baptism existed before the second century AD.[9] Finally, proselyte baptism differs in a few significant ways from Christian baptism. Ferguson summarizes:

> The baptism of proselytes, in spite of some superficial similarities, had basic differences from Christian baptism. Proselyte baptism required witnesses but was self-administered; baptism by John and Christians had an administrator. In proselyte baptism the candidate was freed from pagan impurity; in Christian baptism one received pardon and regeneration as divine grace. The heart of the rabbinic conversion ceremony was circumcision, not baptism; baptism was the central act in Christian conversion. Proselyte baptism was for Gentiles; Christians baptized Jews as well as Gentiles. These differences are significant, even if the chronological difficulty can be overcome.[10]

Considering the difficulties with proselyte baptism, Jewish washing and ceremonial rituals seem to provide a better background to New Testament baptism. Within Jewish Law, there were strict regulations about water use, specifically sprinkling, pouring, and dipping.[11] For example, the high priest was required to immerse himself five times on the day of atonement (cf. *Yoma* 3.3–4). Jewish washings were also commonly mentioned in non-biblical Jewish literature.[12]

Jewish Law also spent considerable effort detailing the need for complete immersion in the cleansing rituals (*Mikwaoth* 8.5; 9.1–4; *b. 'Erubin* 4b). As Ferguson notes, "The requirements of the tractate *Mikwaoth* clearly point to a total submersion. For a valid immersion, water had to touch all

8 Ferguson, *Baptism in the Early Church*, 78.

9 Ibid., 76–77.

10 Ibid., 82.

11 Ferguson writes, "Note especially the tractates *Nega'im* (e.g. 14.10—pouring oil into the hand, dipping the finger in it, and sprinkling the oil) and *Parah* (e.g. 12.11—dipping the hyssop and then sprinkling what adheres to it as distinct from immersing the body). In *Berakoth* 3.5 a person goes down to immerse himself, but if the water is foul, he pours clean water into it" (Ferguson, *Baptism in the Early Church*, 63n17).

12 Among others, Ferguson mentions Tobit washing himself after touching a dead body (Tobit 2.5), a passage from the *Testament of Levi*, where Levi washed himself in living water (*Testament of Levi* 2.3), and Josephus's reference to Leviticus 15:16 and the need to "go down into cold water" and immerse after nocturnal emission (*Antiquities* 3.263) (Ferguson, *Baptism in the Early Church*, 65–67).

parts of the body. Detailed regulations covered the size of an artificial immersion pool to permit a complete immersion and what constituted clean water to fill it."[13]

After reviewing the various information and possibilities, Köstenberger summarizes, "Most likely, John's baptism and Jewish proselyte baptism both harken back to Jewish ritual cleansing and bathing practices."[14] Ferguson comes to a similar conclusion and writes, "Jewish concepts and practices provide a more likely immediate context for Christian baptism than any other antecedents."[15]

In sum, although it is difficult to be dogmatic about the historical background of New Testament baptism, Jewish ritual washings and cleansings provide the most likely scenario. Yet, even so, the Jewish rituals were self-administered and repeated, unlike New Testament baptism.[16]

John the Baptist as a Background to Understanding Baptism

Regardless of the historical backdrop of the baptism ceremony, the New Testament provides ample information on baptism to explain its significance. Baptism in the New Testament first shows up in the ministry of John the Baptist. Therefore, studying his ministry is helpful as a prelude to Christian baptism.

The first thing to observe is that, in John's baptism, the message of repentance was linked with the call to baptism. Mark 1:4 says, "John appeared, baptizing in the wilderness and proclaiming a baptism of repentance for the forgiveness of sins." Matthew writes that all the people of Judea and Jordan were coming to him, being baptized and "confessing their sins" (Matt 3:6). Later, when John described the purpose of his baptism, he said, "I baptize you with water for repentance" (Matt 3:11a). Köstenberger notes, "The references to repentance and the forgiveness of sins make clear that John's baptism is to be understood not merely in terms of ritual purification and religious observance but as essentially *moral* and *ethical*."[17]

---

13 Ibid., 64.

14 Köstenberger, "Baptism in the Gospels," 12.

15 Ferguson, *Baptism in the Early Church*, 60.

16 Köstenberger, "Baptism in the Gospels," 12.

17 Ibid., 13.

Although the Gospels clearly state that John the Baptist proclaimed a baptism connected with repentance and forgiveness of sins, Josephus denies such a connection:

> [John called the Baptist (βαπτιστής)] was a good man and exhorted the Jews to lead righteous lives, practice justice towards one another and piety towards God, and so to participate in baptism [βαπτισμῷ]. In his view this was a necessary preliminary if baptism [βάπτισις, "dipping"] was to be acceptable to God. They must not use it to gain pardon for whatever sins they committed, but for the purity [ἁγνείᾳ] of the body, implying that the soul was already thoroughly cleansed [προεκκεκαθαρμένης] by right behavior (*Antiquities* 18.117).[18]

This may reflect Josephus's attempt to correct the Christian understanding of baptism and bring it more in line with the Jewish understanding.[19] However, John's call to repentance for the forgiveness of sins is an important part of connecting John to the Old Testament prophecies that tie John to the role of preparation for the Messiah.[20]

There have been many attempts to connect John's baptism with the practice of the Essenes. According to Josephus, both the Essenes and John required a life change before experiencing the waters (*Wars of the Jews* 2.138; *Antiquities* 18.117).[21] However, a significant difference is that John's baptism was unrepeatable, while the washings for purification were a daily, repeatable act.

Another notable fact about John's baptism is that it was undoubtedly by immersion. When John baptized Jesus, he did so down in the river. After John baptized Jesus, he "came up out of the water" (Mark 1:10; cf. Matt 3:16). Similarly, John 3:23 says John was baptizing at Aenon near Salim, "because water was plentiful there." This description seems important only if immersion was John's practice. It is also possible that John's title, "the Baptist" (or better, "the Baptizer") also indicates John practiced immersion. If John was simply performing ordinary washings, it would be difficult to see how his title would differentiate him from others.[22]

---

18 Cited in Ferguson, *Baptism in the Early Church*, 84.

19 Ibid.

20 Köstenberger, "Baptism in the Gospels," 15; Jewett, *Infant Baptism and the Covenant of Grace*, 67.

21 Ferguson, *Baptism in the Early Church*, 87.

22 Ferguson writes, "He was doing something different, or else the designation would not have distinguished him" (Ferguson, *Baptism in the Early Church*, 88).

John the Baptist provides the first clear picture of baptism in the New Testament. John's baptism focused on character and the need to repent from one's sins.[23] The biblical authors described his baptism as a "baptism of repentance" (Mark 1:4), and it was unrelated to family genealogy (Luke 3:8; Matt 3:9). These foundational elements make it difficult to argue that John was baptizing infants, since infants themselves are incapable of repentance.[24] Notably, later New Testament references to baptism seem to build on John's baptism. We turn now to explore those connections.

The Connection between John's Baptism and Jesus's Baptism

Some people are not aware of the fact that Jesus and His disciples practiced baptism prior to the Messiah's death and resurrection. However, not only did Jesus and His followers practice baptism, but Scripture links the baptism they practiced with the baptism of John. In John 4:1–3, we see a strong connection between the two:

> Now when Jesus learned that the Pharisees had heard that Jesus was making and baptizing more disciples than John (although Jesus himself did not baptize, but only his disciples) he left Judea and departed again for Galilee.

This text provides early testimony of John's baptism and Jesus's baptism coexisting. It would be difficult to argue that these were two different kinds of baptism. Rather, since we know John's baptism included volitional commitment and repentance from one's sins, it is natural to understand Jesus's baptism in the same way. Given the comparison in John 4:1–3, it is unlikely that the reader should observe significant differences between John's baptism and Jesus's baptism.

Reformed paedobaptist Daniel Doriani acknowledges the connection between John's baptism and Jesus's baptism, admitting that Jesus's disciples did imitate John's baptism. However, Doriani argues without evidence that, since we don't read anything else about Jesus's baptism later in the Gospels, the practice must have quickly stopped.[25] However, this is an argument from silence and breaks one of the primary rules used by the Re-

23 Jewett, *Infant Baptism and the Covenant of Grace*, 66–67.

24 Ibid., 67.

25 Doriani, "Matthew 28:18–20 and the Institution of Baptism," 35.

formed paedobaptist—if Scripture does not explicitly say something has changed, we should assume it continues unabated.

Because of the link between John's baptism and Jesus's baptism, we can connect the idea of baptism and what it means to be a disciple or follower. Being baptized by John or the disciples of Jesus created a close discipleship relationship with that individual. Commenting on John 4:1, Beasley-Murray notes that when John records Jesus made and baptized more disciples than John, this "implies that those baptized at the bidding of Jesus stood in a relation of disciple to Him as those baptized by John did to John. There is no doubt that those baptized under the preaching of Jesus would feel themselves more closely bound to Him than they would to John."[26]

Waymeyer agrees and writes:

> According to this passage there was a direct connection between the making of disciples and the baptizing of them in water. The implication is that one became a disciple of the person with whom his baptism was associated. Those who were baptized by John became disciples of John, and those who were baptized by Jesus (even though He Himself did not do the actual baptizing) became disciples of Jesus. In this way, baptism served as an outward expression of allegiance given to either John the Baptist or Jesus when an individual became a disciple of one or the other.[27]

Waymeyer also notes that it is not possible that infants were baptized by John or Jesus's disciples, since repentance was a vital component of these baptisms.[28] Jewett agrees, "If infants were not baptized by John, with whose baptism Jesus and his disciples (presumably) were baptized, and after whose example they also baptized others (John 3:22–4:3), it is hardly plausible to suppose that at Pentecost the disciples began to do something for which there was no precedent in John's baptism."[29]

When we get to the Great Commission in Matthew 28:18–20, the paedobaptist must make a tough decision. Either he must argue that the baptism Jesus speaks of there is something brand new,[30] or he must try redefining the baptism of John and Jesus's disciples, which likely had been practiced for over two years. When Jesus commanded baptism in Matthew 28:18–20, it would be most natural for the readers of Matthew (and

26 Beasley-Murray, *Baptism in the New Testament*, 72.

27 Waymeyer, *A Biblical Critique of Infant Baptism*, 90–91.

28 Ibid., 91.

29 Jewett, *Infant Baptism and the Covenant of Grace*, 66.

30 Doriani, "Matthew 28:18–20 and the Institution of Baptism," 35–36.

the disciples themselves) to connect Jesus's command to baptize with what they had already been experiencing during Jesus's ministry.

This is not a novel idea. The early Christians regularly viewed John's baptism as the antecedent to Christian baptism. Ferguson notes:

> Christian sources consistently saw the antecedent to Christian baptism in the practice of John the Baptizer. They applied the same distinctive terminology, βάπτισμα (other dippings were designated by the word βαπτισμός), and the same purpose, "forgiveness of sins," to John's baptism as they did to their own. Whether the early disciples of Jesus adopted the terminology of John's disciples or later applied their own terminology to John's practice, the distinctive word usage and description of the ceremony point to where Christians saw the origins of their practice.[31]

Baptism as a Profession of Faith and Repentance

As demonstrated above, John's baptism included repentance from sin and forgiveness (Mark 1:4; Matt 3:11). As argued, there is no reason to claim that the baptism Jesus's disciples practiced differed significantly from John's baptism (cf. John 4:1–2). Furthermore, Christian baptism uses the same language as John's baptism, calling for repentance and forgiveness of sins (cf. Acts 2:38). Since John's baptism and Christian baptism both emphasize the theme of repentance, we should understand baptism as including a profession of faith and repentance.[32]

In 1 Peter 3:21 we find more support for the idea that baptism includes a profession of faith and repentance. As noted in chapter one, some scholars have identified this passage as the most approximate biblical definition of baptism that we have.[33] Although many Baptists shy away from this passage because Peter says baptism saves (an idea that could be used as evidence for baptismal regeneration), this passage is essential to understand what baptism is.

Regarding baptismal regeneration, Peter clarifies that the salvation that comes through baptism is not due to "removal of dirt from the body." By making this clarifying statement, he ensures we do not think it is the use of water that brings salvation. Instead, Peter notes that salvation comes through baptism because baptism is "an appeal to God for a good conscience."

31 Ferguson, *Baptism in the Early Church*, 83.

32 Waymeyer, *A Biblical Critique of Infant Baptism*, 89–91.

33 Dunn, *Baptism in the Holy Spirit*, 219; Waymeyer, *A Biblical Critique of Infant Baptism*, 104.

There are two ways to interpret the word translated as "appeal."[34] Although the ESV and NASB use the word "appeal," we could also translate the word as "pledge" (cf. CSB, NET, NIV). The word under debate is ἐπερώτημα. It is related to the verbal form ἐπερωτάω, which means to ask a question. If we understand the noun as deriving its meaning from the verb, a translation of "ask," "request," or "appeal" would be appropriate.[35] Alternatively, in the Greek papyri, which are from the same general time frame as the New Testament, it is well established that the word ἐπερώτημα was used in a technical sense to create a formal agreement between two parties.[36] The term included not just asking a question, but also the answer when making a pledge or commitment.[37] If we understand the noun in this technical sense, a translation of "pledge" would be appropriate.

Both meanings are possible, but a further question of how these meanings relate to the conscience is also important. If one understands the word as making a request, then baptism is a request or appeal to God for a good conscience. On the other hand, if one understands the word to be a pledge, then the meaning could be either: (a) a pledge to God that flows *from* a good conscience, or (b) a pledge to God to maintain a good conscience. The interpretive options are illustrated in the following chart.

Table 7.1. Meaning of 1 Peter 3:21

Viewpoint	Translation	Meaning	Application
1	"an appeal to God for a good conscience" (ESV)	A request	Baptism is an appeal to God for a good conscience.
2a	"the pledge of a good conscience toward God" (CSB)	A pledge for a good conscience	Baptism is a pledge by the believer to maintain a good conscience before God.
2b	"the pledge of a good conscience toward God" (CSB)	A pledge from a good conscience	Baptism is a pledge by the believer made from a good conscience to live in accordance with baptismal vows.

34 The word ἐπερώτημα is related to the verbal form ἐπερωτάω, which means "to ask a question."

35 Schreiner, *1, 2 Peter, Jude*, 196.

36 Ibid.; D. Edmond Hiebert, *First Peter* (Winona Lake, IN: BMH Books, 1997), 249.

37 Schreiner, *1, 2 Peter, Jude*, 196.

Most interpreters prefer either view 1 (asking for a good conscience) or view 2a (pledging to maintain a good conscience). Although I believe view 2a is slightly preferable,[38] no option fits well with the paedobaptist understanding of baptism. In the words of Schreiner, "What is said here does not fit with infant baptism, for infants cannot appeal to God for a good conscience or pledge to maintain a good conscience before God."[39]

Whichever view one takes, baptism is defined as a volitional act of repentance and confession.[40] In view 1, the one to be baptized appeals to God for a good conscience (a process which *must* include repentance of sins). In view 2, the one to be baptized pledges to live with a good conscience (which would also inherently involve the confession and forsaking of sin). Consequently, in one of the most explicit passages about baptism in Scripture, baptism is clearly defined in terms that support baptism as a voluntary confession.

Surprisingly, noted Reformed paedobaptist John Calvin agrees that baptism is a confession of faith. Calvin writes, "But baptism serves as our confession before men. Indeed, it is the mark by which we publicly profess that we wish to be reckoned God's people; by which we testify that we agree in worshiping the same God, in one religion with all Christians; by which finally we openly affirm our faith."[41]

We find further evidence that baptism expresses faith and commitment in 1 Corinthians 1. In arguing against the factions of Corinth, Paul frames the debate this way: "Is Christ divided? Was Paul crucified for you? Or were you baptized in the name of Paul?" (v. 13). Paul could use the

---

38 Achtemeier notes, "The close association of the aorist form of the verb (ἐπερωτηθείς) with the verb meaning "acknowledge" or "confess" (ὡμολόγησα), and the fact that the baptismal liturgy of the early church included a confession of faith in response to a corresponding question, would support such a view" (Paul J. Achtemeier, *1 Peter: A Commentary on First Peter*, Hermeneia [Minneapolis, MN: Fortress Press, 1996], 271). Additionally, the Jewish community at Qumran also required a pledge as part of their ritual admission (cf. 1QS 1.16; 5.7–8).

39 Schreiner, "Baptism in the Epistles," 71.

40 Waymeyer notes, "In the end, regardless of whether Peter is characterizing baptism as a 'pledge' or an 'appeal,' he clearly views it as an act direct from sinners to God, rather than from God to sinners" (Waymeyer, *A Biblical Critique of Infant Baptism*, 107).

41 Calvin, *Institutes of the Christian Religion*, 1313–14. In a similar statement, Luther writes in 1519, "For in baptism we all make one and the same vow: to slay sin and to become holy through the work and grace of God, to whom we yield and offer ourselves, as clay to the potter.… It is true, then, that there is no vow higher, better, or greater than the vow of baptism" (Martin Luther, "The Holy and Blessed Sacrament of Baptism, 1519," in *Luther's Works: Volume 35 Word and Sacrament I*, trans. Charles M. Jacobs and E. Theodore Bachmann [Philadelphia, PA: Fortress Press, 1960], 41).

argument of baptism because baptism was the way in which individuals expressed their commitment and fidelity to an individual. As Waymeyer notes, "Put simply, to be baptized in the name of a given individual was to declare one's allegiance to that person and thereby identify oneself as that person's disciple."[42] Paul was reminding the Corinthian believers that they had not been baptized in Paul's name. They had not professed their faith or allegiance to Paul, but to Christ.

Lest someone think this is a uniquely Baptist interpretation of this passage, note John Calvin's comments on 1 Corinthians 1 when arguing that baptism is a confession of faith before men. He writes:

> Paul had this in mind when he asked the Corinthians whether they had not been baptized in Christ's name [1 Cor. 1:13]. He thus implied that, in being baptized in his name, they had devoted themselves to him, sworn allegiance to his name, and pledged their faith to him before men. As a result, they could no longer confess any other but Christ alone, unless they chose to renounce the confession they had made in baptism.[43]

In addition to the above texts, Acts 19:1–7 may also be instructive as an example of baptism as an expression of commitment. In Acts 19, Paul arrives at Ephesus and meets 12 individuals who had been baptized into John's baptism (v. 3). However, when they hear of Jesus and the Holy Spirit, they are baptized "in the name of the Lord Jesus" (v. 5). The significance of this narrative is that the disciples switched their allegiance from John to Jesus and communicated this through baptism in the name of the Messiah—a profession of their faith and commitment to Jesus.

Calvin was troubled by Acts 19:1–7, so he adamantly denied that this narrative described rebaptism. Rather, Calvin argued that the baptism mentioned in Acts 19 was simply the laying on of hands by Paul and a Spirit-baptism experience, not water baptism.[44] However, there is no reason not to see water baptism being practiced in Acts 19. It fits well with the New Testament teaching that baptism expresses commitment to an individual.

We are first introduced to baptism in the New Testament through the ministry of John the Baptist. John's baptism included a profession of faith that involved repentance from sins. Jesus's disciples baptized follow-

42 Waymeyer, *A Biblical Critique of Infant Baptism*, 103.

43 Calvin, *Institutes of the Christian Religion*, 1314.

44 Ibid., 1318–19.

ers of Jesus in a similar manner to John's baptism. As the New Testament continues to record the growth of the church, there is no indication that the significance of baptism as a profession of faith and voluntary commitment to discipleship has changed.

The Theological Significance of Baptism

As noted previously, the baptism of John and Jesus's disciples was an initiatory rite by which one confessed his or her sins and became a committed disciple of the one in whose name the person was baptized. Although the Gospels are relatively silent concerning the theological significance of baptism, after the resurrection of Christ the New Testament highlights the significance of the symbolism of this rite.

Therefore, this section will look at the various passages which describe baptism as washing or cleansing. We will also analyze two famous Pauline passages that help us formulate the significance of the symbolism in baptism (Col 2:11–12; Rom 6:3–5). Paul's descriptions of baptism are particularly helpful in understanding the theological significance of baptism.

Passages that Describe Baptism as Washing and Cleansing from Sin

Using water to wash and cleanse is commonplace in every culture.[45] Scripture regularly uses washing and cleansing language that seems to be a reference to baptism. Many of these texts are unambiguous. For example, Ananias commands Paul to be baptized and "wash away your sins" (Acts 22:16). Sometimes, the Bible uses washing language without specifically mentioning baptism. Yet, in many of these cases the reference to baptism seems clear enough. For example, 1 Corinthians 6:11 says, "And such were some of you. But you were washed, you were sanctified, you were justified in the name of the Lord Jesus Christ and by the Spirit of our God." Similarly, Titus 3:5 says, "He saved us, not because of works done by us in righteousness, but according to his own mercy, by the washing of regeneration and renewal of the Holy Spirit." Hebrews 10:22 is often included in this list as well, where the author writes, "Let us draw near with a true heart in full assurance of faith, with our hearts sprinkled clean from an evil conscience and our bodies washed with pure water."

Although not all scholars agree on whether all of these passages refer specifically to baptism, the connection between the washing of baptism

45 John S. Hammett, *40 Questions about Baptism and the Lord's Supper*, 40 Questions Series (Grand Rapids: Kregel Academic, 2015), 117.

and forgiveness of sins is strong. In fact, this is one rare area of unanimous agreement between all baptismal camps. In the words of Hammett, "Thus, while it is worded in slightly different ways, cleansing or purification or forgiveness of sins is one of the most widely agreed upon aspects of the meaning of baptism, included in Catholic, Lutheran, Reformed, and Baptist formulations."[46]

Having looked at a broad survey of texts which show baptism symbolizes the cleansing and washing of sins, we now look specifically at two key Pauline texts which are filled with symbolism as to what baptism represents.

Colossians 2:11-12

> In him also you were circumcised with a circumcision made without hands, by putting off the body of the flesh, by the circumcision of Christ, having been buried with him in baptism, in which you were also raised with him through faith in the powerful working of God, who raised him from the dead.

We have already discussed Colossians 2 in considerable detail in chapter five. However, I want to summarize the theological significance of baptism as described by Colossians 2. As I explained previously, Colossians 2:12 speaks of *how* believers have been "circumcised with a circumcision made without hands." The spiritual circumcision in Colossians 2:11 takes place when believers are "buried with [Christ] in baptism."

Colossians 2:12 describes baptism as the process "in which you were also raised with him through faith." The baptismal process described here pictures the believer buried with Christ, but also raised together with Christ in His resurrection. These are the two primary symbolic elements spelled out by Paul here. When Christians undergo baptism, they are exercising faith (Col 2:12; Gal 3:26), and they are symbolically united in the suffering and death of Christ. Furthermore, they are symbolically united with Christ in His resurrection.[47] Baptism, in the theology of Paul, pictures union with Christ in His death and resurrection. This union comes about through faith.

46 Ibid.

47 Beasley-Murray, *Baptism in the New Testament*, 155.

Romans 6:3–4

> Do you not know that all of us who have been baptized into Christ Jesus were baptized into his death? We were buried therefore with him by baptism into death, in order that, just as Christ was raised from the dead by the glory of the Father, we too might walk in newness of life.

There is significant theological overlap between Romans 6 and Colossians 2. Hence, these passages naturally go together as a detailed explanation of the significance of baptism.[48] Paul's opening phrase, "Do you not know?" assumes that what Paul is about to explain is something well known to the Christians in Rome. Paul's connection between baptism and Christ's death would not have been something completely new but something with which they were familiar.[49]

Some have attempted to argue that Paul was talking about a metaphorical or spiritual baptism in Romans 6.[50] However, by the time Paul wrote Romans, it is unlikely that baptism would have meant anything else to the Christians in Rome. Moo notes, "By the date of Romans, 'baptize' had become almost a technical expression for the rite of Christian initiation by water, and this is surely the meaning the Roman Christians would have given the word."[51]

When looking at Romans 6, there are some important exegetical decisions to make. The first issue centers on what it means to be "baptized into Christ Jesus." There are two main options. First, this phrase could be an abbreviated form of the phrase "into the name of the Lord Christ Jesus."[52] As such, this phrase would reference the allegiance of a believer to Christ—a point which would fit nicely with our previous discussion. Alternatively, baptism "into Christ Jesus" could be interpreted spatially (i.e., into union with Christ).[53] In defense of this second position, Galatians 3:27 is a possible parallel, where believers who have been "baptized into Christ" have also "put on Christ." When Romans 6:4 mentions being "buried with

48 Beasley-Murray goes so far as to say Colossians 2:12 is an exposition of the theology which undergirds Romans 6 (Beasley-Murray, *Baptism in the New Testament*, 152).

49 Moo, *The Epistle to the Romans*, 384; Beasley-Murray, *Baptism in the New Testament*, 126.

50 Wilson, *To a Thousand Generations*, 51.

51 Moo, *The Epistle to the Romans*, 384.

52 Beasley-Murray, *Baptism in the New Testament*, 128–29.

53 Moo, *The Epistle to the Romans*, 385.

Christ in baptism," this makes most sense if union with Christ has already been mentioned. Thus, although both positions have solid arguments, I think it is preferable to take the phrase "baptized into Christ Jesus" as a reference to union with Christ.

Another issue to understand is the statement in Romans 6:4 that believers have been buried with Christ "by baptism into death." Scholars have proposed two primary interpretations of this phrase.[54] First, we could view it as a metaphor for the believer's abandonment of his old life while transitioning to his new life in Christ. Within this view, baptism could either be a metaphor or the actual means by which the believer transitions to a new life with Christ. A second, and preferable view, is that being buried with Christ refers to the believer's participation in Christ's burial. The believer's participation in Christ's burial is symbolized by being submerged in the water through baptism.[55] The passive verbs found throughout the passage support this idea. Hence, baptism is a picture of our representation *in* and union *with* Christ in His death and burial.[56]

Paul spells out the purpose of the being buried with Christ in baptism at the end of verse 4. He writes that Christians have been united with Christ's death and burial so that we might "walk in newness of life."[57] The text clearly specifies that the union of the believer and Christ exists in both death *and* resurrection, "For if we have been united with him in a death like his, we shall certainly be united with him in a resurrection like his" (Rom 6:5). Although it might seem strange that Paul speaks of the believer's future union with Christ's resurrection, this is not denying the symbolism of a *present* union with the resurrection of Christ.[58] Rather, Paul's emphasis seems to be on the final completion of this picture, when the believer will be raised from the dead because of his union with Christ.[59]

Paul's exposition of baptism in Romans 6 explains why believers cannot continue to sin. A believer's old life has ended, having died to sin while being united to Christ's death. Not only is the believer united with Christ's death, but also with His life! The believer has been raised with Christ and

54 Ibid., 386–89.

55 Ibid., 388; Beasley-Murray, *Baptism in the New Testament*, 130.

56 Moo, *The Epistle to the Romans*, 389.

57 Colin G. Kruse, *Paul's Letter to the Romans*, PNTC (Grand Rapids: Eerdmans, 2012), 261.

58 Beasley-Murray, *Baptism in the New Testament*, 139.

59 Moo, *The Epistle to the Romans*, 395.

that new life carries with it an obligation for the believer to "walk in newness of life."[60]

Paul's theology of baptism is clear. Baptism signifies a union with Christ's death, burial, and resurrection. This also helps explain why the mode of baptism is significant. The immersion in the water signifies the death of the believer, being united in the death of Christ. The physical act of rising out of the water in baptism represents the believer's spiritual union with Christ's resurrection and the beginning of a new life. This new life carries with it the obligation and privilege of walking in newness of life.

Although Romans 6 does not speak explicitly about the exercise of faith, it would be unusual to expect Paul to mention every aspect of the baptismal experience in one text. Paul emphasizes the importance of faith in baptism in Galatians 3:26–27 and Colossians 2:12. These texts are more than sufficient to clarify his belief about the necessity of faith in baptism.[61]

In sum, this brief exposition of the theological significance of baptism shows that the New Testament pictures baptism as the washing and cleansing from sin. Additionally, baptism symbolizes the believer's union with Christ in His death *and* in His resurrection. This union with Christ enables and calls the believer to "walk in newness of life."

The Reformed Paedobaptist Understanding of Baptism

It is helpful at this point to briefly sketch the major differences between how the Baptist and Reformed paedobaptist understand the symbolism of baptism. Although there is variation between Reformed paedobaptist interpreters, the following points best summarize the Reformed paedobaptist understanding of baptism according to their own writings.

60 Richard N. Longenecker, *The Epistle to the Romans: A Commentary on the Greek Text*, New International Greek Testament Commentary (Grand Rapids: Eerdmans, 2016), 612.

61 Moo writes, "How, then, can we preserve the cruciality of faith at the same time as we do justice to the mediatorial role of baptism in this text? Here the suggestion of J. D. G. Dunn is helpful. He points out that the early church conceived of faith, repentance, the gift of the Spirit, and water baptism as components of one unified experience, which he calls 'conversion-initiation.' Just as faith is always assumed to lead to baptism, so baptism always assumes faith for its validity. In vv. 3–4, then, we can assume that baptism stands for the whole conversion-initiation experience, presupposing faith and the gift of the Spirit" (Moo, *The Epistle to the Romans*, 390).

Baptism is God's Testimony, not Man's Testimony

Many Reformed paedobaptists believe that Baptists misunderstand the notion of baptism as an individual profession of faith. For example, Booth notes:

> One difference between Baptists and Reformed paedobaptists has been the baptistic notion that baptism is the subjective testimony of the individual believer—his profession of faith—"the Christian man's badge of profession." The Scriptures indicate that the covenant is sovereignly initiated by God, not by man, and therefore that the covenant sign and seal is God's, not the believer's. It is God's message (sign), not man's.[62]

Similarly, Booth also writes, "*It cannot be overstated that baptism is not man's testimony, but God's testimony*. Baptism is not intended as the testimony of the one being baptized that he has personally repented and believed. In fact, baptism is not a sign of anything we do. It is a sign of God's work on our behalf, by means of his gracious covenant, to save his elect people."[63]

It is undoubtedly true that baptism is symbolic of *only* God's work. No honest interpreter can work through Romans 6:3–5 and think baptism signifies any work of man. However, Reformed paedobaptists often exaggerate this point by downplaying the importance of a confession of faith during baptism. While it is true that baptism does not symbolize the work of man, the New Testament demonstrates that a profession of faith belongs with baptism (cf. Acts 2:38; 1 Pet 3:21). This is a fact that even John Calvin would acknowledge as true.[64]

Baptism and Union with Christ

Most paedobaptists agree with Baptists that baptism signifies union with Christ. Murray notes:

> Such passages as Romans 6:3–6; I Corinthians 12:13; Galatians 3:27, 28; Colossians 2:11, 12 plainly indicate that union with Christ is the governing idea. Baptism signifies union with Christ

---

62 Booth, *Children of the Promise*, 112.

63 Ibid., 114. Emphasis in original.

64 I refer here to Calvin's previously quoted statement, "But baptism serves as our confession before men. Indeed, it is the mark by which we publicly profess that we wish to be reckoned God's people; by which we testify that we agree in worshiping the same God, in one religion with all Christians; by which finally we openly affirm our faith" (Calvin, *Institutes of the Christian Religion*, 1313–14).

> in his death, burial, and resurrection. It is because believers are united to Christ in the efficacy of his death, in the power of his resurrection, and in the fellowship of his grace that they are one body. They are united to Christ and therefore to one another. Of this union baptism is the sign and seal. The relationship which baptism signifies is therefore that of union, and union with Christ is its basic and central import.[65]

But what about infants who are unregenerate? Does baptism signify the same reality? Murray says that it does. He writes that baptism "has one import and it bears this same import whether it is dispensed to adults or to infants. It signifies union with Christ, purifying from the pollution of sin by the regeneration of the Spirit, and purifying from the guilt of sin by the blood of Christ. It can have no other import for infants than this."[66] Elsewhere he writes, "If the baptism of infants is of divine institution, baptism must be for them, no less than for adults, the sign and seal of union with Christ in the virtue of his death and power of his resurrection."[67] Similarly, Fesko writes, "Suffice it to say that both adult converts and infants born within the covenant are baptized into union with Christ."[68]

The problem with the above reasoning is that, for the Reformed paedobaptist, baptism does not symbolize *actual* and *present* union with Christ. In the words of Fesko, the timing of water baptism "is not immediately tied to the realities that it signifies and seals."[69] In other words, what baptism symbolizes is not related to *reality*, but to *possibility* of union with Christ.

However, the New Testament knows nothing of baptism symbolizing a general or possible union with Christ. The New Testament assumes that those who are baptized presently enjoy a real and specific union with Christ. This is a major dilemma for Reformed paedobaptists. If they embraced such a meaning and applied it to infant baptism, they would be guilty of holding to a form of baptismal regeneration. Therefore, they must either redefine union with Christ and its significance, or they must say baptism speaks of what is possible, not what is actual.

---

65 John J. Murray, "Christian Baptism," *Westminster Theological Journal* 13, no. 2 (1951): 109. Fesko writes that "being baptized 'into Christ' signifies union with Him. This union is in His death, burial, resurrection, and ascension" (Fesko, *Word, Water, and Spirit*, 321).

66 Murray, *Christian Baptism*, 41.

67 John J. Murray, "Christian Baptism: Second Article," *Westminster Theological Journal* 14, no. 1 (1951): 1.

68 Fesko, *Word, Water, and Spirit*, 323.

69 Ibid.

Baptism Signifies Cleansing of Sin

The Heidelberg Catechism illustrates this point in the 69th question:

> Q: How is it signified and sealed unto you in Holy Baptism, that you have part in the one sacrifice of Christ on the cross?
>
> A: Thus: that Christ instituted this outward washing with water and joined therewith this promise: that I am washed with His blood and Spirit from the pollution of my soul, that is, from all my sins, as certainly as I am washed outwardly with water, whereby commonly the filthiness of the body is taken away.

As noted previously, Scripture uses the language of washing away sins frequently concerning baptism (cf. Acts 22:16; 1 Cor 6:11; Titus 3:5). This is an area where all theological camps agree. The New Testament describes baptism as washing away sin. But this is because the symbol is intimately connected to reality. To put it another way, any time a New Testament believer was baptized, he vividly demonstrated his union with Christ, the washing away of his sins, and the beginning of a new life.

The major disagreement I have with the Reformed paedobaptist is in his attempt to connect this theme of washing with circumcision. For example, Ross states, "So we see that both circumcision in the Old Testament and baptism in the New Testament signify a cleansing from sin, a removal of the uncleanness of sin. In neither case does the sign produce such cleansing; rather, the signs testify to the truth that God cleanses from sin when one believes."[70]

We have already discussed at length in chapter five how circumcision does not symbolize a washing or a cleansing, and I will leave that discussion there. However, the idea that the New Testament presents baptism as washing away sin is a valid point and something we can add to the symbolic picture of baptism.

Baptism Is a Sign of God's Ownership

In order to understand the significance of this point, we must remember that the Reformed paedobaptist views circumcision and baptism as identical in almost every way. Thus, according to Ross, "Abraham's circumcision thus functioned as a mark of ownership upon him, marking him as belonging to God and under obligation to do God's will. Baptism in the New Testament carries an identical meaning."[71] Again, later in his chap-

70 Ross, "Baptism and Circumcision as Signs and Seals," 103.

71 Ibid., 106.

ter, Ross notes, "I conclude that baptism and circumcision have the same meaning. Both signify and seal that by faith we are cleansed from our sins, and that we have been consecrated to God to be his own."[72]

Because paedobaptists often assume baptism and circumcision are related, there is little defense of the idea that baptism is a seal of God's ownership. However, we would do well to note that nowhere is baptism alluded to as a seal of the believer, and the Bible only describes circumcision as a seal of righteousness for Abraham specifically (cf. Rom 4:11).[73] We have examined Romans 4:11 in chapter five and will not repeat that discussion here. It is enough to say that the evidence for seeing baptism as a seal or sign of God's ownership is lacking, and the attempt seems to be systematically driven rather than exegetically derived. Scripture seems rather clear in its presentation of the Spirit as the seal of the believer (cf. 2 Cor 1:22; 5:5; Eph 1:13–14; 4:30). Regardless, I still think it is helpful to assess the logic of the paedobaptist argument on this point.

To explain the significance of baptism being a sign and seal, Ross gives the following illustration about engagement to show the difference that baptism makes in one's life:

> Take two young ladies. Both have special young men in their lives. Both men are talking about marriage, making big promises: lifelong faithfulness, joint ownership of all that the man possesses, etc. (all on the condition, of course, of marriage and faithfulness from her). The ladies are treated equally in every respect but one: one lady has received an engagement ring, while the other has not. Now what does the engaged lady have that the other does not? The answer is obvious. The engaged lady has a ring. Does that make a difference? Well, just ask any lady without one.[74]

Ross goes on to explain the significance of this illustration:

> The visible token of the ring does not alter the promises made, but it surely makes those promises more firm in the mind of the recipient. Likewise, the ring makes more firm the duties owed. For the engaged lady, receiving the ring has brought home to her both the promises and the duties in a much more tangible way. It is just this way that the baptized child has something that the unbaptized child does not. Baptism signifies and seals truths that are most precious. It shows that we do have a place within God's

72 Ibid.

73 Waymeyer, "Romans 4:11 and the Case for Infant Baptism," 239.

74 Ross, "Baptism and Circumcision as Signs and Seals," 109.

> covenant, that we are called by his name, that his promises have indeed been given to us. The baptism does not guarantee that we have possession of what is promised. That can only be guaranteed by faith. But the baptism can assure us that faith is enough. As a visible token of God's promise, it gives tangible expression to the certainty of God's promise to us, and that is something more than just the promise itself.[75]

Thus, according to Ross and other paedobaptists, baptism is a visible token, a reminder of a conditional promise—that those who respond in faith to Christ will be saved. However, I believe this viewpoint has significant problems that can be summarized in two critiques.

First, the Reformed paedobaptist understanding of baptism focuses on *potentiality* not on *actuality*. This is a similar critique to my point about union with Christ. In Ross's description above, baptism has no real or objective significance, only symbolic potential. For the Reformed paedobaptist, baptism is the promise of salvation conditioned upon faith. It is a sign of potentiality which is sometimes effectual, but in many cases is unrealized.[76] Viewing baptism as a sign of potential salvation or potential union with Christ differs significantly from the way the New Testament describes baptism.

Second, on a related point, there is a problem with the logic of the paedobaptist system. Reformed paedobaptists like Mark Ross give extended illustrations about engagements and rings because the looming question is, "What does baptism actually give to a child?"

According to Ross, baptism is a visible token of God's promise. But what is the difference between a non-baptized child and a baptized child? Both have access to the same promise—that those who respond in faith will be saved. Reformed paedobaptists will argue about the importance of baptism for the covenant child, but they cannot demonstrate how baptism affects a covenant child differently than a child outside the covenant. In the words of Waymeyer:

> Baptizing an infant may indeed be a tangible reminder of God's promises and therefore personally meaningful to those who witness the baptism. But none of this changes the fact that every unbaptized infant has the same conditional promise extended to

75 Ibid.

76 I say "often" because if one counts all the infant baptisms in broader Christendom, including Catholicism, most infants who are baptized do not embrace Christ through faith alone.

> him, and therefore baptism—specifically as a seal of the covenant promise of justification (Rom. 4:11)—fails to distinguish in any objective way the infant who is baptized from the one who is not.[77]

In summary, the Reformed paedobaptist understanding of baptism as a sign or seal of God's ownership is questionable. I do not deny that baptism *can* and *should* be a motivation for holy living that is sanctified to the Lord. That is the way Paul uses the argument in Romans 6. However, the assumption in Romans 6 is that there is an objective reality behind baptism, not potentiality. Those Christians referred to in Romans 6 have *actually* been united with Christ in His death, burial, and resurrection. Therefore, they cannot return to sin because they have died to it! This is far different from the Reformed paedobaptist understanding of baptism as a picture of potential salvation and potential union. The New Testament never speaks of baptism as potential at all. Instead, the New Testament describes baptism as a reality currently enjoyed by those who participate in it.

The Significance of the Mode of Baptism

Whether we baptize by immersion or affusion is of little to no importance to the paedobaptist. In fact, Reformed churches will regularly accept immersed believers, and some pastors will immerse those who want to be baptized that way. Typically, paedobaptists view the mode of baptism as a non-essential part of the discussion. In contrast, the mode of baptism is an issue of great significance for a Baptist. This section will examine the significance of the mode of baptism by first examining the biblical and historical evidence for immersion. Then we will talk about why the mode of baptism matters for believers.

The Lexical Information

The English word "baptize," is a transliteration of a Greek term, βαπτίζω (*baptizo*). By using the word "baptize" in our English translations, we do not solve the issue since we still need to know what the word for baptism means.

The Greek words related to baptism come from the same root (βαπτ-) and occur regularly in Classical and Hellenistic Greek. Although the noun forms (βάπτης, βαπτισμός, βαπτιστήριον) and the adjective (βαπτός) occur infrequently, the two verbs (βάπτω and βαπτίζω) occur often, giv-

77 Waymeyer, "Romans 4:11 and the Case for Infant Baptism," 239n24.

ing us insight into their usage and meaning. Baptism scholar, Everett Ferguson, has done us a great service by cataloging the use of the Greek verbs βάπτω and βαπτίζω. I will highlight many of his findings below.[78]

In Classical Greek, the verb βάπτω carries with it the basic idea of "to plunge" or "to dip" in a substance (usually a liquid). This is readily illustrated in Homeric Greek and other Classical writings and is supported by all the major lexical work by Greek scholars.[79] Because of the inherent idea of dipping or immersing, βάπτω also took on a few metaphorical meanings which corresponded to that use, such as "to temper" metals or "to dye" clothing. Ferguson notes, "Since a common practice was to dye by dipping an object in the coloring agent, a secondary meaning of *baptō* was "to dye," and this meaning almost replaced the primary meaning."[80]

To support the idea that baptism can mean sprinkling, some paedobaptists have pointed out that in some metaphorical uses in Classical literature, the term βάπτω can be understood as sprinkling.[81] However, as Ferguson has noted, we should understand these uses as metaphorical, with an emphasis on the result (coloring/dying), not on the action (sprinkling/immersing).[82] In other words, the metaphorical use points to what happened, not how it happened.

Let me give an illustration. The English verb "to drink" is easy to understand. To drink something (usually a liquid) is to ingest it through the mouth. The connotation of drinking liquid is occasionally used to communicate metaphorically. Thus, "to drink in the sights" means to mentally absorb or ingest what is being seen with the eyes. However, nobody would argue that this means we can drink with our eyes! In cases like this, a word's secondary, metaphorical usage emphasizes the result. Or, to say it another way, nobody is arguing that one drinks through the eyes. We

78 Ferguson, *Baptism in the Early Church*, 38–59.

79 For example, see the lexical entries in Henry George Liddell, Robert Scott, Henry Stuart Jones, and Roderick McKenzie. *A Greek-English Lexicon* (Oxford: Clarendon Press, 1996), 306; William Arndt, Frederick W. Danker, Walter Bauer, and F. Wilbur Gingrich. *A Greek-English Lexicon of the New Testament and Other Early Christian Literature* (Chicago: University of Chicago Press, 2000), 165–66; Franco Montanari, *The Brill Dictionary of Ancient Greek*, ed. Madeleine Goh and Chad Schroeder (Leiden; Boston: Brill, 2015), βάπτω.

80 Ferguson, *Baptism in the Early Church*, 43.

81 For example, Scott gives examples from the Homeric poem, *The Battle of the Frogs and Mice* (v. 220), Lucian's *True History* 17, and *Iliad* 18.329. He writes, "In each of these passages quoted the verb must mean to sprinkle, or, what is really the same thing, to color by sprinkling, and in no one of them can the idea of submerge or immerse be obtained even by the most forced interpretation" (John A. Scott, "The Meaning of the Verb Βάπτω, Βαπτίζω," *The Classical Journal* 16, no. 1 [1920]: 54).

82 Ferguson, *Baptism in the Early Church*, 45–46.

understand that drinking is done through the mouth but can be metaphorically applied elsewhere.

The simple point of the above illustration is that in Classical literature, the verb βάπτω signifies immersion or dipping; but it also carries a widespread metaphorical meaning of dying clothing. Dying of clothing could be achieved through a variety of means (dipping, sprinkling, etc.). This is not problematic and is common in language. Therefore, the classical usage of βάπτω cited by some paedobaptists cannot be used to argue against the basic idea of immersion or dipping.

We move on now to analyze the Jewish usage of the baptism terminology. A helpful observation is that in translating the Hebrew Bible, βάπτω most often translates the Hebrew term טבל (*taval*), which means "to dip something into."[83] The Greek translation of the Hebrew Scriptures regularly preserves a distinction between dipping and sprinkling. For example, Leviticus 4:17 gives the following instruction, "And the priest will dip his finger [βάπτω] into the blood of the young bull and sprinkle it [ῥαίνω] seven times before the Lord in front of the veil of the holy place."[84] Leviticus 4:6 is similar, though there is a different word for sprinkling: "And the priest will dip his finger [βάπτω] in the blood and sprinkle [προσραίνω] some of the blood seven times down along the holy veil before the Lord."

We also observe this distinction between dipping and sprinkling in the purification ritual for those who have touched a dead body. Numbers 19:18 says, "And a clean man will take hyssop and dip it [βάπτω] in water and will sprinkle [περιρραίνω] the house and the various vessels and the persons, whoever may be there, and the one who touched the bone of a human or a fatally wounded man or a corpse or a grave marker."

The usage of βάπτω in the Greek Old Testament provides confirmation of the meaning of dipping or immersing. Out of the 16 uses of βάπτω in the Greek Old Testament, there are only a few that require additional comment. Deuteronomy 33:24 says, "Blessed with children is Asher, and he shall be acceptable to his brothers; he shall immerse [βάπτω] his foot in olive oil." This is clearly a metaphor for blessing, and not intended to be taken literally (although dipping one's feet in olive oil is clearly the picture

83 Ludwig Koehler et al., *The Hebrew and Aramaic Lexicon of the Old Testament* (Leiden: E.J. Brill, 1994–2000), 368, טבל. According to Logos Bible Software, out of the 16 uses of טבל in the Old Testament, all but two are translated by βάπτω. Μολύνω (Gen 37:31) and βαπτίζω (2 Kgs 5:14) are the two exceptions.

84 References to the Greek translation will use *The Lexham English Septuagint*, 2nd ed. (Bellingham, WA: Lexham Press, 2020).

represented here). In Job 9:31, Job complains, "You dip [βάπτω] me fully in filth, and my clothing feels loathing for me."[85] This is also clearly a metaphor to communicate the overwhelming experience of Job.

Although βάπτω is the verb used most frequently in the Greek Old Testament for dipping or immersion, there are also four uses of βαπτίζω, with two of them occurring in the Apocrypha (cf. 2 Kgs 5:14; Jdt 12:7; Sir 34:25; Isa 21:4). These uses of βαπτίζω match with our observations of βάπτω. The only occurrence that does not refer to literal dipping is Isaiah 21:4, "My heart goes astray, and lawlessness immerses me [βαπτίζω]; my life stands in fear." Here βαπτίζω is used metaphorically for the idea of overwhelming, similar to βάπτω in Job 9:31.

Outside of the biblical literature, Josephus provides some helpful detail on the usage of βάπτω and βαπτίζω. In Josephus, βάπτω occurs exclusively with its secondary meaning, "to dye."[86] Thus, when Josephus refers to Numbers 19:18 and the purification rituals about coming into contact with a dead body, he substitutes βαπτίζω for βάπτω (*Antiquities* 4.81). Ferguson notes that Josephus represents the tendency in later Greek to substitute βαπτίζω for βάπτω. The most likely reason for this substitution is that βάπτω began to be associated primarily with dyeing or coloring.[87] Throughout his writings, Josephus uses βαπτίζω mainly in a literal sense, often referring to the submersion of a ship or of a drowning person (e.g., *Antiquities* 9.212, *Jewish War* 3.423, *Life* 3.15, *Jewish War* 3.368, *Jewish War* 2.556, *Antiquities* 15.55).[88]

Similar to βάπτω, the verb form βαπτίζω developed a metaphorical usage. To illustrate this, Ferguson focuses on the uses of βαπτίζω by Plutarch (ca. 50–120 AD). He summarizes, "Continuing with Plutarch, we find that he represents classical usage of *baptizō* not only in a literal sense with reference to ships sinking, persons drowning, objects submerged, and dipping in a liquid (water, blood, or wine), but also in a metaphorical sense

---

85 But it is perhaps evidence of a shift from βάπτω to βαπτίζω that in the second century AD Aquila uses βαπτίζω in his translation of Job 9:31. See Ferguson, *Baptism in the Early Church*, 57.

86 Ibid., 47.

87 Ferguson writes, "The-ίζω form tended to replace βάπτω, in accord with the tendency in languages for strengthened forms of words to replace the root form and to lose their intensified meaning, in this case a development likely related also to *baptō* being ordinarily used for 'to dye.'" Ferguson goes on to give examples of how βαπτίζω is used in parallel with βάπτω to communicate a more intensive or significant submersion (Ferguson, *Baptism in the Early Church*, 47).

88 Ibid., 57–58.

of being overwhelmed whether with drunkenness, affairs of life, or debts."[89] This metaphorical usage of βαπτίζω is also used by the first century Jewish philosopher, Philo. Ferguson notes that Philo does not use βάπτω, but uses βαπτίζω exclusively in its metaphorical sense of being overwhelmed.[90] In addition to the many literal uses of βαπτίζω, Josephus also uses it in a metaphorical sense. For example, Josephus uses the word figuratively to speak of a city being overwhelmed (*Jewish War* 4.137), or a storm overwhelming a group of young men (*Jewish War* 1.535).

Summarizing his 21-page analysis of the lexical information, Ferguson concludes with the following statement:

> *Baptizō* meant to dip, usually a thorough submerging, but it also meant to overwhelm and so could be used whether the object was placed in an element (which was more common) or was overwhelmed by it (often in the metaphorical usages). The secular usage for "destroy" or "perish," as in a person drowning or a ship sinking, did not make this the primary connotation; such was the effect of the submerging and one could substitute the effect for the act, but that was a secondary application. As will be seen, Christian sources maintained the basic meaning of the word. Pouring and sprinkling were distinct actions that were represented by different verbs, and this usage too continued in Christian sources. When the latter speak of the pouring out of the Holy Spirit or the sprinkling of blood, they do not use *baptizō* for these actions.[91]

The Immersions of John the Baptist and Early Christian Precedent

The lexical data of the preceding section is overwhelming. The usage of baptismal language signifies dipping or immersion. Furthermore, any of the possible Jewish antecedents to John's baptism—washings for purity, Qumran washings, or proselyte baptism—would all have been a full immersion experience.[92] That baptism was practiced through immersion is also supported by the details we read about John the Baptist, who functions as the New Testament's introduction to baptism.

For example, when we are told about John's baptismal practice, we read that "John also was baptizing at Aenon near Salim, because water

89 Ibid., 52.

90 Ibid., 57–58.

91 Ibid., 59.

92 Ibid., 95.

was plentiful there, and people were coming and being baptized" (John 3:23). Some have suggested that Aenon could be located seven miles south of Beisan, where there are seven springs that are active within a quarter of a mile.[93] Regardless, the point of John 3:23 is that John chose this location because of the abundance of water—a moot point if John's baptism was not immersion.

We read additional insight into John's mode of baptism in the Synoptics. Mark 1:5 says, "And all the country of Judea and all Jerusalem were going out to him and were being baptized by him in the river Jordan, confessing their sins." The phrase, "in the river Jordan," shows that the individuals were being baptized while in the river—something unnecessary if immersion was not being practiced. This point is confirmed by the details of Jesus's own baptism a few verses later. "And when he came up out of the water, immediately he saw the heavens being torn open and the Spirit descending on him like a dove" (Mark 1:10; cf. Matt 3:16). Coming up out of the water likely does not refer to raising someone out of the water post-immersion. However, it does mean that they were down in the waters of the Jordan River while the baptism was taking place.

We have previously discussed the connection between the baptism performed by Jesus's disciples and the baptism of John found in John 4:1–2. It is improbable that Jesus's followers used a different method than John's baptism, which was immersion. The evidence we have shows that there was continuity between the practice of John and the Christians. For example, the book of Acts reveals that those baptized "went down into the water" (Acts 8:38), just like John's baptism. Combining the clear lexical information with the descriptions of baptism in the New Testament, we conclude that both John the Baptist and early Christians practiced baptism by immersion.

The Early Church's Testimony

We have seen that the lexical information clearly supports the idea that baptism was performed through immersion or dipping. Additionally, the New Testament descriptions support the view that baptism was practiced by immersion. We now look at the testimony of church history.

One of the earliest sources we have on baptism is from the *Didache* (7:1–4). We have talked briefly about the *Didache* in chapter one, but here I want to emphasize that this early church source puts an emphasis on immersion. Consider how the *Didache* describes baptism:

---

93 Morris, *The Gospel According to John*, 210.

> Concerning baptism, baptize in this way: after you have reviewed all these things, baptize into the name of the Father and of the Son and of the Holy Spirit in running water. If you do not have running water, baptize in some other water. If you are not able [to baptize] in cold water, then in warm water. If you have neither, pour water upon the head three times in the name of the Father and Son and Holy Spirit. Prior to baptism, let the one who baptizes and the baptizand fast, and others if they are able. Instruct the baptizand to fast one or two days beforehand.[94]

There are a variety of observations that help us here. First, the location of the baptism is in the water (like the New Testament picture). It was to be in "running water" (i.e., flowing water like a river). However, cold water was permissible if there was no running water, and warm water was permissible if neither running nor cold water was available. Importantly, these instructions only make sense if one is to be immersed or dipped in the water, because they would have to be standing in water.

Another important observation is that pouring water on the head three times was viewed as an exception. This exception was in contrast to the normal process of baptism. If pouring water on the head was the normal process of baptism, why would the author list it as an exception to be practiced *only* if there was insufficient water?

We discussed the church father, Tertullian, in the first chapter. He was a prolific Latin author of the early third century, and he produced the most extensive early writings on baptism that we have. We have already talked about how he provides the first undisputed evidence that the early church practiced infant baptism during his time, although it is highly debatable whether that was viewed as the norm at that time (Tertullian seems to speak against infant baptism). But for our purposes, Tertullian also gives powerful testimony that immersion was the practice of the church during his time. He writes:

> After His resurrection He promises in a pledge to His disciples that He will send them the promise of His Father; and lastly, He commands them to baptize into the Father and the Son and the Holy Ghost, not into a unipersonal God. And indeed it is not once only, but three times, that we are immersed into the Three Persons, at each several mention of Their names.[95]

94 Translation from Wilhite, *The Didache*, xxxvii.

95 Tertullian, "Against Praxeas," in *Latin Christianity*, 623.

Similarly, elsewhere Tertullian writes:

> To deal with this matter briefly, I shall begin with baptism. When we are going to enter the water, but a little before, in the presence of the congregation and under the hand of the president, we solemnly profess that we disown the devil, and his pomp, and his angels. Hereupon we are thrice immersed, making a somewhat ampler pledge than the Lord has appointed in the Gospel.[96]

In both texts, Tertullian says that the Christians practiced immersion three times (once for each member of the Trinity). Tertullian's testimony is also important because he is writing in Latin. Thus, he is a very early testimony, describing baptism as immersion in a language other than Greek.

Another Latin father, Cyprian, provides helpful insight into the issue, but from a unique angle. In his *Epistle to Magnus (LXXV)*, Cyprian discusses how Christians should think about those who are too weak or sick to be baptized by the normal process:

> You have asked also, dearest son, what I thought of those who obtain God's grace in sickness and weakness, whether they are to be accounted legitimate Christians, for that they are not to be washed, but sprinkled, with the saving water. In this point, my diffidence and modesty prejudges none, so as to prevent any from feeling what he thinks right, and from doing what he feels to be right. As far as my poor understanding conceives it, I think that the divine benefits can in no respect be mutilated and weakened; nor can anything less occur in that case, where, with full and entire faith both of the giver and receiver, is accepted what is drawn from the divine gifts. For in the sacrament of salvation the contagion of sins is not in such wise washed away, as the filth of the skin and of the body is washed away in the carnal and ordinary washing, as that there should be need of saltpetre and other appliances also, and a bath and a basin wherewith this vile body must be washed and purified. Otherwise is the breast of the believer washed; otherwise is the mind of man purified by the merit of faith. In the sacraments of salvation, when necessity compels, and God bestows His mercy, the divine methods confer the whole benefit on believers; nor ought it to trouble any one that sick people seem to be sprinkled or affused, when they obtain the Lord's grace ...[97]

---

96 Tertullian, "The Chaplet, or De Corona," in *Latin Christianity*, 94.

97 Cyprian of Carthage, "The Epistles of Cyprian," in *Fathers of the Third Century*, 400–401.

The important takeaway of Cyprian's text is that it was exceptional to sprinkle or practice affusion in his day. Cyprian makes a difference between the normal washing that Christians undergo in baptism, and the sprinkling which weak or sick Christians undergo. Like the *Didache*, Cyprian believed it was appropriate to allow sprinkling or affusion when someone could not practice normal baptism by immersion.

Another helpful confirmation of the early church's practice of immersion comes from Leo I. Also known as Leo the Great, Leo I was bishop of Rome from 440 to 461 AD.[98] In his argument for why baptisms should occur on Easter, he writes the following (*Letter* 16.4):

> As the blessed Apostle says: "Are ye ignorant that all we who were baptized in Christ Jesus, were baptized in His death? We were buried with Him through baptism into death; that as Christ rose from the dead through the glory of the Father, so we also should walk in newness of life. For if we have become united with the likeness of His death, we shall be also (with the likeness) of His resurrections," and the rest which the Teacher of the Gentiles discusses further in recommending the sacrament of baptism: that it might be seen from the spirit of this doctrine that that is the day, and that the time chosen for regenerating the sons of men and adopting them among the sons of God, on which by a mystical symbolism and form, what is done in the limbs coincides with what was done in the Head Himself, *for in the baptismal office death ensues through the slaying of sin, and threefold immersion imitates the lying in the tomb three days, and the raising out of the water is like Him that rose again from the tomb.*[99]

Leo provides another reference to threefold immersion, and we also have a clear connection to the biblical theology of Romans 6. In agreement with my exegesis of Colossians 2 and Romans 6, Leo argues that the baptismal picture of immersion corresponds with Christ's death, and the raising up of Christ in resurrection corresponds with the raising up out of the water.

The quotations above are just a sampling of the many early church sources that support the idea that immersion was the main practice of

98 Ferguson, *Baptism in the Early Church*, 761.

99 Leo the Great, "Letters," in *Leo the Great, Gregory the Great*, ed. Philip Schaff and Henry Wace, trans. Charles Lett Feltoe, vol. 12a of *A Select Library of the Nicene and Post-Nicene Fathers of the Christian Church, Second Series* (New York: Christian Literature Company, 1895), 28. Emphasis added.

the early church.[100] The evidence that the early church practiced baptism through immersion is overwhelming. Lexicography, biblical description, and church history all point to this reality.

The Paedobaptist Conundrum

As we have seen, the evidence is compelling that the early church practiced baptism through immersion. Historically, many notable paedobaptists have also acknowledged this. Note, for example, Luther's words:

> Baptism [*Die Taufe*] is *baptismos* in Greek, and *mersio* in Latin, and means to plunge something completely into the water, so that the water covers it. Although in many places it is no longer customary to thrust and dip infants into the font, but only with the hand to pour the baptismal water upon them out of the font, nevertheless the former is what should be done. It would be proper, according to the meaning of the word *Taufe*, that the infant, or whoever is to be baptized, should be put in and sunk completely into the water and then drawn out again. For even in the German tongue the word *Taufe* comes undoubtedly from the word *tief* [deep] and means that what is baptized is sunk deeply into the water. This usage is also demanded by the significance of baptism itself. For baptism, as we shall hear, signifies that the old man and the sinful birth of flesh and blood are to be wholly drowned by the grace of God. We should therefore do justice to its meaning and make baptism a true and complete sign of the thing it signifies.[101]

Luther goes on in the same treatise on baptism to note that the significance of baptism is "the dying or drowning of sin," which is pictured by immersion. Subsequently, the lifting one out of the water signifies "the spiritual birth."[102] Apparently, Luther would be in significant agreement with much of the exegesis of this chapter.

Other paedobaptists have also acknowledged that immersion was the ancient form practiced by the church. Perhaps the most famous paedobaptist, John Calvin, said it this way:

---

100 Chris Whisonant has compiled a helpful chronological list of sources that support baptism meaning immersion. See the list at https://cwhisonant.wordpress.com/baptism-in-the-early-church/.

101 Luther, "The Holy and Blessed Sacrament of Baptism, 1519," 29.

102 Ibid., 30–31.

> But whether the person being baptized should be wholly immersed, and whether thrice or once, whether he should only be sprinkled with poured water—these details are of no importance, but ought to be optional to churches according to the diversity of countries. Yet the word "baptize" means to immerse, and it is clear that the rite of immersion was observed in the ancient church.[103]

As both Calvin and Luther acknowledge, the mode of baptism is not hidden or mysterious. The lexical details, biblical descriptions, and historical precedent all show that the normal mode of baptism was immersion in the early church. However, Calvin voices the opinion of most paedobaptists when he says, "these details are of no importance." The Westminster Confession of Faith also downplays the importance of the mode of baptism when it says, "Dipping of the person into the water is not necessary; but baptism is rightly administered by pouring or sprinkling water upon the person" (28.3).

Herein lies the dilemma for the paedobaptist. The evidence is overwhelming that the early church practiced baptism through immersion. That picture of immersion matches with what baptism itself signifies—union with the death of Christ and being raised in the newness of life (Rom 6:4). So, why do paedobaptists have the freedom to depart from this biblical prescription and pattern? This presents a significant dilemma for paedobaptist interpreters, who regularly appeal to continuity and the need to follow biblical patterns if God has not explicitly changed them. If the paedobaptist recognizes the biblical pattern of baptism by immersion, and if he recognizes that God has not explicitly changed that pattern, then he must also recognize that his theological system has been in substantial error from the outset.

Perhaps an illustration will help highlight the significance of this dilemma. As discussed in chapter five, the Reformed paedobaptist argument rests heavily upon the connection between circumcision and baptism. Since the mode of baptism is not significant, can we not also argue that the mode of circumcision also does not matter?

In fact, Reformed paedobaptists argue that the blood is a significant part of the circumcision sign. So, would an Old Testament Israelite have been able to prick his finger and sprinkle the blood upon his foreskin to fulfill the purpose of the sign of circumcision? Or perhaps if sprinkling the blood was not enough, an Old Testament Israelite could have made just a

103 John Calvin, *Institutes of the Christian Religion*, 1320.

tiny incision in the foreskin to draw blood? To put it candidly, I am not aware of anyone who would argue that the mode of circumcision was not crucial to the Old Testament Israelite, nor was there flexibility in how circumcision was to take place. The Israelites practiced circumcision that was precise and calculated. So, if baptism and circumcision are similar, as the Reformed paedobaptist argues, then why is the mode of baptism insignificant in contrast to circumcision? Reformed paedobaptists have no satisfactory answer to this dilemma.

Mode Matters because Symbolism Matters

In contrast to the paedobaptist, like Calvin, who argues that the mode of baptism is "of no importance," I would argue that immersion in baptism is important for two reasons. First, that is what Jesus has commanded the church to do. When Jesus commands His followers to "go therefore and make disciples of all nations, baptizing them in the name of the Father and of the Son and of the Holy Spirit" (Matt 28:19), He means something by what He says. The command to baptize is most naturally read as a command to immerse. Just like a command to circumcise is a command to circumcise.

Second, immersion is the picture of what baptism signifies. Being submerged in water symbolizes the death of an individual, uniting him with the death of Christ. The raising up out of the water signifies the new life of that individual, uniting him with the resurrection of Christ. Scripture is clear about this picture, and we lose that picture when we practice sprinkling or affusion. As the quotes from Leo and Luther demonstrate, immersion contributes significantly to the picture of what baptism signifies.

Conclusion

While analyzing the New Testament description of baptism, we saw that John's baptism is foundational for understanding later Christian baptism. Even if they are not identical, one has to acknowledge that the disciples were unlikely to perform baptisms that were thought to be radically different from that of their prophetic predecessor.

The Gospels and Acts clearly connect baptism and discipleship. Thus, confession of sin and a profession of faith are integral to the baptismal process. The early church would have known nothing about a baptized individual who had not also made a profession of allegiance to Christ.

The New Testament also paints a vivid picture of what baptism signifies. Colossians 2:11–12 and Romans 6:3–4 define baptism as being united to the death, burial, and resurrection of Christ. This is why the mode of baptism is significant. In baptism, the believer is picturing his actual union with the death of Christ (the immersion in the water) and with His resurrection (coming up out of the water).

Having analyzed the New Testament's view of baptism, this is the strongest argument against paedobaptism. Given the descriptions and definition of baptism in the New Testament, it is simply not possible for infants to qualify for baptism. Only those who put their faith in Christ and confess their sins are granted entrance into the church through the ordinance of baptism.

Chapter 8

Embracing the Biblical Picture of Baptism

When I set out to write this book, I did so for two reasons. First, I wanted to reignite an appreciation for biblical baptism. Unfortunately, due in part to the debates surrounding baptism, many Christians misunderstand or undervalue baptism. But biblical baptism is a beautiful and symbolically rich picture of our union with Christ, His death, and His resurrection. I pray God uses the information in this book to encourage your heart and excite you about the beauty of baptism.

Second, I wanted to provide a loving challenge to my Reformed paedobaptist friends. Baptists and paedobaptists have drastically different views of baptism, and both cannot be correct. Both views have drastic implications for how one views the church—an assembly of believers, or an assembly of believers and unbelievers. We owe it to our Lord to search the Scriptures to make sure we are following His commands and establishing His church the way He wants. Challenging one another to compare our theological systems to Scripture can be very beneficial in this process.

Obviously, there are serious ramifications for what one believes about infant baptism. In this regard, the paedobaptist has much more to lose than the Baptist. I fully acknowledge that if a paedobaptist changes his or her mind on baptism, this will inevitably lead to making some uncomfortable decisions. For example, it could mean being baptized as a believer. Or it could mean not baptizing one's children, even though it has been a family practice for generations. Therefore, I tried to be as thorough as possible in addressing the arguments put forward by Reformed paedobaptists. I want the reader to understand and evaluate the Reformed position on infant baptism and be confident in what Scripture teaches.

I believe Scripture is clear on baptism. Although Reformed paedobaptism is a logically coherent system, it does not have biblical support. If we prioritize the biblical evidence over theological systems and tradition, we will inevitably embrace the biblical picture of baptism. The Bible teaches that those who embrace Christ in faith are baptized as a profession of that faith. Therefore, we call it believer's baptism. But we could simply call it biblical baptism.

Bibliography

Achtemeier, Paul J. *1 Peter: A Commentary on First Peter*. Hermeneia. Minneapolis, MN: Fortress Press, 1996.

Alexander, T. Desmond. *Exodus*. Apollos Old Testament Commentary 2. Downers Grove, IL: InterVarsity Press, 2017.

———. *From Eden to the New Jerusalem: An Introduction to Biblical Theology*. Grand Rapids: Kregel Publications, 2008.

———. "Genesis 22 and the Covenant of Circumcision." *Journal for the Study of the Old Testament* 25 (1983): 17–22.

Allen, Leslie C. *Jeremiah: A Commentary*. The Old Testament Library. Louisville, KY: Westminster John Knox Press, 2008.

Aristides of Athens. "The Apology of Aristides." In *The Ante-Nicene Fathers*. Vol. 9, *The Gospel of Peter, the Diatessaron of Tatian, the Apocalypse of Peter, the Visio Pauli, the Apocalypses of the Virgil and Sedrach, the Testament of Abraham, the Acts of Xanthippe and Polyxena, the Narrative of Zosimus, the Apology of Aristides, the Epistles of Clement (Complete Text), Origen's Commentary on John, Books I–X, and Commentary on Matthew, Books I, II, and X–XIV*. Edited by Allan Menzies. Translated by D. M. Kay, 257–80. New York: Christian Literature Company, 1897.

Arndt, William, Frederick W. Danker, Walter Bauer, and F. Wilbur Gingrich. *A Greek-English Lexicon of the New Testament and Other Early Christian Literature*. Chicago: University of Chicago Press, 2000.

Arnold, Clinton E. *Ephesians*. Zondervan Exegetical Commentary on the New Testament. Grand Rapids: Zondervan, 2010.

Augustine of Hippo. "On Baptism, against the Donatists." In *A Select Library of the Nicene and Post-Nicene Fathers of the Christian Church,*

First Series. Vol. 4, *St. Augustin: The Writings against the Manichaeans and against the Donatists*. Edited by Philip Schaff. Translated by J. R. King, 407–514. Buffalo, NY: Christian Literature Company, 1887.

Augustine of Hippo. "A Treatise on the Merits and Forgiveness of Sins, and on the Baptism of Infants." In *A Select Library of the Nicene and Post-Nicene Fathers of the Christian Church, First Series*. Vol. 5, *Saint Augustin: Anti-Pelagian Writings*. Edited by Philip Schaff. Translated by Peter Holmes, 11–78. New York: Christian Literature Company, 1887.

Barcellos, Richard C., ed. *Recovering a Covenantal Heritage: Essays in Baptist Covenant Theology*. Palmdale, CA: RBAP, 2014.

Barrick, William D. "The Kingdom of God in the Old Testament." *The Master's Seminary Journal* 23, no. 2 (2012): 173–92.

Bartchy, S. Scott. "Slaves and Slavery in the Roman World." In *The World of the New Testament: Cultural, Social, and Historical Contexts*. Edited by Joel B. Green and Lee Martin McDonald, 169–78. Grand Rapids: Baker Academic, 2013.

Basil of Caesarea, "The Book of Saint Basil on the Spirit." In *A Select Library of the Nicene and Post-Nicene Fathers of the Christian Church, Second Series*. Vol. 8, *St. Basil: Letters and Select Works*. Edited by Philip Schaff and Henry Wace. Translated by Blomfield Jackson. New York: Christian Literature Company, 1895.

Bateman, Herbert W. "Introducing the Warning Passages in Hebrews: A Contextual Orientation." In *Four Views on the Warning Passages in Hebrews*. Edited by Herbert W. Bateman, 23–85. Grand Rapids: Kregel Academic, 2007.

Beale, G. K. *A New Testament Biblical Theology: The Unfolding of the Old Testament in the New*. Grand Rapids: Baker Academic, 2011.

Beasley-Murray, G. R. *Baptism in the New Testament*. New York: St Martin's Press, 1962.

Beeke, Joel R. "'Only for His Believers': Paedocommunion and the Witness of the Reformed Liturgies." In *Children and the Lord's Supper*. Edited by Guy Waters and Ligon Duncan, 163–80. Ross-shire, UK: Christian Focus Publications, 2011.

Beeke, Joel R., and Ray B. Lanning. "Unto You, and to Your Children." In *The Case for Covenantal Infant Baptism*. Edited by Gregg Strawbridge, 49–69. Phillipsburg, NJ: P&R Publishing, 2003.

Berkhof, Louis. *Systematic Theology*. Grand Rapids: Eerdmans, 1938.

Bierma, Lyle D. *German Calvinism in the Confessional Age: The Covenant Theology of Caspar Olevianus*. Grand Rapids: Baker, 1996.

Blaurock, George. "The Beginnings of the Anabaptist Reformation Reminiscences of George Blaurock." In *Spiritual and Anabaptist Writers*. Edited by George H. Williams and Angel M. Mergal, 41–46. Philadelphia, PA: Westminster Press, 1957.

Boice, James Montgomery. *Romans: God and History (Romans 9–11)*. Vol. 3. Grand Rapids: Baker Books, 1991.

———. *Romans: Justification by Faith (Romans 1–4)*. Vol. 1. Grand Rapids: Baker Books, 1991.

Booth, Randy. "Covenant Transition." In *The Case for Covenantal Infant Baptism*. Edited by Gregg Strawbridge, 175–200. Phillipsburg, NJ: P&R Publishing, 2003.

Booth, Robert R. *Children of the Promise: The Biblical Case for Infant Baptism*. Phillipsburg, NJ: P&R Publishing, 1995.

Brinkel, Karl. *Die Lehre Luthers von der fides infantium bei der Kindertaufe*. Berlin: Evangelische Verlagsanstatt, 1958.

Brownson, James V. *The Promise of Baptism: An Introduction to Baptism in Scripture and the Reformed Tradition*. Grand Rapids: Eerdmans, 2007.

Bruce, F. F. *The Epistles to the Colossians, to Philemon, and to the Ephesians*. New International Commentary on the New Testament. Grand Rapids: Eerdmans, 1984.

Busenitz, Irvin A. "Introduction to the Biblical Covenants: The Noahic Covenant and the Priestly Covenant." *The Master's Seminary Journal* 10, no. 2 (1999): 173–89.

Calvin, John, and William Pringle. *Commentaries on the Epistles of Paul the Apostle to the Corinthians*. Bellingham, WA: Logos Bible Software, 2010.

———. *Commentaries on the Epistles of Paul to the Galatians and Ephesians.* Bellingham, WA: Logos Bible Software, 2010.

———. *Institutes of the Christian Religion.* The Library of Christian Classics 1. Edited by John T. McNeill. Translated by Ford Lewis Battles. Louisville, KY: Westminster John Knox Press, 2011.

Campbell, Douglas A. "Participation and Faith in Paul." In *"In Christ" in Paul: Explorations in Paul's Theology of Union and Participation.* Edited by Michael J. Thate, Kevin J. Vanhoozer, and Constantine R. Campbell, 37–60. Wissenschaftliche Untersuchungen zum Neuen Testament 2. Reihe 384. Tübingen, Germany: Mohr Siebeck, 2014.

Carson, D. A. "Matthew." In *The Expositor's Bible Commentary: Matthew, Mark, Luke.* Edited by Frank E. Gaebelein, 1–600. Grand Rapids: Zondervan, 1984.

Chapell, Bryan. "A Pastoral Overview of Infant Baptism." In *The Case for Covenantal Infant Baptism.* Edited by Gregg Strawbridge, 9–29. Phillipsburg, NJ: P&R Publishing, 2003.

Collins, Adela Yarbro. *Mark: A Commentary on the Gospel of Mark.* Hermeneia. Minneapolis, MN: Fortress Press, 2007.

———, and John J. Collins. *King and Messiah as Son of God: Divine, Human, and Angelic Messianic Figures.* Grand Rapids: Eerdmans, 2008.

Collins, Brian. "The Covenants of Grace." In *Lexham Survey of Theology.* Edited by Mark Ward et al. Bellingham, WA: Lexham Press, 2018.

Cotrell, Jack. *Baptism: A Biblical Study.* Joplin, MO: College Press Publishing, 1989.

Coxe, Nehemiah. *A Discourse of the Covenants That God Made with Men before the Law: Wherein, the Covenant of Circumcision Is More Largely Handled, and the Invalidity of the Plea for Paedobaptism Taken from Thence Discovered.* London: John Darby, 1681.

Craigie, Peter C. *Jeremiah 1–25.* Word Biblical Commentary 26. Dallas, TX: Word, 1991.

———. *Psalms 1–50.* 2nd ed. Word Biblical Commentary 19. Nashville, TN: Thomas Nelson, 2004.

Cross, Anthony R. "Faith-Baptism: The Key to an Evangelical Baptismal Sacramentalism." In *Truth That Never Dies*. Edited by Nigel G. Wright, 19–42. Cambridge, UK: The Lutterworth Press, 2014.

Cyprian of Carthage. "The Epistles of Cyprian." In *The Ante-Nicene Fathers*. Vol. 5, *Fathers of the Third Century: Hippolytus, Cyprian, Novatian, Appendix*. Edited by Alexander Roberts, James Donaldson, and A. Cleveland Coxe. Translated by Robert Ernest Wallis, 275–420. Buffalo, NY: Christian Literature Company, 1886.

DeRouchie, Jason S. "Circumcision in the Hebrew Bible and Targums: Theology, Rhetoric, and the Handling of Metaphor." *Bulletin for Biblical Research* 14, no. 2 (2004): 175–203.

Doriani, Daniel M. "Matthew 28:18–20 and the Institution of Baptism." In *The Case for Covenantal Infant Baptism*. Edited by Gregg Strawbridge, 30–48. Phillipsburg, NJ: P&R Publishing, 2003.

Dunn, James D. G. *Baptism in the Holy Spirit*. London: SCM Press Ltd, 1970.

———. *The Epistles to the Colossians and to Philemon*. New international Greek Testament Commentary. Grand Rapids: Eerdmans, 1996.

Edwards, James R. *The Gospel According to Mark*. Pillar New Testament Commentary. Grand Rapids: Eerdmans, 2002.

Elliot, J. K. *The Apocryphal New Testament: A Collection of Apocryphal Christian Literature in an English Translation*. Oxford: Clarendon Press, 1993.

Engnell, Ivan. *Studies in Divine Kingship in the Ancient Near East*. 2nd ed. Oxford: Basil Blackwell, 1967.

Essex, Keith. "The Abrahamic Covenant." *The Master's Seminary Journal* 10, no. 2 (1999): 191–212.

Estelle, Bryan D. "Passover and the Lord's Supper: Continuity or Discontinuity?" In *Children and the Lord's Supper*. Edited by Guy Waters and Ligon Duncan, 31–58. Ross-shire, UK: Christian Focus Publications, 2011.

Fee, Gordon D. *The First Epistle to the Corinthians*. New International Commentary on the New Testament. Grand Rapids: Eerdmans, 1987.

Ferguson, Everett. *Baptism in the Early Church: History, Theology, and Liturgy in the First Five Centuries*. Grand Rapids: Eerdmans, 2009.

———. "Exhortations to Baptism in the Cappadocians." In *The Early Church at Work and Worship*. Vol. 2, *Catechesis, Baptism, Eschatology, and Martyrdom,* 100–109. London: James Clarke, 2014.

———. "Spiritual Circumcision in Early Christianity." In *The Early Church at Work and Worship*. Vol. 2, *Catechesis, Baptism, Eschatology, and Martyrdom,* 144–54. London: James Clarke, 2014.

Ferguson, Sinclair B. *The Holy Spirit*. Downers Grove, IL: InterVarsity Press, 1997.

Fesko, J. V. *Word, Water, and Spirit: A Reformed Perspective on Baptism*. Grand Rapids: Reformation Heritage Books, 2010.

Fox, Michael V. "The Sign of the Covenant: Circumcision in the Light of the Priestly ʾôt Etiologies." *Revue Biblique* 81 (1974): 557–96.

Frame, John. *Systematic Theology: An Introduction to Christian Belief*. Phillipsburg, NJ: P&R Publishing, 2013.

Garrett, Duane A. *A Commentary on Exodus*. Kregel Exegetical Library. Grand Rapids: Kregel Academic, 2014.

Gentry, Kenneth L. "Postmillennialism." In *Three Views on the Millennium and Beyond*. Edited by Darrell L. Bock, 11–57. Grand Rapids: Zondervan, 1999.

———. *The Greatness of the Great Commission*. Tyler, TX: Institute for Christian Economics, 1990.

Gentry, Peter J., and Stephen J. Wellum. *Kingdom through Covenant: A Biblical-Theological Understanding of the Covenants*. Wheaton, IL: Crossway, 2012.

Gibson, David. "Sacramental Supersessionism Revisited: A Response to Martin Salter on the Relationship between Circumcision and Baptism." *Themelios* 37, no. 2 (2012): 191–208.

Goeman, Peter J. "Implications of the Kingdom in Acts 3:19–21." *The Master's Seminary Journal* 26, no. 1 (2015): 75–93.

———. "Towards a New Proposal for Translating the Conjunction כִּי in Deuteronomy 4.29." *The Bible Translator* 71, no. 2 (2020): 158–78.

Gräbe, Peter. "The New Covenant and Christian Identity in Hebrews." In *A Cloud of Witnesses: The Theology of Hebrews in Its Ancient Contexts*. Edited by Richard Bauckham, Daniel Driver, Nathan MacDonald, and Mark Goodacre, 118–27. New York: T&T Clark, 2008.

Grant, Robert M. "Aristides." In *The Anchor Yale Bible Dictionary*. Vol. 1, edited by David Noel Freedman, 382. New York: Doubleday, 1992.

———. "Justin Martyr." In *The Anchor Yale Bible Dictionary*. Vol. 3, edited by David Noel Freedman, 1133–34. New York: Doubleday, 1992.

Green, Joel B. *The Gospel of Luke*. New International Commentary on the New Testament. Grand Rapids: Eerdmans, 1997.

Gregory Nazianzen. "Select Orations of Saint Gregory Nazianzen." In *A Select Library of the Nicene and Post-Nicene Fathers of the Christian Church, Second Series.* Vol. 7, *S. Cyril of Jerusalem, S. Gregory Nazianzen.* Edited by Philip Schaff and Henry Wace. Translated by Charles Gordon Browne and James Edward Swallow, 202–434. New York: Christian Literature Company, 1894.

Gregory of Nyssa, "The Great Catechism." In *A Select Library of the Nicene and Post-Nicene Fathers of the Christian Church, Second Series.* Vol. 5, *Gregory of Nyssa: Dogmatic Treatises, Etc.* Edited by Philip Schaff and Henry Wace. Translated by William Moore. New York: Christian Literature Company, 1893.

———. "On the Baptism of Christ." In *A Select Library of the Nicene and Post-Nicene Fathers of the Christian Church, Second Series.* Vol. 5, *Gregory of Nyssa: Dogmatic Treatises, Etc.* Edited by Philip Schaff and Henry Wace. Translated by William Moore. New York: Christian Literature Company, 1893.

Grudem, Wayne A. "Perseverance of the Saints: A Case Study of Hebrews 6:4–6 and the Other Warning Passages in Hebrews." In *The Grace of God, The Bondage of the Will: Biblical and Practical Perspectives on Calvinism, Volume One*. Edited by Thomas R. Schreiner and Bruce A. Ware, 133–82. Grand Rapids: Baker, 1995.

Hamilton Jr., James M. *God's Indwelling Presence: The Holy Spirit in the Old & New Testaments*. New American Commentary Studies in Bible and Theology. Nashville, TN: B&H Academic, 2006.

Hamilton Jr., James M., and Fred G. Zaspel. "A Typological Future-Mass-Conversion View." In *Three Views on Israel and the Church: Perspectives on Romans 9–11*. Edited by Andrew Naselli and Jared Compton, 97–140. Grand Rapids: Kregel Academic, 2019.

Hammett, John S. *40 Questions about Baptism and the Lord's Supper*. 40 Questions Series. Grand Rapids: Kregel Academic, 2015.

Hays, Hunter. "The Meaning and Significance of Circumcision." ThM Thesis, Shepherds Theological Seminary, 2022.

Helopoulos, Jason. *Covenantal Baptism*. Blessings of the Faith. Phillipsburg, NJ: P&R Publishing, 2021.

Hiebert, D. Edmond. *First Peter*. Winona Lake, IN: BMH Books, 1997.

Hodge, Charles. *A Commentary on the Epistle to the Romans*. Philadelphia, PA: Alfred Martien, 1873.

———. *Systematic Theology*. Vol. 3. Oak Harbor, WA: Logos Research Systems, 1997.

Hoeksema, Herman. *The Biblical Ground for the Baptism of Infants*. Grand Rapids: First Protestant Reformed Church, 1998.

Holladay, William Lee. *Jeremiah 1: A Commentary on the Book of the Prophet Jeremiah, Chapters 1–25*. Hermeneia. Philadelphia, PA: Fortress Press, 1986.

Horton, Michael. *Introducing Covenant Theology*. Grand Rapids: Baker Books, 2006.

———. "'The Lord and Giver of Life': The Holy Spirit in Redemptive History." *Journal of the Evangelical Theological Society* 62, no. 1 (2019): 47–63.

Hubmaier, Balthasar. "Ein Gespräch (1526)." In *Quellen zur Geschichte der Täufer*. Gütersloh, Germany: Gerd Mohn, 1962.

Huey, Jr., F.B. *Jeremiah, Lamentations*. New American Commentary 16. Nashville, TN: Broadman & Holman, 1993.

Hunt, J. P. T. "Colossians 2:11–12, The Circumcision/Baptism Analogy, and Infant Baptism." *Tyndale Bulletin* 41, no. 2 (1990): 227–44.

Jeremias, Joachim. *Infant Baptism in the First Four Centuries*. Translated by David Cairns. London: SCM Press, 1960.

Jewett, Paul K. *Infant Baptism and the Covenant of Grace: An Appraisal of the Argument That as Infants Were Once Circumcised, so They Should Now Be Baptized*. Eugene, OR: Wipf and Stock Publishers, 1999.

Johnson, Jeffrey D. *The Fatal Flaw of the Theology Behind Infant Baptism*. Conway, AR: Free Grace Press, 2010.

Jordan, James B. "Children and the Religious Meals of the Old Creation." In *The Case for Covenant Communion*. Edited by Gregg Strawbridge, 49–68. Monroe, LA: Athanasius Press, 2006.

Kaiser Jr., Walter C. "The Indwelling Presence of the Holy Spirit in the Old Testament." *Evangelical Quarterly* 82, no. 4 (2010): 308–15.

———. *Walking the Ancient Paths: A Commentary on Jeremiah*. Bellingham, WA: Lexham Press, 2019.

Köhler, Ludwig, Walter Baumgartner, M. E. J. Richardson, and Johann Jakob Stamm, eds. *The Hebrew and Aramaic Lexicon of the Old Testament*. 2 vols. Leiden, The Netherlands: Brill, 1994.

Köstenberger, Andreas J. "Baptism in the Gospels." In *Believer's Baptism: Sign of the New Covenant in Christ*. Edited by Thomas R. Schreiner and Shawn D. Wright, 11–34. NAC Studies in Bible & Theology. Nashville, TN: B & H Academic, 2006.

Kruse, Colin G. *Paul's Letter to the Romans*. Pillar New Testament Commentary. Grand Rapids: Eerdmans, 2012.

Lane, William L. *Hebrews 1–8*. Word Biblical Commentary 47a. Nashville, TN: Thomas Nelson, 1991.

Leithart, Peter J. "Infant Baptism in History: An Unfinished Tragicomedy." In *The Case for Covenantal Infant Baptism*. Edited by Gregg Strawbridge, 246–62. Phillipsburg, NJ: P&R Publishing, 2003.

Leo the Great. "Letters." *A Select Library of the Nicene and Post-Nicene Fathers of the Christian Church, Second Series*. Vol. 12a, *Leo the Great, Gregory the Great*. Edited by Philip Schaff and Henry Wace. Translated by Charles Lett Feltoe, 1–114. New York: Christian Literature Company, 1895.

The Lexham English Septuagint. 2nd ed. Bellingham, WA: Lexham Press, 2020.

Liddell, Henry George, Robert Scott, Henry Stuart Jones, and Roderick McKenzie. *A Greek-English Lexicon*. Oxford: Clarendon Press, 1996.

Lightfoot, Joseph Barber, and J. R. Harmer. *The Apostolic Fathers*. London: Macmillan, 1891.

Lillback, Peter A. *The Binding of God: Calvin's Role in the Development of Covenant Theology*. Grand Rapids: Baker Academic, 2001.

Lincoln, Andrew T. *Ephesians*. Word Biblical Commentary 42. Dallas, TX: Word, 1990.

Longenecker, Richard N. *Galatians*. Word Biblical Commentary 41. Dallas, TX: Word, 1990.

———. *The Epistle to the Romans: A Commentary on the Greek Text*. New International Greek Testament Commentary. Grand Rapids: Eerdmans, 2016.

Luther, Martin. "A Treatise on the New Testament, That Is, the Holy Mass, 1520." In *Luther's Works: Volume 35 Word and Sacrament I*. Translated by Jeremiah J. Schindel and E. Theodore Bachmann, 75–112. Philadelphia, PA: Fortress Press, 1960.

———. "Concerning Rebaptism, 1528." In *Luther's Works: Volume 40 Church and Ministry II*. Translated by Conrad Bergendoff, 225–62. Philadelphia, PA: Fortress Press, 1958.

———. "The Babylonian Captivity of the Church, 1520." In *Luther's Works: Volume 36 Word and Sacrament II*. Translated by A. T. W. Steinhäuser, Frederick C. Ahrens, and Abdel Ross Wentz, 11–126. Philadelphia, PA: Fortress Press, 1959.

———. "The Holy and Blessed Sacrament of Baptism, 1519." In *Luther's Works: Volume 35 Word and Sacrament I*. Translated by Charles M. Jacobs and E. Theodore Bachmann, 29–44. Philadelphia, PA: Fortress Press, 1960.

Marcel, Pierre. *The Biblical Doctrine of Infant Baptism: Sacrament of the Covenant of Grace*. Translated by Philip Edgcumbe Hughes. London: James Clarke, 1953.

Martyr, Justin. "The First Apology of Justin." In *The Ante-Nicene Fathers.* Vol. 1, *The Apostolic Fathers with Justin Martyr and Irenaeus.* Edited by Alexander Roberts, James Donaldson, and A. Cleveland Coxe, 163–87. Buffalo, NY: Christian Literature Company, 1885.

Mathews, Kenneth A. *Genesis 11:27–50:26.* New American Commentary 1B. Nashville, TN: Broadman & Holman, 2005.

McCabe, Robert V. "Were Old Testament Believers Indwelt by the Spirit?" *Detroit Baptist Theological Seminary Journal* 9 (2004): 215–64.

Meade, John D. "Circumcision of Flesh to Circumcision of Heart: The Typology of the Sign of the Abrahamic Covenant." In *Progressive Covenantalism: Charting a Course between Dispensational and Covenant Theologies.* Edited by Stephen J. Wellum and Brent E. Parker, 127–58. Nashville, TN: B&H Academic, 2016.

———. "The Meaning of Circumcision in Israel: A Proposal for a Transfer of Rite from Egypt to Israel." *Southern Baptist Journal of Theology* 20, no. 1 (2016): 35–54.

Migne, Jacques-Paul, ed. *Patrologia Graeca* [= *Patrologiae Cursus Completus:* Series Graeca]. Vol. 46. Paris, 1863. Cited in Everett Ferguson, *Baptism in the Early Church: History, Theology, and Liturgy in the First Five Centuries.* Grand Rapids: Eerdmans, 2009.

Milgrom, Jacob. *Leviticus 23–27: A New Translation with Introduction and Commentary.* Anchor Yale Bible 3B. New York: Doubleday, 2001.

Montanari, Franco. *The Brill Dictionary of Ancient Greek.* Edited by Madeleine Goh and Chad Schroeder. Leiden; Boston: Brill, 2015.

Moo, Douglas. *The Epistle to the Romans.* 2nd ed. New International Commentary on the New Testament. Grand Rapids: Eerdmans, 2018.

Morris, Leon. *The Gospel According to John.* New International Commentary on the New Testament. Grand Rapids: Eerdmans, 1995.

Murray, John. *Christian Baptism.* Phillipsburg, NJ: P&R Publishing, 1980.

———. *The Epistle to the Romans.* New International Commentary on the New Testament. Grand Rapids: Eerdmans, 1968.

Murray, John J. "Christian Baptism." *Westminster Theological Journal* 13, no. 2 (1951): 105–50.

———. "Christian Baptism: Second Article." *Westminster Theological Journal* 14, no. 1 (1951): 1–45.

Naselli, Andrew, and Jared Compton, eds. *Three Views on Israel and the Church: Perspectives on Romans 9–11*. Grand Rapids: Kregel Academic, 2019.

Niehaus, Jeffrey J. "An Argument Against Theologically Constructed Covenants." *Journal of the Evangelical Theological Society* 50, no. 2 (2007): 259–73.

———. *Biblical Theology: The Common Grace Covenants*. Vol. 1. Bellingham, WA: Lexham Press, 2014.

———. "God's Covenant with Abraham." *Journal of the Evangelical Theological Society* 56, no. 2 (2013): 249–71.

Niell, Jeffrey D. "The Newness of the New Covenant." In *The Case for Covenantal Infant Baptism*. Edited by Gregg Strawbridge, 127–55. Phillipsburg, NJ: P&R Publishing, 2003.

O'Brien, Peter T. *Colossians, Philemon*. Word Biblical Commentary 44. Dallas, TX: Word, 1982.

Ortlund, Gavin. "Why Not Grandchildren? An Argument against Reformed Paedobaptism." *Themelios* 45, no. 2 (2020): 333–46.

Osborne, Grant R. "Baptism." In *Baker Encyclopedia of the Bible*. Vol. 1, edited by W. A. Elwell, 257–59. Grand Rapids: Baker, 1988.

———. *Matthew*. Zondervan Exegetical Commentary on the New Testament 1. Grand Rapids: Zondervan, 2010.

Owen, John. *The Works of John Owen*. Vol. 11, *The Doctrine of the Saints Perseverance Explained and Confirmed* [1654]. Edited by W. G. Gould. London: Johnstone & Hunter, 1850–53; reprint, Edinburgh: Banner of Truth Trust, 1965.

Pao, David W. *Colossians and Philemon*. Zondervan Exegetical Commentary on the New Testament. Grand Rapids: Zondervan, 2012.

Peterson, David G. *The Acts of the Apostles*. Pillar New Testament Commentary. Grand Rapids: Eerdmans, 2009.

Pettegrew, Larry. *The New Covenant Ministry of the Holy Spirit*. The Woodlands, TX: Kress Biblical Resources, 2013.

Pettegrew, Larry D. "Israel and the Dark Side of the Reformation." In *Forsaking Israel: How It Happened and Why It Matters*. 2nd ed., 75–106. The Woodlands, TX: Kress Biblical Resources, 2021.

Polhill, John B. *Acts*. New American Commentary 26. Nashville, TN: Broadman & Holman, 1992.

Porter, Stanley E. *The Apostle Paul: His Life, Thought, and Letters*. Grand Rapids: Eerdmans, 2016.

Pratt Jr., Richard L. "Infant Baptism in the New Covenant." In *The Case for Covenantal Infant Baptism*. Edited by Gregg Strawbridge, 156–74. Phillipsburg, NJ: P&R Publishing, 2003.

Rainbow, Jonathan H. "'Confessor Baptism': The Baptismal Doctrine of the Early Anabaptists." In *Believer's Baptism: Sign of the New Covenant in Christ*. Edited by Thomas R. Schreiner and Shawn D. Wright, 189–206. NAC Studies in Bible & Theology. Nashville, TN: B & H Academic, 2006.

Ramsey, D. Patrick. "Sola Fide Compromised? Martin Luther and the Doctrine of Baptism." *Themelios* 34, no. 2 (2009): 179–93.

Robertson, O. Palmer. *The Christ of the Covenants*. Phillipsburg, NJ: P&R Publishing, 1980.

Ross, Mark E. "Baptism and Circumcision as Signs and Seals." In *The Case for Covenantal Infant Baptism*. Edited by Gregg Strawbridge, 85–111. Phillipsburg, NJ: P&R Publishing, 2003.

Rutherford, Samuel. "On the Baptism of the Children of Adherents." In *A Peaceable and Temperate Plea for Paul's Presbytery in Scotland*. London: John Bartlet, 1642.

Salter, Martin. "Does Baptism Replace Circumcision? An Examination of the Relationship between Circumcision and Baptism in Colossians 2:11–12." *Themelios* 35, no. 1 (2010): 15–29.

Sarna, Nahum M. *Exodus*. JPS Torah Commentary. Philadelphia: Jewish Publications Society, 1991.

———. *Genesis*. JPS Torah Commentary. Philadelphia: Jewish Publications Society, 1989.

Schaff, Philip. *The Creeds of Christendom, with a History and Critical Notes: The Evangelical Protestant Creeds, with Translations*. New York: Harper & Brothers, 1882.

Schreiner, Thomas R. *1, 2 Peter, Jude*. The New American Commentary 37. Nashville, TN: Broadman & Holman, 2003.

———. “Baptism in the Epistles: An Initiation Rite for Believers.” In *Believer’s Baptism: Sign of the New Covenant in Christ*. Edited by Thomas R. Schreiner and Shawn D. Wright, 67–96. NAC Studies in Bible & Theology. Nashville, TN: B&H Academic, 2006.

———. *Galatians*. Zondervan Exegetical Commentary on the New Testament. Grand Rapids: Zondervan, 2010.

———. *Paul, Apostle of God’s Glory in Christ*. Westmont, IL: IVP Academic, 2006.

———. “Perseverance and Assurance: A Survey and a Proposal.” *The Southern Baptist Journal of Theology* 2, no. 1 (1998): 32–62.

Schreiner, Thomas R., and Ardel B. Caneday. *The Race Set before Us: A Biblical Theology of Perseverance & Assurance*. Downers Grove, IL: IVP Academic, 2001.

Scott, John A. “The Meaning of the Verb Βάπτω, Βαπτίζω.” *The Classical Journal* 16, no. 1 (1920): 53–54.

Sproul Jr., R. C. “In Jesus’ Name, Amen.” In *The Case for Covenantal Infant Baptism*. Edited by Gregg Strawbridge, 303–10. Phillipsburg, NJ: P&R Publishing, 2003.

Sproul, R. C. *What Is Baptism?* The Crucial Questions Series 11. Orlando, FL: Reformation Trust, 2011.

———. *Who Is the Holy Spirit?* The Crucial Questions Series 13. Orlando, FL: Reformation Trust, 2012.

Strawbridge, Gregg. “Introduction.” In *The Case for Covenantal Infant Baptism*. Edited by Gregg Strawbridge, 1–8. Phillipsburg, NJ: P&R Publishing, 2003.

———, ed. *The Case for Covenant Communion.* Monroe, LA: Athanasius Press, 2006.

———. "The Polemics of Anabaptism from the Reformation Onward." In *The Case for Covenantal Infant Baptism.* Edited by Gregg Strawbridge, 263–85. Phillipsburg, NJ: P&R Publishing, 2003.

Stuart, Douglas. *Exodus.* New American Commentary 2. Nashville, TN: Broadman & Holman, 2006.

Taylor, Mark. *1 Corinthians.* New American Commentary. Nashville, TN: Broadman & Holman, 2014.

Tertullian. "Against Praxeas." In *The Ante-Nicene Fathers.* Vol. 3, *Latin Christianity: Its Founder, Tertullian.* Edited by Alexander Roberts, James Donaldson, and A. Cleveland Coxe. Translated by Peter Holmes, 597–632. Buffalo, NY: Christian Literature Company, 1885.

———. "On Baptism." In *The Ante-Nicene Fathers.* Vol. 3, *Latin Christianity: Its Founder, Tertullian.* Edited by Alexander Roberts, James Donaldson, and A. Cleveland Coxe. Translated by S. Thelwall, 669–80. Buffalo, NY: Christian Literature Company, 1885.

———. "The Chaplet, or De Corona." In *The Ante-Nicene Fathers.* Vol. 3, *Latin Christianity: Its Founder, Tertullian.* Edited by Alexander Roberts, James Donaldson, and A. Cleveland Coxe. Translated by S. Thelwall, 93–104. Buffalo, NY: Christian Literature Company, 1885.

———. "On Repentance." In *The Ante-Nicene Fathers.* Vol. 3, *Latin Christianity: Its Founder, Tertullian.* Edited by Alexander Roberts, James Donaldson, and A. Cleveland Coxe. Translated by S. Thelwall, 657–6668. Buffalo, NY: Christian Literature Company, 1885.

Thiselton, Anthony C. *The First Epistle to the Corinthians.* The New International Greek Testament Commentary. Grand Rapids: Eerdmans, 2000.

Thorsell, Paul R. "The Spirit in the Present Age: Preliminary Fulfillment of the Predicted New Covenant According to Paul." *Journal of the Evangelical Theological Society* 41, no. 3 (1998): 397–413.

Treat, Jay Curry. "Barnabas, Epistle Of." In *The Anchor Yale Bible Dictionary*. Vol. 1, edited by David Noel Freedman, 611–14. New York: Doubleday, 1992.

Ursinus, Zacharias. *The Commentary of Zacharias Ursinus on the Heidelberg Catechism*. Translated by G. W. Williard. Cincinnati, OH: T. P. Bucher, 1851.

VanderKam, James C. *Jubilees: A Commentary on the Book of Jubilees, Chapters 1–50*. Vol. 1. Hermeneia. Minneapolis, MN: Fortress Press, 2018.

Venema, Cornelis P. "Covenant Theology and Baptism." In *The Case for Covenantal Infant Baptism*. Edited by Gregg Strawbridge, 201–29. Phillipsburg, NJ: P&R Publishing, 2003.

Verduin, Leonard. *The Reformers and Their Stepchildren*. Grand Rapids: Eerdmans, 1964.

Vlach, Michael J. "A Non-Typological Future-Mass-Conversion View." In *Three Views on Israel and the Church: Perspectives on Romans 9–11*. Edited by Andrew Naselli and Jared Compton, 21–76. Grand Rapids: Kregel Academic, 2019.

———. *Has the Church Replaced Israel? A Theological Evaluation*. Nashville, TN: Broadman & Holman, 2010.

———. *He Will Reign Forever: A Biblical Theology of the Kingdom of God*. Silverton, OR: Lampion Press, 2017.

Waldron, Samuel E. "A Brief Response to Richard L. Pratt's 'Infant Baptism in the New Covenant.'" *Reformed Baptist Theological Review* 2 (2005): 105–10.

Walvoord, John F. *The Holy Spirit*. 3rd ed. Grand Rapids: Zondervan, 1958.

———. "The Work of the Holy Spirit in the Old Testament." *Bibliotheca Sacra* 97, no. 388 (1940): 410–34.

Ware, Bruce A. "Believers' Baptism View." In *Baptism: Three Views*. Edited by David F. Wright, 19–50. Downers Grove, IL: InterVarsity Press, 2009.

Warfield, Benjamin Breckinridge. "The Polemics of Infant Baptism." In *Studies in Theology*, 389–410. New York: Oxford University Press, 1932.

———. "The Spirit of God in the Old Testament." *Biblical and Theological Studies*. Philadelphia, PA: Presbyterian and Reformed, 1952.

Watt, Jonathan M. "The Oikos Formula." In *The Case for Covenantal Infant Baptism*. Edited by Gregg Strawbridge, 70–84. Phillipsburg, NJ: P&R Publishing, 2003.

Watts, John D. W. *Isaiah 1–33*. Rev. ed. Word Biblical Commentary 24. Nashville, TN: Thomas Nelson, 2005.

Waymeyer, Matt. *A Biblical Critique of Infant Baptism*. The Woodlands, TX: Kress Christian Publications, 2008.

———. "Romans 4:11 and the Case for Infant Baptism." *The Master's Seminary Journal* 29, no. 2 (2018): 233–55.

Wellum, Stephen J. "Baptism and the Relationship between the Covenants." In *Believer's Baptism: Sign of the New Covenant in Christ*. Edited by Thomas R. Schreiner and Shawn D. Wright, 97–162. NAC Studies in Bible & Theology. Nashville, TN: B&H Academic, 2006.

Wenham, Gordon J. *Genesis 16–50*. Word Biblical Commentary 2. Waco, TX: Word, 1998.

White, James R. "The Newness of the New Covenant (Part 2)." In *Recovering a Covenantal Heritage: Essays in Baptist Covenant Theology*. Edited by Richard C. Barcellos, 357–82. Palmdale, CA: RBAP, 2014.

Wilhite, Shawn J. *The Didache: A Commentary*. Eugene, OR: Cascade Books, 2019.

Wilson, Douglas. "Baptism and Children: Their Place in the Old and New Testaments." In *The Case for Covenantal Infant Baptism*. Edited by Gregg Strawbridge, 70–84. Phillipsburg, NJ: P&R Publishing, 2003.

———. *To a Thousand Generations: Infant Baptism—Covenant Mercy for the People of God*. Moscow, ID: Canon Press, 1996.

Zwingli, Ulrich. "Friendly Exegesis (1527)." In *Huldrych Zwingli: Writings*. 2 vols. Edited by E. J. Furcha and H. Wayne Pipkin. Allison Park, PA: Pickwick, 1984.

———. *Selected Works of Huldreich Zwingli*. Edited by Samuel Macauley. Translated by Lawrence A. McClouth, Henry Preble, and George W. Gilmore. Philadelphia, PA: University of Pennsylvania, 1901.

———. *Antwort über Balthasar Hubmaiers Taufüchlein*. In *Huldreich Zwinglis Sämtliche Werke*. Vol. 4. Edited by Emil Egli et al. Leipzig: Verlag von Heinsius Nachfolger, 1927.

———. "Of Baptism." In *Zwingli and Bullinger*. Translated by G. W. Bromiley. Library of Christian Classics 24. Philadelphia, PA: Westminster, 1953.

Scripture Index

Romans

Made in the USA
Middletown, DE
31 March 2024

52376118R00136